Dynamics Of Marginality

Trends in Classics – Supplementary Volumes

Edited by
Franco Montanari and Antonios Rengakos

Volume 143

Dynamics Of Marginality

Liminal Characters and Marginal Groups
in Neronian and Flavian Literature

Edited by
Konstantinos Arampapaslis, Antony Augoustakis,
Stephen Froedge and Clayton Schroer

DE GRUYTER

ISBN 978-3-11-162848-6
e-ISBN (PDF) 978-3-11-106394-2
e-ISBN (EPUB) 978-3-11-106410-9
ISSN 1868-4785

Library of Congress Control Number: 2023932650

Bibliographic information published by the Deutsche Nationalbibliothek
The Deutsche Nationalbibliothek lists this publication in the Deutsche Nationalbibliografie;
detailed bibliographic data are available on the internet at http://dnb.dnb.de.

www.degruyter.com

Acknowledgments

The present collection was conceived, many years ago, by three members of the editorial team (all students of the fourth) as they were enjoying beer and each other's company during one of those hot, halcyon summer evenings of Champaign, Illinois. The camaraderie and intellectual environment they found in that place and time — and in one another — are things they will not soon find elsewhere. Many years, not to mention a global pandemic, have come and gone since then, but the idea is now made flesh.

Clayton would like to thank, in particular, his former colleagues in the Classics Department and Interlibrary Loan Office at Colorado College, where much of his work on the volume was completed. Jen's constant support and friendship deserves more thanks than he can give. Kostas is deeply grateful to Stavros Frangoulides, Angeliki Tzanetou, and Craig Williams for offering their acumen at different levels of this project.

It is also our privilege to thank the editorial team at De Gruyter, especially Antonios Rengakos, for their early and constant support of this project. Finally, we thank the contributors for sharing and developing their work, particularly at a time when COVID-19 made our personal and professional lives more precarious and uncertain.

Konstantinos Arampapaslis, Antony Augoustakis,
Stephen Froedge, and Clayton Schroer
Thessaloniki, Urbana, Toledo, and Atlanta
August 2022

https://doi.org/10.1515/9783111063942-202

Contents

Abbreviations

All journal abbreviations follow the system of *L'Année Philologique*. Here are any other abbreviations used:

CP	Kytzler, B. (ed.) (1978), *Carmina Priapea*, Zurich.
D-K	Diels, H. and Kranz, W. (eds.) (1960–1961), *Die Fragmente der Vorsokratiker*, 3 vols., Berlin.
LIMC	*Lexicon Iconographicum Mythologiae Classicae* (1981–99), 8 vols., Zurich.
Migne, *PG*	Migne, J.P. (ed.) (1858), *Patrologiae Cursus, series Graeca*, Vol. XXXVI.
OCD	Hornblower, S., Spawforth, A., and Eidinow, E. (eds.) (2012), *The Oxford Classical Dictionary*, Oxford.
OLD	Glare, P.G.W. (ed.) (2012), *Oxford Latin Dictionary*, 2nd ed., Oxford.
PGM	Preisendanz, K. and Henrichs, A. (eds.) (1974), *Papyri Graecae Magicae*, 2nd ed., 2 vols., Stuttgart.

https://doi.org/10.1515/9783111063942-204

Konstantinos Arampapaslis, Antony Augoustakis,
Stephen Froedge, and Clayton Schroer
Marginality in Neronian and Flavian Literature

Introduction

Latin literature in the 1st century CE celebrates imperial expansion and contraction, as well as the anxiety that comes with an empire *sine fine*. This period is characterized by contradictory senses of belatedness and new possibilities, at once after (and, by popular sensibility, "less than") the Augustan age, but also reaching a geographical expanse far beyond what Augustus had imagined (viz. Augustus' clear demarcation between the "inside" and "outside" of his ideal empire as reported in Tac. *Ann.* 1.11). This is a century of shifting borders and definitions — the margins, in other words, are not where they used to be. When we read Petronius, Lucan, Statius, or their coevals, we often sense that we are (1) reading from the outside (of literary prestige, of imperial boundaries) looking in,[1] and that (2) the "outside", be it notional or geographic, is more distant from the "inside" than it once had been. As a result, the 1st century CE is a period of marginalization or rather a period that can be viewed quite well from the margins. In this volume, we aim to embrace the inherently protean nature of these margins, embracing a broad understanding of the people who inhabit these liminal places: people and characters who, from their positions at the margins of their moments, can help define and clarify the moment itself as a whole. What follows — rather than some rigid definition to be embraced, abandoned, or qualified by the chapters that follow — situates marginalization as a category of thought, both within the Neronian and Flavian (literary-)historical periods and within the scholarly criticism of Latin literature in recent decades.

---

[1] So, for instance, Statius' enjoinder in the sphragis of the *Thebaid* that his poem only follow in the footsteps of the *Aeneid* "at a distance", *longe* (Stat. *Theb.* 12.817). Such an intertextual rhetoric of belatedness in Flavian epic is identified by Hardie 1993, 1, given a sense that the *Aeneid* had in some completed the aim of epic, which "strives for totality and completion"; more recently on the *sphragis* of Statius' *Thebaid*, see Gervais 2020.

https://doi.org/10.1515/9783111063942-001

Marginality

As a concept of modern criticism, the term marginality has been applied to the connection between the uprooted experience of immigrant communities and the subsequent diasporas these groups formed in their new homes. The concept also covers individuals or groups who were barred from access to resources and equal opportunities based on their deviation from a "normal" or dominant culture or ideology. This definition speaks to the societal framework of marginality with regard to religion, culture, class, ethnicity, and gender — as well as economics and politics — as factors which can lead to marginalization. However, sociologists have also recognized another framework, namely the spatial, which focuses on geographical location both as a factor that can negatively influence the lives of people and the space itself: according to such architectures of thought, marginalized spaces produce marginalized peoples who in turn reinforce the marginalized status of the spaces they inhabit. Marginality is a state which develops and changes over time under different social, economic, cultural, political, and geographical environments.

"Marginal", or the more common noun in ancient literature, *margo*, were entirely unknown to the ancients as a term of literary criticism.[2] The word does not appear at all in the *Rhetorica ad Herennium* or Cicero's rhetorical treatises; Quintilian uses it only once to define a device for teaching students to write within a defined space (*Inst.* 1.1.27), although we might also compare the (presumably marginal) mark, *censoria quadam virgula*, he says critics used to excise authors and works from the canon (1.4.3). Similarly, Servius (ad Virg. *Ecl.* 5.7, *Aen.* 1.724) only uses the word in a descriptive function rather than a literary-critical one. For that matter, *margo* is a relatively rare word in the Latin literary canon more broadly considered, occurring some 120 times according to a search of the PHI database. Even still, the diachronic dynamics of its usage in Latin literature demonstrate the importance of marginality in Neronian and Flavian literature. Take, for instance, its use in Latin hexameter poetry, where *margine* regularly appears after a bucolic caesura in the fifth foot paired with a disyllable (e.g., *margine ripae*: Ov. *Met.* 1.729, 5.598; Stat. *Theb.* 4.703; Sil. *Pun.* 6.165).[3] Neither Virgil nor Lucretius, however, ever use *margo*; the language of margin-

---

2 Edmunds 2010, 31, discussing the concept of "minor" poetry, dismisses concerns over the anachronism of modern critical terms in the discussion of ancient texts, although he offers no further investigation of the term in ancient criticism.

3 Indeed, Ovid can be credited with creating a poetics of marginality in his exilic poetry; see, e.g., Fulkerson 2016.

ality then, strictly defined, becomes markedly more prominent in the so-called imperial age of Latin literature — the time period under investigation in this volume.

Yet, as the examples just cited testify, there is one prominent marginal figure whose work and displacement exerts an outsized influence on the literary imaginings of marginalization during the Neronian and Flavian periods. The poet Ovid's removal by Augustus to Tomis in the year 8 CE fundamentally changed the way that poets, in particular, talked about living at and beyond the boundaries of the Roman world. More broadly considered, of course, Ovid's influence on the poets of the period is well studied.[4] However, the poet's exile and exilic poetry, more germane to this collection,[5] is only recently beginning to receive substantial attention in Flavian literature.[6]

Likewise, marginality has not received a substantial amount of systematic investigation within the field of Classics. As Edmunds suggests in an important article on defining the qualities (and examples) of "minor" Latin poetry, marginality is a more important critical concept in postcolonial theory than in Classical studies.[7] At first glance, these fields can seem antithetical to, or at the very least in tension with, one another: after all, postcolonial criticism often defines literary marginality as being outside a Eurocentric canon that, whether explicitly or not, derives its authority from the ancient Greek and (especially) Roman textual traditions.[8] As Formisano admits in the introduction to the only other volume devoted to marginality in ancient literature, this fact makes it difficult to analyze Greek and Latin literature with such tools given the diachronic "cultural, ideological, and political implications".[9] Edmunds and Formisano, therefore, attempt to define marginality through the idea of the Classical canon, variously identified either through ancient theories of genre and literary criticism (Ed-

---

4 See, e.g., Bruère 2016; Keith 2002; Keith 2004–5; Marks 2022.
5 See the contribution of Roumpou in this volume.
6 See recently Marks 2020 and Schroer 2022.
7 Edmunds 2010, 30.
8 See, e.g., Said 1979, 56–58, tracing the marginalization of the Orient to Aeschylus, Euripides, and the "geographers, historians, public figures like Caesar, orators, and poets" of Greece and Rome, who "added to the fund of taxonomic lore separating races, regions, nations, and minds from each other".
9 Formisano and Kraus 2018, 5. A difficult, but by no means impossible challenge; the forthcoming "Routledge Handbook on Postcolonial Theory in Classical Studies" by Blouin and Akrigg is eagerly awaited. The articles on Neronian and Flavian literature that do make use of postcolonial theory — see Keith 2010 and Lowrie 2015 — point to exciting new interpretive possibilities.

munds) or reception (Formisano). As Edmunds suggests, canons tend to evade definition, and renewed scholarly interest can often remove a poet from "marginal" to canonical status;[10] complementarily, Formisano analyzes the dynamics of such changing scholarly appreciation through the lens of the hazards and contingencies of the modern academy.

The Neronian and Flavian Periods Examined

The collected chapters herein illuminate the identification of marginalized individuals and groups in the Roman Empire of the second half of the 1st century CE, their living conditions, and the reasons which may have led to their marginalization. At the same time this collection features studies of marginalized authors, as well as marginalized approaches to those authors. Indeed, these chapters, taken as a whole, offer a timely addition to the scholarship on imperial literature, responding to the so-called "spatial turn"[11] and revising our understanding of many understudied authors, texts, and topics by questioning the essentialist distinctions scholars of the Neronian and Flavian ages tend to draw between the center/canonical and periphery/marginal.[12] Collectively, these chapters offer a timely, even if not exhaustive, and necessary reading of 1st century Rome from the outside in.

Our study begins with Caligula's Rome in the mid-first century CE. Victoria Pagán opens this collection with a study on the gloss of *impudicitiam* in Tacitus *Annales* 6, thus illustrating the diverse 'phenomenalization' of the notion of marginality. Applying the 'genettean' context of the paratext, she explores the possibilities of reading the text through such margins and suggests that *marginalia* might offer valuable information for the partial reconstruction of lost sections of Tacitus' account. Pagán aptly classifies Philo as a paratext based on the author's position between the Roman and the alien, the Jewish and the 'other', as well as his historical proximity, but physical and social distance from Caligula's Rome. Focusing on two narratives, the mock-crowning of Carabas from Philo's *In Flaccum* and the meeting of the Jewish legates with Caligula in the gardens of Agrippina from the *De Legatione*, Pagán traces diverse aspects of

---

10 Edmunds' 2010, 33–34 citation of the case of Silius Italicus, for instance, seems prophetic given the current renaissance of studies on the *Punica*; see Antoniadis and Roumpou in this volume.

11 Fitzgerald and Spentzou 2018.

12 E.g., Bexley 2009; Rimell 2015; Pogorzelski 2016.

marginality in the binaries Caligula/Carabas and Agrippina's gardens/theater. The emperor and the pauper, both characterized by their mental instability, are sketched as outcasts, and are turned into a "spectacle" in the fringe, which is exemplified by the garden and the theater. These parallels allow Pagán to supplement the portrayal of Caligula, thus shedding further light on the history of a period which itself lies in the margins of textual sources.

The next three chapters examine marginality as a phenomenon connected, in various ways, to life in the Roman countryside in diverse authors, such as Pliny the Elder, the anonymous author of the *Moretum*, and Persius; chronologically, these chapters cover a wider period from the Julio-Claudians to the Flavians. First, Eleni Manolaraki addresses grafting in Pliny's *Natural History* to show how the Roman author extends the process of *insitio* beyond its agronomic context, and aptly applies it to his "botanical politics". She suggests that grafting in Pliny's encyclopedic work mirrors the story of the new emperor Vespasian, the first member of a new dynasty succeeding the Julio-Claudians and especially Nero. Manolaraki submits that Vespasian's life course epitomises the concept of integration, which finds the perfect reflection in grafting: the new emperor is grafted onto the system of the empire, while he also innovates within this same system through policies that close gaps between different social and ethnic groups as well as geographical spaces; his persona is characterized by traditional Italian values and rural simplicity, while his policies succeeded in the interpolation of the provincial/Italian and the Roman. As Manolaraki shows, Vespasian's governing policy, which relied on selection, adoption, and fosterage on the basis of meritocracy and values instead of birthrights, is analogous to the process of grafting. Manolaraki employs the examples of the people from Spain, for instance, where imagery of grafting offers the means to explain their provincial, but simultaneously also Roman, identity. She also discusses Syria in this same context as another province that exemplifies the course from the social and geographic margin to Rome but also Vespasian's "reverse outreach" from the capital to the furthest corners of the Empire.

Then, Jonathan Master brings the brief and anonymous *Moretum* to this study of marginality, which features the daily tasks of a man named Simulus. Master shifts away from traditional arguments which focus on the things Simulus produces. Instead, he analyzes a previously disregarded topic, namely Simulus' physical and sensory experience in this anonymous poem from the mid-first century CE. As Master submits, Simulus' physicality and tactile experience emerge as prevalent themes in this poem, as the readers are invited to see themselves in Simulus and his daily difficulties. Simulus' work may be divine, but he is still a sweaty and undignified individual, marginalized and yet so central. The

poem is ultimately about life and death, and the all-consuming work for survival; Simulus and Scybale's lives are very difficult, and their only reward is living
to struggle another day.

Following this fresh analysis of the *Moretum*, the chapter by Paul Roche
treats the marginalized, decentralized identity of the speaker of Persius' *Satires*.
Roche argues that the marginal position claimed by the poet corresponds to a
performed social isolation. He shows how the poetic persona's marginalized
voice and identity are mirrored in the interiority of the broader world of the
Satires. Persius avoids full social inclusion by identifying as a *semipaganus*, a
half-member of the *pagus* ("country community"), a term that may place him in
the reader's mind at the margins of Rome's boundaries with its rural surroundings or at the margins of community. Such social alienation promoted by Persius is matched by his own poetic position at the periphery of contemporary
(Neronian) tastes. But the speaker's social status, the position from which he
speaks, is gradually revealed as a pretense: it develops from an unelaborated
position as an outsider into a portrait of a conservative aristocrat whose intellectual inclinations have alienated him from the mainstream he rejects.

The next two chapters explore the theme of marginality in Petronius' *Satyrica* as it manifests in both the human and the divine sphere. While framing the
text as a story of miscreants and outlaws — marginalized figures — Christopher
Star argues that the law plays a central role in outlining marginality in the *Satyrica*. Encolpius' violation of laws, both human and divine, is instrumental in
framing the novel's confused world. For Star, the *Satyrica* revolves around Encolpius' status as a criminal whose deeds lead him to wander from place to
place, abandoning every time a community, only to find himself in a different
marginal setting. But the importance of law, Star maintains, is also evident in
discussions concerning legal education, the law of slaves and inheritance law
which are found throughout the narrative, and whose hyperbolic presentations
guide the reader to compare them with real-life forms of law. Contrary to Seneca
who examines the function of law from a philosophical and political perspective, Petronius uses it as a tool to build up a liminal space in which his protagonists live and act. It is this "other world", the marginal one, different from the
society of the elite that the *Satyrica* explores.

Following and expanding upon Encolpius' marginality asserted by Star,
Kostas Arampapaslis focuses on the god Priapus in the *Satyrica*. While ac-
knowledging the divinity's traditionally marginal status, he argues for the god's
centrality in the *Satyrica* itself. Ultimately, this perspective highlights the *Satyrica* as a pilgrimage narrative. Encolpius' expulsion from Massilia marks the
beginning of his travels, and at the same time places the protagonist in the mar-

gins of society. But it also assimilates him with Priapus, a deity who was mythologically marginalized by the gods due to his deformities and lewdness. Arampapaslis views the *Satyrica* as the author's effort to reflect contemporary anxieties, when people would frequently travel and resettle for better life conditions. The mythological *vita* of the god who belongs to the margins of Roman religious life served as a general model for the adventures of the anti-hero, Encolpius, perhaps reflecting the anxieties of low-class people during the Imperial period who would become marginalized through their wanderings in search of a better future. Similarly, Encolpius travels essentially for the same purpose, and his adventures fall under the auspices of Priapus as the marginal character of the religious events of the narrative also indicate. The marginality of Priapus might also be reflected in the title through the deity's frequent association in art and literature with the Satyrs, a creature that is half-human, half-animal and which lives outside the boundaries of human society.

The final two chapters of this collection take us to the end of the 1st century CE and Domitianic Rome, as they are devoted to the process leading to the marginalization of characters in Silius Italicus' *Punica*. Theodore Antoniadis examines how Hercules, typically a dominant figure is, in various ways, marginalized within the poem's narrative. He uses this figure at the margins, a "preeminent outsider", to assess some of the more central questions of the moment. Antoniadis focuses on Hercules' emotional imbalance as the cause for his marginal status in Flavian literature and argues that such depictions are not alien to the hero's earlier portrayals, even when he serves as a symbol of regal power and worldwide dominance (Virg. *Aen.* 8.362–368; 6.801–803). The diverse personality traits of Silius' Hercules, scattered in individual narrative scenes, essentially function as a point of reference for judging Silius' protagonists positively (Scipio) or negatively (Hannibal), and the schizophrenic characters might allude to Nero's own psychological profile. Hercules' marginal status is exemplified by his powerlessness to assist his priest Theron, whose demise can be viewed as the demigod's own defeat, while the vocabulary of violence permeating the description of the temple doors at Gades underscores him as a ravager of female beings, and through Pyrene's rape, further marginalizes him. Antoniadis asserts that, even when Silius brings to the foreground a positive assessment of Hercules, justified on Domitian's preference to identify with the demi-god, through the hero's assimilation with Scipio, his figure still remains "effectively marginal".

Similarly, Angeliki Roumpou's focuses on the question of marginality as it relates to characters in the *Punica*. She finds new significance in assessing the marginality of Silius' Hannibal, primarily a central figure in that text. She argues that his absence from the battlefield near the text's conclusion moves him to the text's margins and challenges the closure of the entire epic. The Flavian poet builds Hannibal's figure as the driving force behind the epic's development and narrative in Book 1, when he aspires to attack Rome and is described as the only one capable of reaching close to Rome. To succeed in his mission, Hannibal has to break boundaries, thus affirming his movement from the margins of his ethnic identity to the center of the epic narrative. This sketching of Hannibal as the instigator of the war renders him the 'raison d'être' of the poem, and his removal from the final battle and placement in the pastoral landscape renders him a liminal figure again, this time one that exists between life and death simultaneously within and outside the epic setting. From a metapoetic perspective, the hero's limbo mirrors the literary liminality between conclusion and commencement. His marginal position is also emphasized at the end when Silius turns Hannibal from a protagonist to a spectator of the events, as the boundaries between Roman and Carthaginian become indistinguishable. Hannibal's tendency to transgress boundaries reaches its climax at the end of the poem, when his removal from the battle creates another threshold set by the limits of the narrative, leaving the reader wondering with the expectation of further events.

***

Marginality is an inherently protean concept, its definition a relational one prone to diachronic, geographic, and ideological changes; furthermore, as Rimell has argued, understanding changing dynamics such as these only becomes more difficult when confronting an empire like Rome that could claim to itself to have no boundaries in either time or space (Virg. *Aen.* 1.279).[13] In such an imagining of empire, is there simply no marginal space, or does marginal space threaten to expand infinitely? In this volume, we aim to control for one of these variables, time, thereby bringing the margins of Neronian and Flavian Rome into clearer focus. It will become evident on reading the essays in this volume that very few of the authors (ancient or modern) identify the same geographical or ideological margins; nonetheless, though few are in agreement of where those margins are, all agree that they exist and exert an identifiable and significant impact on the texts under investigation.

Although the chapters here provide a timely and useful analysis of marginality in Latin literature of the first century, the topic remains understudied, and our selection of these texts only touches the surface. We hope that these chapters offer insight and impetus for further insightful analysis of central concerns which start from the margins.

---

13 Rimell 2015.

Victoria Emma Pagán
Marginality and Philo of Alexandria

Abstract: Using Genette's theories of the paratext, this chapter illustrates the phenomenology of marginality in the important — but understudied — source for Caligula's reign, Philo of Alexandria. Based on the slippage of his identity as Roman and non-Roman, Jewish and non-Jewish, Philo is a kind of paratext, embodying the physical and social distance between his station in Egypt and Caligula's in Rome. Examination centers on the mock-coronation of one Carabas from Philo's *In Flaccum* and Caligula's reception of a Jewish embassy in his gardens from the *De Legatione*. On these readings, the marginalized mental instability of prince Caligula and pauper Carabas as well as the liminal space of the garden poised between culture and untamed nature become proxies for tracing the earliest development of the stereotyped characterization of Caligula found in Josephus, Suetonius, and Cassius Dio.

Introduction

Tacitus' *Annals* Book 6 breaks off after the obituary of Tiberius in the year 37 CE. After recording Tiberius' ancestry and rivals to power, Tacitus describes his tumultuous marriage to Julia the Elder: "[Tiberius] enduring his wife's unchastity, or avoiding it" (*impudicitiam uxoris tolerans aut declinans, Ann.* 6.51.2). The last inscribed page of the First Medicean manuscript (Plut. 68.1.138r) contains only eighteen out of the usual twenty-four lines; the text stops abruptly at the beginning of the line not because of a lack of space on the page but because of a lack of material to copy. The only gloss on the page is *impudicitiam,* a prescient noun for all that is lost before the Second Medicean resumes in the middle of *Annals* Book 11, ten years later in the year 47. This gloss, written in the margin of the text, provides tangible, material access to a study of marginality. This solitary word, *impudicitiam,* is at the same time syntactically connected to, but physically separated from, *Annals* 6.51.2, which thus appears partial and incomplete, but only once the marginalia is perceived. Of course, the allographic note was added to the text of Tacitus by a later scribe; it is posthumous, external, and in no way involves the responsibility of the author. Genette notes that even glosses that derive from textual transmission are an extension of what he calls the paratext: "if the paratext is an often indefinite fringe between text and off-text, the note — which, depending on type, belongs to one or the other or lies

https://doi.org/10.1515/9783111063942-002

between the two — perfectly illustrates this indefiniteness and this slipperiness".[1] The contributions in this volume on marginality explore precisely manifold illustrations of this indefinite and slippery phenomenon.

The principate of Caligula lies between the two manuscripts, whose lacuna renders the narrative of Caligula indefinite and slippery. The modern perception of the mad, profligate Caligula depends on the embellishments and exaggerations of Suetonius and Cassius Dio. The lost books that would have recounted the reign of Caligula with examples of his *impudicitia* are supplemented easily enough by recourse to Suetonius, although he begins the biography with seven full paragraphs devoted to Caligula's storied father Germanicus before commencing with his birth in 12 CE (Suet. *Calig.* 8.1). The later historian Cassius Dio describes Caligula's behavior in this way: "For Gaius invariably went so by contraries in every matter, that he not only emulated but even surpassed his predecessor's [i.e., Tiberius'] licentiousness and bloodthirstiness, for which he used to censure him" (οὕτω γὰρ καὶ πρὸς πάντα ἐναντίος ἐπεφύκει ὥστε τὴν μὲν ἀσέλγειαν καὶ τὴν μιαιφονίαν αὐτοῦ, ἐφ' οἷσπερ καὶ διέβαλλεν αὐτόν, οὐ μόνον ἐζήλωσεν ἀλλὰ καὶ ὑπερέβαλεν, 59.4.1).[2] Memorable are his pointless bridge from Puteoli to Baiae (59.17); chests filled with ridiculous seashells, booty from his sham military expedition (59.25); his hubristic assumption of divine attributes, dress, and insignia (59.26). However, at least one modern biographer cautions that Caligula "probably behaved no better or worse than his successors".[3]

We might also consult Josephus, born in 37 CE, the year Caligula became emperor. He was a Jewish priest of royal descent and a leader in the Jewish Revolt of 66–73 CE against Rome. He commanded forces in Galilee against Vespasian and survived the forty-seven-day siege of Jotapata in Northwestern Galilee and was taken prisoner. Because his prophecy that Vespasian would become emperor was fulfilled, Josephus was released and granted freedom. He followed Vespasian to Rome where he was given a villa and a generous pension. Under these circumstances, he produced an immense literary corpus; all his writing thus post-dates the reign of Caligula. The *Jewish War* was originally composed in Aramaic but translated into Greek to reach a broader audience (*BJ* 1.3). After the successful publication of the *Jewish War*, Josephus undertook the ambitious task of writing a history of the Jews. The voluminous *Jewish Antiquities* was written in Greek under Domitian and published in 93 (*AJ* 20.267). It begins with the story of the Jews from the creation of the world to the administration of the

---

1 Genette 1997, 343.
2 Texts and translations of Cassius Dio are from Cary 1924.
3 Barrett 1989, xxiii; interestingly, this is a comment on Nero not Tiberius.

last procurators before the war with Rome. It falls into two halves, the first of which records Jewish history until the time of the first destruction of Jerusalem, concluding with the prophecy of Daniel. These first ten books rely heavily on Scripture. The second half of the work includes the post-exilic and Hellenistic periods, the rise and fall of the Herodian kingdom, and three final books on Roman imperial history.

Josephus begins Book 18 with the census conducted by Sulpicius Quirinius, governor of the province of Syria, to which Augustus had annexed Judaea.[4] The census provoked a rebellion, which prompts a digression on the ancient Jewish philosophies of the Pharisees, Sadducees, Essenes, and a fourth, recent school (18.11–25). Josephus then lists the succession of Roman procurators and high priests (18.31–35). At every turn, the histories of the Jews and the Romans are inextricably intertwined, as he narrates the Parthian civil war between Vonones and Artabanus swiftly followed by the poisoning of Germanicus (18.46–54). After the death of Tiberius (18.224), the rest of the book is taken up with the reign of Caligula, thus providing an external source by which to measure other narratives. Although Josephus fully covers the reign of Caligula and affords the most detailed account of his assassination, he conveys a moral purpose for the Jewish people, often at the expense of historical accuracy.

In all fairness, Josephus, Suetonius, and Cassius Dio had already received a negative tradition, which can be traced to at least one contemporary extant source.[5] Seneca the Younger wrote from the center of Roman imperial politics, from an elite position, although upon the succession of Claudius he was sent into exile (only to be recalled by Agrippina the Younger in 49 CE). Seneca's portrayal of Caligula is consistent. The princeps is the ultimate paradigm of cruelty, anger, greed, luxury, pride, and deceit.[6]

Philo of Alexandria (20 BCE – *circa* 50 CE), on the other hand, wrote from the periphery, with somewhat more limited access to imperial centers of power, although he was well-educated and from a prominent and wealthy family.[7] Among our historical sources, Philo is a sort of paratext, in Genette's formulation. He is an "indefinite fringe" between Roman and non-Roman, between Jewish and non-Jewish. To the extent that he "belongs to one or the other or lies

---

4 The date of the census in Josephus *AJ* 18.1–6 does not align with the Gospel of Luke (Luke 2:1–5); see Dąbrowa 2011.
5 Cluvius Rufus likely wrote about Caligula and would have been an available source, to some degree; Wiseman 1991, xii–xiv and 113–117, with the perspicacious review by Mason 2016.
6 Griffin 1976, 213–215.
7 See the biography by Niehoff, 2018.

between the two", he "perfectly illustrates this indefiniteness and this slipperiness". His brother Alexander Lysimachus held offices for Rome in Egypt (Josephus calls him an alabarch, *AJ* 18.159) and loaned money to Herod Agrippa I. Alexander's son Marcus married Bernice, the daughter of Herod Agrippa I (*AJ* 19.276–277); his other son Tiberius Iulius Alexander was procurator of Judaea (46–48 CE) and a prefect of Egypt (66–70 CE). These activities brought his brother and nephews into close contact with Rome; Philo, on the other hand, lived his life in Alexandria, leaving only as ambassador. From this, Christoforou observes, "Philo's own position as a prominent member of the Alexandrian Jewish community and an ambassador to Rome itself elevates his position as an interlocutor between worlds".[8] In his thoroughgoing study of Philo's views on Roman emperorship and his ideal of an emperor, Christoforou explores the connections between Philo's self-presentation as a negotiator of mutually exclusive and antagonistic worlds[9] and the historical reality that Philo was in fact a mediator, "someone positioned between worlds".[10] Philo's marginality derives from the fact that he is simultaneously historically connected to but socially, and even physically separated from the Roman world of Caligula.

Yet Philo was by no means concerned with narrating the principate of Caligula, the Julio-Claudian principate, or even Roman history more generally. Most of Philo's works were written mainly to explicate religious tradition and are essentially exegetical or philosophical in nature. His literary output is mainly concerned with Moses, either his writings or the biblical texts (e.g., *On Abraham, On the Decalogue, On Joseph, On the Life of Moses, On the Creation, On Rewards and Punishments, On the Special Laws, On the Virtues*). Philo also concentrated on allegorical commentaries on the book of Genesis and wrote philosophical works, but even in these Moses figures prominently. Only four of his works can be categorized as historical.[11] Even the *In Flaccum* and *De Legatione ad Gaium*, two historical works that treat events that took place during the reign of Caligula, convey fundamental principles of Jewish faith and philosophy. Although contemporary with the reign of Caligula, these two works raise more problems than solutions for the political historian seeking to pin down events or even for the cultural historian seeking a schema for understanding contact among Greeks, Jews, and Romans in Alexandria. Because of his Jewish perspective and his philosophical agenda, Philo's reliability for historical facts is easily

---

8 Christoforou 2021, 87.
9 Christoforou 2021, 110.
10 Christoforou 2021, 89.
11 Scholer 1993, x.

called into question,[12] although this is not surprising since none of our ancient sources are ever what we want them to be.

In the study of Julio-Claudian history, Philo is an underappreciated author who tends to receive less attention. Yet the *In Flaccum* and *De Legatione ad Gaium* are rich sources for the study of marginality. The *In Flaccum* was composed certainly after 38 and was probably published as late as 40 or even 41, after the death of Caligula. It describes the persecution of the Jews in Alexandria under the governor Flaccus and his subsequent punishment.[13] The *De Legatione* begins with the accession of Caligula and his reign and describes the extreme violence that took place in Alexandria and the embassy Philo led to Rome in 38, which was received by Caligula in 39. Philo continued to negotiate with Claudius after Caligula's assassination in 41, thus providing the *terminus ante quem* for the *De Legatione*.[14] These two works are unusual within the corpus of Philo's writing, because they address current events. Philo was not able to ignore the extraordinary violence against the Jews. Although the two works document a particular historical moment, they are designed to deliver a clear message of faith to the Jews of Alexandria. Both are thus unique specimens of a generic hybrid of philosophy, rhetoric, and historiography. The *In Flaccum*, or "Against Flaccus", carries a title such as that of a prosecutorial speech; the title *De Legatione ad Gaium*, on the other hand, narrates the embassy in a format resembling the ancient monograph.

Philo is our only literary source for information about the life of Aulus Avillius Flaccus. He was born *circa* 15 BCE and educated at Rome in the company of Gaius, Lucius, and Agrippa Postumus, the grandsons of Augustus (*In Flacc.* 158). In addition to this proximity to the ruling family, he was also a friend of Aemilius Lepidus, husband of Caligula' sister Drusilla, and Macro, the prefect of the praetorian guard (*In Flacc.* 151, 11). In these social circles he became one of Tiberius' closest friends. Thanks to the *In Flaccum*, we know more about the last year of Flaccus' life than any other time. The treatise is arranged in two parts of equal length.

Part 1 (1–96) describes the persecution of the Jews. Tiberius appointed Flaccus prefect of Egypt in 32 and for six years he governed well (1–7) until the death of Tiberius brought changes that threatened Flaccus' position. He was in a bad spot because he had supported Tiberius Gemellus, rival to Caligula in the imperial succession; he had participated actively in the prosecution of Caligula's

---

12 Gruen 2016, 397–412.

13 See van der Horst 2003, 1–53 for introduction to the text.

14 On chronology, see Decharneux 2003, 22–23.

mother, Agrippina the Elder; and his friend Macro was forced to suicide (8–20). To gain Caligula's favor, Flaccus began to heed anti-Jewish factions who were treating the Jews poorly. The initial cause of the ensuing violence was the arrival of Herod Agrippa, grandson of Herod the Great, whom Caligula had made king of Palestine. Agrippa stopped in Alexandria on his way from Rome and was greeted enthusiastically by the Jews, but their enemies were angered that Agrippa enjoyed such imperial favor (25–35). Young men flocked to the local theater and staged a coronation mocking Agrippa, played by an unwitting Carabas, a local man known for his mental illness. Flaccus ignored the public display of insult and instead used it as an opportunity to erect statues of the emperor in Jewish synagogues (36–44). The desecration of Jewish places of worship was followed by a decree that Jews were foreigners and aliens, without a right to trial. This set the stage for wide-spread plundering of the Jewish quarters of the city that escalated to evictions and violence (45–96). The second half (97–191) of the work is taken up with the punishment and death of Flaccus. Agrippa informed Caligula that Flaccus had failed to deliver a declaration of loyalty to the new emperor from the Jewish community; Caligula sent an undercover detail to arrest Flaccus. He was tried in Rome and condemned; his property was confiscated; and he was exiled to the island of Andros, where he lived until Caligula ordered his execution. "Such was the end of Flaccus, who suffered thus, being made the most manifest evidence that the nation of the Jews is not left destitute of the providential assistance of God" (*In. Flacc.* 191).

Like Sallust's *Bellum Catilinae*, the *De Legatione ad Gaium* is a unified narrative covering just one historical event that occurred within the author's lifetime, although of course Philo was much more directly involved than Sallust. However, we do well to remember that the full title of the work is *De Virtutibus Prima Pars, Quod Est De Legatione ad Gaium*. In this context, the *De Legatione* itself becomes a paratext of sorts and is marginal insofar as it is separate from, but an integral part of, the larger work on virtue. The last sentence situates the *De Legatione* vis-à-vis the conception for the larger work: "So now I have told in a summary way the cause of the enmity which Gaius had for the whole nation of the Jews, but I must also describe the palinode" (Εἴρηται μὲν οὖν κεφαλαιωδέστερον ἡ αἰτία τῆς πρὸς ἅπαν τὸ Ἰουδαίων ἔθνος ἀπεχθείας Γαΐου· λεκτέον δὲ καὶ τὴν παλινῳδίαν, *Leg.* 373).[15] However, without the "palinode", the *De Legatione* remains suspended, an "indefinite fringe between text and off-text", that "belongs to one or the other or lies between the two", a "perfect illustration of the "indefiniteness and slipperiness" that characterizes marginality.

---

15 Texts and translations of Philo are from Colson 1941 and 1963.

This chapter examines two iterations of marginality, broadly conceived. In the *In Flaccum*, the bizarre story of the mock-crowning of Carabas, a man afflicted with mental illness, provides a window into the experience of an individual living on the fringes of society. In the *De Legatione*, the meeting with Caligula takes place in the gardens of Agrippina in Rome, a space embedded within but distinct from the city that serves to make perceptions of marginality into lived reality. Yet by now it should be clear that my larger concern is the historiography of the reign of Caligula, and the ways that this period of history, with all its indefiniteness and slipperiness, resides in the margins of our sources.

Madness on the Margins

In the modern imagination, Caligula is the mad emperor; so too in antiquity. Suetonius summarizes neatly: he was weak in both body and mind (*valitudo ei neque corporis neque animi constitit, Calig.* 50.2). He was aware of his mental infirmity and often thought of retiring to clear his mind (*Calig.* 50.2). His poor sleep patterns attested to his mental instability (*Calig.* 50.3). Suetonius ventures a reason for his madness: "Not without warrant can I attribute to this mental weakness the extremely diverse vices within the same man, the highest confidence and on the other hand far too much fear" (*non inmerito mentis valitudini attribuerim diversissima in eodem vitia, summam confidentiam et contra nimium metum, Calig.* 51.1). Josephus prefaces his account of the assassination of Caligula with "the madness of hubris" (τῆς ὕβρεως τὴν μανίαν, *AJ* 19.1). Following suit, Cassius Dio remarks, "As he [Caligula] continued to play the madman in every way, a plot was formed against him by Cassius Chaerea and Cornelius Sabinus" (ὡς οὖν πάντα τρόπον ἐξεμαίνετο, ἐπεβούλευσαν αὐτῷ Κάσσιός τε Χαιρέας καὶ Κορνήλιος Σαβῖνος, 59.29.1). Tacitus speaks of Caligula's impulsive behavior (*impetus C. Caesaris, Ann.* 11.3.2), and Seneca describes his physical ugliness, an emblem of his deranged immorality ("he had such a foulness of pallor that belied his insanity", *tanta illi paloris insaniam testantis foeditas erat, Constant.* 18.1). Barrett catalogues the reception of the madness of Caligula from the nineteenth century with its insistence on derangement, depravity, and cruelty beyond the norms of human behavior, to the twentieth century with "a more sophisticated quasi-clinical diagnosis of his mental state".[16] As recently as April 2021, medical explanations still proliferate. Charry-Sánchez, Velez-van-

---

16 Barrett 1989, 215.

Meerbeke, and Palacios-Sánchez provide a chart listing possible physical illnesses that may have contributed to his madness: epilepsy, insomnia, encephalitis, lead poisoning, neurosyphilis, bipolar disorder, hyperthyroidism, anxiety disorder, personality disorder (sociopathy), schizophrenia, and alcoholism.[17] For the more circumspect Barrett, however, satire is the key to understanding this emperor whose perverse sense of humor and ironic view of the world were misunderstood then and now.[18] The incomplete and unscientific reports of Caligula's mental instability will resist medical explanation, and their sensationalism can be tempered with source criticism. Their ubiquity across all sources, however, means that they cannot be ignored. As the maternal great-grandson of Augustus and paternal great-grandson of Tiberius Claudius Nero (husband of Livia and father of her children), Caligula was the first emperor to embody the Julio-Claudian connection, yet his mental instability, regardless of its causes, pushed him to the margins of the very elite ruling society to which he so redundantly belonged.

Philo also uses the language of madness to describe Caligula's "insane desire" to be worshipped as a god (παραπληξίας, *Leg.* 76), which only increased: "So great a frenzy possessed him, so wild and delirious an insanity that leaving the demigods below he proceeded to advance upwards and armed himself to attack the honors paid by their worshippers to the deities held to be greater and divine on both sides, Hermes, Apollo, and Ares" (Τοσαύτη δέ τις περὶ αὐτὸν ἦν λύττα καὶ παράφορος καὶ παράκοπος μανία, ὥστε καὶ τοὺς ἡμιθέους ὑπερβὰς ἐπανῄει καὶ ἐπαπεδύετο τοῖς τῶν μειζόνων καὶ ἀμφιθαλῶν εἶναι δοκούντων σεβασμοῖς Ἑρμοῦ καὶ Ἀπόλλωνος καὶ Ἄρεως, *Leg.* 93). Overall, Philo's Caligula is a familiar portrait of tyranny characterized by arrogance, cruelty, restricted access, and megalomania. Tyrants live in fear of losing power, which causes them to become greedy and thereby debased, with disastrous effects on society: such is the description of the stock tyrant in Tacitus by Walker, applicable to both Tiberius and Nero.[19] When reading Philo, we may begin to discern the portrait of Caligula lost from the *Annals*.

The madness of Caligula can be compared and contrasted with another description of mental illness in the *In Flaccum*. At Rome, Caligula invested Herod Agrippa, the grandson of Herod the Great, with the royal title of King of Judaea. Such an arrangement underscores the asymmetrical political relationship between Rome and Judaea, which was not a province in its own right but was not

---

17 Charry-Sánchez *et al.* 2021, 344.
18 Barrett 1989, 216–218.
19 Walker 1952, 204–215.

autonomous either. Caligula advised Agrippa to take the speedy route, via Alexandria (*In Flacc.* 25). Agrippa was careful to enter the city after nightfall so as to avoid crowds. Philo attributes such behavior to his modesty. However, news of Agrippa's arrival and new position was soon divulged, and members of the community, jealous that a Jew would receive such imperial favor, approached Flaccus with a view to stirring up his animosity (*In Flacc.* 28–31). While he pretended friendship with Agrippa, he secretly encouraged the mob to ridicule the king. Agrippa was the subject of abuse in poems, puppet shows, and public gatherings (*In Flacc.* 33–35).

Flaccus turned a blind eye to the abuse, which reached a boiling point in the following incident (*In Flacc.* 36–38):

Ἦν τις μεμηνὼς ὄνομα Καραβᾶς οὐ τὴν ἀγρίαν καὶ θηριώδη μανίαν — ἄσκηπτος γὰρ αὕτη γε καὶ τοῖς ἔχουσι καὶ τοῖς πλησιάζουσιν —, ἀλλὰ τὴν ἀνειμένην καὶ μαλακωτέραν. οὗτος διημέρευε καὶ διενυκτέρευε γυμνὸς ἐν ταῖς ὁδοῖς οὔτε θάλπος οὔτε κρυμὸν ἐκτρεπόμενος, ἄθυρμα νηπίων καὶ μειρακίων σχολαζόντων. συνελάσαντες τὸν ἄθλιον ἄχρι τοῦ γυμνασίου καὶ στήσαντες μετέωρον, ἵνα καθορῷτο πρὸς πάντων, βύβλον μὲν εὐρύναντες ἀντὶ διαδήματος ἐπιτιθέασιν αὐτοῦ τῇ κεφαλῇ, χαμαιστρώτῳ δὲ τὸ ἄλλο σῶμα περιβάλλουσιν ἀντὶ χλαμύδος, ἀντὶ δὲ σκήπτρου βραχύ τι παπύρου τμῆμα τῆς ἐγχωρίου καθ᾽ ὁδὸν ἐρριμμένου ἰδών τις ἀναδίδωσιν. ἐπεὶ δὲ ὡς ἐν θεατρικοῖς μίμοις τὰ παράσημα τῆς βασιλείας ἀνειλήφει καὶ διεκεκόσμητο εἰς βασιλέα, νεανίαι ῥάβδους ἐπὶ τῶν ὤμων φέροντες ἀντὶ λογχοφόρων ἑκατέρωθεν εἱστήκεσαν μιμούμενοι δορυφόρους. εἶθ᾽ ἕτεροι προσῄεσαν, οἱ μὲν ὡς ἀσπασόμενοι, οἱ δὲ ὡς δικασόμενοι, οἱ δ᾽ ὡς ἐντευξόμενοι περὶ κοινῶν πραγμάτων.

There was a certain lunatic named Carabas, whose madness was not of the fierce and savage kind, which is dangerous both to the madmen themselves and those who approach them, but of the easy-going, gentler style. He spent day and night in the streets naked, shunning neither heat nor cold, made game of by the children and the lads who were idling about. The rioters drove the poor fellow into the gymnasium and set him up on high to be seen of all and put on his head a sheet of byblus spread out wide for a diadem, clothed the rest of his body with a rug for a royal robe, while someone who had noticed a piece of the native papyrus thrown away in the road gave it to him for his scepter. And when as in some theatrical farce he had received the insignia of kingship and had been tricked out as a king, young men carrying rods on their shoulders as spearmen stood on either side of him in imitation of a bodyguard. Then others approached him, some pretending to salute him, others to sue for justice, others to consult him on state affairs.

The first thing to note in this highly detailed description is the explicit distinction Philo makes between dangerous and blameless madness, which allows the reader to draw an implicit distinction between Caligula and Carabas, emperor and pauper, Roman and Alexandrian. As we shall see in the next section, roads are significant indicators of the spatial connection between the center and periphery; here, Caraba's interstitial position is further reinforced by his living in the streets and his ability to dwell between extreme cold and heat. His scepter is an object retrieved from the side of the road; his cloak, a doormat, is a liminal object.

Once outfitted, Carabas is likened to an actor in a theater. The young boys in their mockery also take on the roles of bodyguards and intercessors in a spectacle that parodies the crowning of Agrippa. As Catharine Edwards convincingly argues, Roman attitudes toward actors and the theater were often contradictory; "for the Roman elite", she says, "the theater was both alluring and threatening".[20] Actors were among the lowest members of society, and yet they were often celebrities. The persistent hostility toward actors betrays an underlying anxiety about the threat that they posed to social order.[21] Theaters were places where dangerous social tensions (for example, between slaves and masters so readily seen in the plays of Plautus) could be safely displayed. The laughter in Philo's account is generated not only by the mismatch of the actor (the lowly Carabas) and the character he portrays (the royal Agrippa), but by the ridicule that aggressively attacks Agrippa with its bungle and slapstick.

Through this theatrical representation, a stark reality is revealed, that Agrippa is in fact nothing more than a puppet king. The crowd makes this clear (*In Flacc.* 39):

> εἶτ᾽ ἐκ τοῦ περιεστῶτος ἐν κύκλῳ πλήθους ἐξήχει βοή τις ἄτοπος Μάριν ἀποκαλούντων — οὕτως δέ φασι τὸν κύριον ὀνομάζεσθαι παρὰ Σύροις —· ᾔδεσαν γὰρ Ἀγρίππαν καὶ γένει Σύρον καὶ Συρίας μεγάλην ἀποτομὴν ἔχοντα, ἧς ἐβασίλευε.

> Then from the multitudes standing around him there rang out a tremendous shout hailing him as Marin, which is said to be the name for "lord" in Syria. For they knew that Agrippa was both a Syrian by birth and had a great piece of Syria over which he was king.

However, the real actor in this scene is Flaccus himself. He does not punish the crowd; he does not even try to stop the mockery. Instead, he allows it to continue, "pretending not to see what he did see, and not to hear what he did hear" (προσποιούμενος ἅ τε ἑώρα μὴ ὁρᾶν καὶ ὧν ἤκουε μὴ ἀκούειν, *In Flacc.* 40). The entire event provoked the crowd to erect statues in the synagogues. The language of madness persists, as Flaccus is described as having a "mad desire for glory" (δοξομανής, *In Flacc.* 41). Throughout the episode, Philo redirects the mockery away from its original target, Agrippa and the Jews, and aims it subtly

---

20 Edwards 1993, 100.
21 Edwards 1993, 131.

but unmistakably toward Flaccus and the Alexandrians.[22] And as Decharneux observes, the real spectacle of Carabas is "the tragedy of a city ruled by a 'madman' who takes the stage".[23]

For Philo, the situation in Alexandria risks becoming an example to the rest of the world, for Jews live everywhere in great numbers. His description of the relationship between the Jews of Alexandria and elsewhere once again models the simultaneous connection and separation that defines marginality (*Flacc.* 45–46).

Ἰουδαίους γὰρ χώρα μία διὰ πολυανθρωπίαν οὐ χωρεῖ. ἧς αἰτίας ἕνεκα τὰς πλείστας καὶ εὐδαιμονεστάτας τῶν ἐν Εὐρώπῃ καὶ Ἀσίᾳ κατά τε νήσους καὶ ἠπείρους ἐκνέμονται μη- τρόπολιν μὲν τὴν ἱερόπολιν ἡγούμενοι, καθ᾽ ἣν ἵδρυται ὁ τοῦ ὑψίστου θεοῦ νεὼς ἅγιος, ἃς δ᾽ ἔλαχον ἐκ πατέρων καὶ πάππων καὶ προπάππων καὶ τῶν ἔτι ἄνω προγόνων οἰκεῖν ἕκα- στοι πατρίδας νομίζοντες, ἐν αἷς ἐγεννήθησαν καὶ ἐτράφησαν· εἰς ἐνίας δὲ καὶ κτιζομένας εὐθὺς ἦλθον ἀποικίαν στειλάμενοι, τοῖς κτίσταις χαριζόμενοι.

For so populous are the Jews that no one country can hold them, and therefore they settle in very many of the most prosperous countries in Europe and Asia both in the islands and on the mainland, and while they hold the Holy City where stands the sacred Temple of the most high God to be their mother city, yet those which are theirs by inheritance from their fathers, grandfathers, and ancestors even further back, are in each case accounted to them to be their fatherland in which they were born and reared, while to some of them they have come at the time of their foundation as immigrants to the satisfaction of the founders.

It is anachronistic to refer to a Jewish diaspora in the reign of Caligula since the destruction of the Temple in 70 CE by the Flavians is regarded as the principal catalyst for what we today call the diaspora. However, as Gruen notes, the conquests of Alexander the Great stimulated settlements of Greeks deep into the eastern Mediterranean, and Jews followed: "A Greek diaspora, in short, brought the Jewish one in its wake".[24] Furthermore, it cannot be the case that Jews who settled thousands of miles from Jerusalem consistently sought to return; communities prospered across the Mediterranean world. Although biblical texts recall the sufferings under Assyrians and Babylonians, Hellenistic Jews were able to thrive.[25] According to Gruen, "Jews formed stable communities in the diaspora, entered into the social, economic, and political life of the nations they

---

22 See Weitzman 2005, 55–78 for a close reading of Philo's portrayal of Agrippa and the politics of friendship between Jews and the emperor.
23 Decharneux 2003, 25.
24 Gruen 2016, 284.
25 Gruen 2016, 294.

joined, aspired to and often obtained citizen privileges in the cities of the Hellenistic world".[26] And as this passage of Philo shows, Jews were marginalized by virtue of their connection to their local communities but simultaneous separation from Jerusalem.

The Topography of Marginalization

Caligula makes his first appearance in the *Annals* of Tacitus at 1.41.2: "an infant born in the camp, brought up in the company of the legions, whom they called 'Little Boots,' using a military term because he often put on such coverings for the feet to obtain the goodwill of the commoners" (*iam infans in castris genitus, in contubernio legionum eductus, quem militari vocabulo Caligulam appellabant, quia plerumque ad concilianda vulgi studia eo tegmine pedum induebatur*). Seneca had used much the same language concerning Caligula's birthplace and name: "born in the camp and reared as the child of the legions, he used to be called [Caligula], with no name was he more familiar to the soldiers; but now he judged 'Caligula' a reproach and an insult" (*hoc enim in castris natus et alumnus legionum vocari solebat, nullo nomine militibus familiarior umquam factus, sed iam Caligulam convicium et probrum iudicabat coturnatus, Constant.* 18.4). Suetonius also explains the origin of the nickname and provides evidence of what Tacitus called the *vulgi studia*, since during the mutiny after the death of Augustus in 14 CE the soldiers became contrite at the mere sight of Caligula (*solus haud dubie ex conspectu suo flexit, Calig.* 9). The substitution of a military term for his personal name creates a realistic intimacy between the common soldiers and the great-grandson of Augustus. Yet at the same time, the nickname creates a theoretical distance between the signifier, Caligula, and the signified, Gaius, incidentally the name of his uncle who died when traveling through Armenia in 4 CE, possibly at the hands of Livia (Tacitus, *Ann.* 1.3, 53; see also *Ann.* 2.4). As for the birthplace, however, Suetonius refutes the assertions that Caligula was born at Tibur (as per Lentulus Gaetulicus) or in a Treveran village called Ambitarvium (as per Pliny the Elder); instead, he trusts the *acta* which record Antium (*Calig.* 8). Yet such positivism cannot preclude the slipperiness and indefiniteness of a birthplace *in castris*. The topography of marginality is at the heart of Caligula's lost story.

---

26 Gruen 2016, 299.

Embassies crystalize the separation of one community and its simultaneous connection to another community. The embassy of Jews arrive in Rome and are finally granted an audience with Caligula: "After first greeting us in the plain by the Tiber, as he issued from the gardens left him by his mother" (δεξιωσάμενος γὰρ ἡμᾶς ἐν τῷ πρὸς Τιβέρει πεδίῳ τὸ πρῶτον — ἔτυχε δὲ ἐκ τῶν μητρῴων ἐξιὼν κήπων, *Leg.* 181). The gardens of Agrippina are described similarly in the only other extant literary testimony: "in the courtyard of his mother's gardens which separate the portico from the riverbank" (*in xysto maternorum hortorum qui porticum a ripa separat*, Sen. *Ira* 3.18.4). The reference to Agrippina as mother (and not by name) suggests Caligula's rehabilitation of her image after the death of Tiberius and his emphasis on his dynastic lineage as direct grandson of Augustus — in stark contrast to Tiberius, merely adopted by Augustus. The only other evidence of these gardens of Caligula's mother is an inscription that alludes to gardens of Germanicus (*Germanici ... hortos*, *CIL* VI 4346).[27] According to Grimal, there were gardens across the Tiber that were owned in Cicero's time by Germanicus' father, Drusus the Elder. Grimal proposes that given the dramatic conditions under which Germanicus died and the notorious devotion with which Agrippina honored his memory, she came to be associated with the gardens.[28]

So much for the name of the gardens; for location, the evidence of Seneca shows that the gardens were bordered by the Tiber. According to Grimal, to the north they would have been limited by a line passing through the (later) Mausoleum of Hadrian and heading west, following what was to become the Via Cornelia. It is generally assumed that the gardens of Agrippina occupied the northern slopes of the Janiculum and the depression that separates that hill from the Vatican. Today this site is occupied by Saint Peter's Basilica, where the circus of Caligula and Nero was located. Although likely, there is no explicit evidence attesting that the circus was included within the compass of the gardens; it may be the case that Caligula enlarged the original, more modest area.[29] Grimal proposes that the gardens may have been connected to the *Pons Neronianus*, a few remains of which can be seen from the Ponte Vittorio Emanuele II, since it was built immediately below the modern bridge but at a slightly different angle. Dating to Nero and possibly as far back as to Caligula, the bridge was built to connect the western part of the Campus Martius to the Vatican valley where the imperial family owned land (along the Via Cornelia, which does not seem to

---

27 Grimal 1984, 141 n. 3.
28 Grimal 1984, 141.
29 Grimal 1984, 141–142.

have existed before the reign of Vespasian). The bridge would have been essentially private and would have connected mainly to the gardens and not to a broader network of roads across the river for public use.[30]

Gardens are liminal spaces. Originally set just beyond the *atrium* of a private house, between the dwelling and its uncultivated surroundings, the *hortus* occupied a space between nature and culture. Later, the grand *horti* of the Republic were built on the edges of the city. Neither completely urban nor truly rural, the gardens that survived and flourished in the first century CE formed a ring around the crowed urban spaces of Rome. Thus, both the simple *hortus* and the grand *horti* are characterized by peripheral locations. This position in the landscape recapitulates the etymological origins of *hortus* meaning enclosure. In Roman gardens, the boundaries marked with a stone, herm, or statue were regarded as sacred. Such boundaries limit, surround, define, and reassure by asserting ownership and imposing cultivated order on a chaotic natural world. Located on the edge of the city and even across the limit imposed by the Tiber River, the gardens formed a boundary between city and country. As they developed into luxurious pleasure retreats, these gardens came to symbolize extravagance. The etymology of extravagance resonates if we consider the behavior of the wealthy who, in 'wandering beyond' the forum, the place of duty and *negotium*, find ways to spend their *otium* and to display their wealth, the fruits of their ambition — in ornamental, sterile gardens. Gardens are very real, palpable spaces (in their own time, for we shall not be able to stroll in the gardens of Agrippina even as we stroll the streets of Trastevere and the Vatican) that reflect the beliefs, myths, fictions, and illusions of their creators. In effect, a garden is an ongoing dialogue between nature and culture, a dialogue shaped by, but distinct from, its interlocutors.

For these reasons, the gardens of Agrippina are a place freighted with symbolic meaning. Our marginalized Caligula spends his time on the outskirts of the city in a place that is both natural and cultivated. There he receives the embassy of Alexandrian Jews, who are part of the Roman empire but also forever bound to Judaea. And there he plays the role of a benevolent monarch, for he greets them, waves his right hand in a gesture of protection, gives tokens of his goodwill, and promises to listen to them (*Leg.* 181). Members of the embassy were encouraged and believed they had come to achieve their goal. But Philo was wary. He wondered why, when so many ambassadors come from all corners of the world, would Caligula assent to meet with them, with Jews? To Philo's mind, Caligula was more interested in helping the Alexandrians (*Leg.* 183). The em-

---

30 Grimal 1984, 142–143.

bassy then followed Caligula to Dicaearchia (Puteoli, on the bay of Naples), where the terrible news arrived that Caligula had ordered a colossal statue of himself to be erected in the temple (*Leg.* 187).[31]

As Flaccus played the role of the innocent governor, ignorant of the insults to Herod Agrippa and the rapidly ensuing violence perpetrated against the Jews in Alexandria, so Caligula played the role of innocent ruler, simply receiving foreign emissaries and leaving the details to his secretary (Philo names him: Homilus, Ὅμιλον, *Leg.* 181). Later, the ambassadors plead with Caligula, reminding him of their sacrifices on his accession; when he recovered from illness; and when he set out on his German campaigns. But Caligula was not satisfied, for they had not sacrificed to him (*Leg.* 356–357). Philo then likens the encounter to a theatrical spectacle (*Leg.* 359–360):

εἶτα ἡμεῖς ἐλαυνόμενοι παρηκολουθοῦμεν ἄνω κάτω, χλευαζόμενοι καὶ κατακερτομούμενοι πρὸς τῶν ἀντιπάλων ὡς ἐν θεατρικοῖς μίμοις· καὶ γὰρ τὸ πρᾶγμα μιμεία τις ἦν· ὁ μὲν δικαστὴς ἀνειλήφει σχῆμα κατηγόρου, οἱ δὲ κατήγοροι φαύλου δικαστοῦ πρὸς ἔχθραν ἀποβλέποντος, ἀλλ᾽ οὐ τὴν φύσιν τῆς ἀληθείας. ὅταν δὲ αἰτιᾶται κρινόμενον δικαστὴς καὶ τοσοῦτος, ἀνάγκη σιωπᾶν·

Then driven along we followed him up and down mocked and reviled by our adversaries, as they do in the mimes at the theatres. For indeed the business was a sort of mime; the judge had taken on the role of accuser, the accusers the role of a bad judge who had eyes only for his enmity and not for the actual truth. But when the person on trial is accused by a judge and that one of such eminence, he must needs hold his peace.

As Beard has observed, Philo's theatrical imagery is part of a discourse in which gardens are conceived as stages, especially formed to humiliate the Jews: "within the *horti* they [the Jews] became the object of the spectator's scornful gaze".[32] But the gardens were also places for the emperor to put himself on display, not only to the world but perhaps more importantly to himself. Gardens are sites of self-fashioning.[33] More recently, von Stackelberg has explored the transformative potential of gardens as performative spaces, a phenomenon to be observed in Philo's embassy.[34] No doubt the luxurious Roman *horti* bore historical and topographical importance; the gardens of Agrippina were part of an inheritance of wealth, status, and power. Ownership was everything. But the gardens are

---

31 This statue provoked popular movements against Caligula in Judaea and Galilee; see Taylor 2001.
32 Beard 1998, 31.
33 Beard 1998, 31–32.
34 von Stackelberg 2009.

also part of the matrix of imperial ideology, places where the emperor could perform his role. Flaccus dissimulated his sympathies toward the Jews but harmed them for petty reasons. Caligula on the other hand openly imitated the gods, with significant consequences for the Jews not just in Alexandria but across the empire.[35]

Although I have made no mention of the extreme violence against the Jews that Philo so graphically describes, I do not mean to downplay the testimony of this episode in the millennia-long history of anti-Semitism. In both treatises, Philo is painfully explicit (*inter alia*, In *Flacc.* 53–96; *Leg.* 120–126). Nor have I engaged with the socio-political status of the Alexandrian Jews, their citizen status, or local rights. Missing too is a discussion of the relationship between the different groups living in Alexandria, and the question of the difference between Greek, Roman and Egyptian attitudes towards the Jews, or Jewish attitudes towards Greeks and Romans.[36] Instead, I have tried to excavate the margins of the texts for some possible ways of supplementing our understanding of the portrait of Caligula missing from Tacitus' *Annals*. Madness is a permanent part of that portrait, and the episode of Carabas allows for fruitful comparison. The poor, homeless, mentally ill Carabas contrasts in every way with the wealthy, powerful, mad Caligula. Yet both men are outcasts even as they are made into grand spectacles, and as liminal sites of contest theaters and gardens are ideal sites for such displays. The margins still hold much information about the "often indefinite fringe" that "belongs to one or the other or lies between the two".

---

35 Decharneux 2003, 27.
36 Gruen 2004; Pearce 2007, 45–80; Gambetti 2009, 195–212 on the cultural and religious background of the events; Tuori 2021 on the larger context of the dispute between Greek and Jewish elites in Alexandria.

Eleni Hall Manolaraki
Grafting and the Marginal in Pliny's *Natural History*

Abstract: This chapter studies grafting in Pliny's *Natural History*. Noting grafting's metaphorical suitability to represent social relations, Manolaraki argues that Pliny's use of grafting can be seen as crafting a narrative of Vespasian and critical aspects of his reign. Contextualizing previous arboreal castings of imperial power, specifically as an apt metaphor for Julio-Claudian succession, Manolaraki discusses how Pliny's use of grafting suggests Vespasian as a 'splice' into that Julio-Claudian tree. This Vespasianic graft corresponds both to Vespasian's peripheral background and his innovations as emperor. As the progenitor of a new dynasty and one who projected Italic traditions at Rome, his reign finds a fiting expression in grafting. Pliny's use of grafting in the *Natural History* parallels Vespasian's assertion of his peripheral, marginal, characteristics into the center of Rome and Roman politics.

Introduction

From Cato's *De agricultura* to Palladius' *De re rustica*,[1] agronomic works elucidate social and political aspects of Roman thought.[2] Arboriculture is one such cultural register, especially valuable because it draws direct analogies between humans and trees.[3] Of all arboricultural practices expounded in prose and poetry, grafting (*insitio*) stands out as a remarkable phenomenon: its mysterious origins, its combination of natural process and human fabrication, and its life-sustaining fruits exalt *insitio* into a veritable *miraculum*.[4] Furthermore, the con-

---

1 For Pliny, I use the Teubner text of von Jan and Mayhoff 1870–1909; I have edited minimally the Loeb translation of Pliny's *Natural History*.
2 White 1970, 224–261; Frass 2006; Cima and Talamo 2008; Lowe 2010; Jones 2014.
3 Perutelli 1985; Telford 1991, 290–296, 302; Baldwin 2005, 73; Lowe 2010; Gowers 2011, 87–88; Manolaraki 2015; Hunt 2016, 29–71.
4 Discovered around the first millennium BCE, grafting enabled the domestication of forest trees, hence improving nutrition with fundamentals such as olives, grapes, and apples. Grafting is marvelous already in Theophrastus: Cofer 2015, 243–249 and 259–260. In Latin, the *locus classicus* is the Virgilian *exit ad caelum ramis felicibus arbos | miratastque novas frondes et non sua poma* (*G.* 2.81–82: "the tree shoots up to the sky with joyous branches and marvels at its strange, new leaves and fruits not its own"), on which see discussion below pp. 26–27. Grafting

https://doi.org/10.1515/9783111063942-003

joining and ameliorating function of grafting make it representational of human relations: the limits of compatibility between rootstock and scion, their fragile alignment, their gradual fusion, their composite offspring, and their binding scar metaphorize encounters between establishments (rootstock) and margins (scion) of all stripes. Premised in the above, this essay explores *insitio* in the Elder Pliny, an author explicitly invested in botanical politics.[5] I submit that in the *Natural History* grafting is attuned to the social atmosphere of Vespasianic Rome, and it constructs a narrative about the emperor.

My notion that Vespasian could be discursively abstracted by grafting is grounded in Roman cultural history. To Pliny's contemporaries, arboreal thinking about monarchs traced from the Romulean *Ficus Ruminalis* to the Julio-Claudian orchards that allegedly died with Nero.[6] The dynastic change, too, was framed by tree lore predicting Vespasian as a godsend for the empire. According to Suetonius, each time his mother gave birth, an oak tree in the family yard put out new branches. The first branch died in a short time, the second grew sturdy, and the third one — Vespasian — grew as big as a tree. Similarly, a cypress in his grandfather's estate was mysteriously uprooted one night, but it grew even more robust a day later. Vespasian's foundational feat was commemorated on coins featuring *Judaea Capta* under a palm, the trademark Syrian tree; and flora imported from around the empire dotted the grounds of his Temple of Peace.[7]

Within this mindset, imperial power was troped as *insitio* long before Pliny. In a well-studied instance, Virgil recounts six grafting combinations, most of which are among incompatible genera and therefore unviable (*G.* 2.32–34, 69–82).[8] Richard Thomas has read those unsustainable grafts as deliberate misalignments literalizing the Roman lust for violence and possession.[9] Conversely, for Dunstan Lowe and Clay Coffer, the same grafts evoke the hybridized plants

---

in Greek and Roman antiquity: Garner 1979, 39–48; Cofer 2015; Mudge *et al.* 2009, 452–458; Lowe 2010.

5 Lao 2008, 154–163; Pollard 2009; Manolaraki 2015. Grafting is presented positively in the *Natural History*, as an advancement in knowledge (Lowe 2010, 465–467).

6 Totelin 2012. See examples in Gowers 2011, 87–88.

7 Tree stories: Suet. *Vesp.* 5.2, 5.4 (and Lowe 2010, 485 for the *topos*). *Judaea Capta*: Stevenson 2010, 188–189; Temple of Peace: Pollard 2009.

8 These are apple onto pear (*G.* 2.33), cornel onto plum (*G.* 2.34), walnut and arbutus (*G.* 2.69), plane and apple (*G.* 2.70), pear and elm (*G.* 2.71–72), chestnut and beech (*G.* 2.71). Of these, only the first and the last are biologically possible. Ancient authors recognize that grafting combinations are restricted by compatibility: Varro, *Rust.* 1.40.5; Columella, *Rust.* 5.11.1 and *Arb.* 26.1; Plin. *HN* 17.103; Plut. *Mor.* 640b–c.

9 Thomas 1988a, 167–170; 1988b, 271–172; see similarly Ross 1980.

of the *Ara Pacis*, reifying an imperial utopia of peaceful abundance.[10] With similar positivism, Emily Gowers argues that Virgil's grafts admonish Augustus to maximize his heirs through adoption; this argument is appealing given the alternate usage of *adoptio* and *insitio* as equivalents in agronomic narratives and beyond.[11] Narratives of Julio-Claudian succession certainly illustrate the parallel between grafting and adopting. In Suetonius, Tiberius is assured a privileged descent when his maternal grandfather is 'planted' into the Livii (Suet. *Tib.* 3: *insertus … Liviorum familiae*). Tacitus has Agrippina remind Nero that Britannicus is the genuine successor to Claudius, while he is but an interloper (Tac. *Ann.* 13.14: *insitus et adoptivus*; ps.-Sen. *Oct.* 249: *Nero insitivus*).[12]

In this vein, I contend that Plinian *insitio* suggests the imperial persona, especially since Vespasian's trajectory activates notions of interpolation. The equestrian son of a Sabine tax collector, a sometime mule trader, a provincial general declared emperor outside Europe, the first to lord the army over the senate in his *dies imperii*, Vespasian was a splice into the tree of the Caesars and a pariah compared to the consular families of Galba, Otho, and Vitellius.[13] However, instead of whitewashing his *novitas*, the emperor made it into cultural policy. His projection of Italic traditionalism and rustic austerity, his appointment (*adlectio*) of Italian and provincial nobles into senatorial and equestrian offices, and his attention to provincial management, were projects bridging geographical, ethnic, and social margins with and within Rome.[14] By *Rome*, I understand both the imperial state and the metropolis that served as the physical, administrative, and symbolic center of the power wielded by the state.[15]

Vespasian's assimilation of peripheral entities to Rome, and his favoring of competence and loyalty over ancestry and rank, relied on a dynamic of selec-

---

10 Lowe 2010, 465; Cofer 2015, 556–562, 782–826. Other positivist readings of the Virgilian passage include Pucci 1998, 99–108; Hinds 1998, 104; Bovey 1999; Clément-Tarantino 2006; Deremetz 2009; Henkel 2014, 58–62.

11 Gowers 2011, 116–118. On *adoptio/adoptivus* used for *insitio/insitivus/insiticius*, see Cofer 2015, 299 and 400.

12 On the overlap between *insero/insertus* and *insero/insitus*, see below n. 21.

13 Vespasian's humble origins: Levick 1999, 4–8 and 28; *dies imperii*: Hurlet 1993. *Sulpicii Galbae*: Eck 1991; *Salvii*: Roche 2003; Collins 2009, 94–97; *Vitellii*: Master 2009, 191–193.

14 Traditionalist persona, rustic mannerisms: Luke 2010b; Milns 2010; urban restoration after the civil war: Lindsay 2010; *adlectio* of Italian and provincial worthies, improved management of the provinces: Houston 1977; Levick 1999, 63–64, 124–151, 171–172; den Hollander 2014, 128–129.

15 I borrow the double meaning of 'Rome' from Lavan 2020, 46. Lavan explores how scholarship on Roman identity is erroneously filtered through the modern experience of nationality and citizenship.

tion, adoption, and fosterage paralleling the process of grafting. Pliny, a Transpadane equestrian given four provincial procuratorships and an admiralship by Vespasian, was well positioned to impart to his audience imperial inclusivity and social advancement as the hallmark of the times.[16] By *his audience* I understand Pliny's eminent dedicatee, Titus, as well as members of a broad social circle revolving around Vespasian and his sons: consular, senatorial, and equestrian *amici*, newly adlected magistrates, and urban and Latian elites, in sum a sophisticated constituency oriented to the Palatine for political and social capital.[17] Whether empirically or vicariously familiar with grafting, this metropolitan cross section would grasp the subtexts of *insitio* in Pliny's politicized botany.

Illustrating the cultural inflections of Plinian graftage aims at a historicist and a formalist contribution to the theme of marginality. First, interpreting Pliny's *insitio* along structuralist lines adds to the historicity of his work and, consequently, to his value as a source for Vespasian along the likes of Josephus, Suetonius, and Tacitus. Second, my discussion parses Pliny's seemingly objective prose to display his authorial consciousness; recovering his subjectivity ties his *insitio* to the thematic coherence of the *Natural History*, and generally to the recognition of ancient technical treatises as literary products.[18] Finally, processing Pliny's vegetal politics reaffirms his place in the continuum of botanical imperialism, a monarchical practice stretching from Achaemenid hunting parks to Victorian greenhouses.[19] To lay the groundwork for the *Natural History*, let us outline semantic associations of *insitio* in its precursors.

Plants, Transplants, Implants

When in mid-second century BCE Cato urges his readers to think of a working farm as a living body (*Agr.* 1.6), he relies on their recognition of parallels be-

---

16 On Pliny's four procuratorships from 70 CE and his *officia* in Rome (culminating with his fateful command of the fleet at Misenum), see Syme 1991, esp. 503–510; Syme 1969, esp. 211–218, and 226–227.

17 This audience includes the individuals discussed by Syme 1991; Levick 1999, 82–88; Lao 2008, 18–37; Acton 2011; Doody 2011, 124–129.

18 Doody 2007 focuses this question on Pliny. See further Taub and Doody 2009.

19 I understand *botanical imperialism* as the literal and symbolic appropriation of flora to normalize political power (Pollard 2009). On this practice in antiquity, see Totelin 2012; Cofer 2015, 277–280, 479–488; for later empires, see Schiebinger and Swan 2005.

tween humans and plants. Within this intuitive concept, grafting figures social bonds throughout the literature produced over the subsequent two centuries.

A few highlights make the point. Ovid warns that a new romance is volatile, likening the lovers to a scion tentatively rooting in the stock. Strengthened by time, however, the relationship bears combined riches (*Ars am.* 2.649–652: *adoptivas ... opes*).[20] In a declamatory scenario, relatives of a childless rich turn against his adopted heir (Sen. *Controv.* 2.1.21.17: *insitivum heredem*). Cicero exposes the lowly origins of an Atilius Serranus, which he claims were masked when he was adopted by the Atilii (*Sest.* 72: *in ... Atilios insitus*). By contrast, the biological and adopted progenies of the Scipios are a fine stock, "onto which the wisdom of many has been grafted, like manifold scions on the same tree" (*Brut.* 213: *tamquam in unam arborem ... sic in istam domum multorum insitam ... sapientiam*).

The inoculation of indigenous stocks with imported cultivars, which leads to the geographic dispersion of trees, amplifies graftage as transplantation.[21] Consequently, the familial connotations of *insitio* extend to encounters between heterogeneous communities, with desirable outcomes or otherwise. In pseudo-Sallust, the urban poor are a parasitic graft on the nobles (ps.-Sall. *Rep.* 2.11.3: *multitudo ... insiticia sit*), and even Cicero an opportunist upstart "only recently grafted into this city" (ps.-Sall. *Cic.* 1.1: *paulo ante insitus huic urbi*). The Ciceronian Scipio acknowledges Greek influences in early Rome as a civilizing cultivar, admitting that the city "first appears to have become more educated through a certain grafted discipline" (*Rep.* 2.34.1: *primum videtur insitiva ... disciplina doctior ... civitas*). In a neat agricultural pun, the Ovidian Cadmus is warned by the Spartoi to not plant himself amidst their civil war (*Met.* 3.117: *nec te civilibus insere bellis*).

Among many such instances, let us review three that together highlight the stakes of *insitio* in discourses of autochthony, ethnicity, and class. When the Livian consul Manlius Vulso exhorts his legions to fight the Galatian Gauls, he

---

20 Grafting and familial relationships: Gowers 2005 and 2011 (and cf. Wilson 2012 for the trope in Shakespeare); erotics of *insitio* in Ovid: Hunt 2010; von Stackelberg 2014; substitution of *adoptio* for *insitio*: above p. 27.

21 Grafting enabled the movement of fruit trees fruits from Central Asia to Europe (Mudge *et al.* 2009, 438–439). Common vocabulary of grafting and (trans)planting: τὰς φυτείας καὶ τὰς ἐμφυτείας (Theophr. *Hist.* pl. 1.16.10); *serito aut inserito* (Cat. *Agr.* 7.3–4); *sationis et insitionis origo* (Lucr. 5.1361); *serendis inserendisque* (Plin. *HN* 17.140). Note the overlap between *insero* (*insevi, insitum*, "to graft") and *insero* (*inserui, insertum*, "to plant") with Clément-Tarantino 2006, 7 n. 17; Lowe 2010, 469; Gowers 2011, 89 n. 9; Cofer 2015, 298.

belittles the enemy's collective character.[22] The natives, he mocks, are but the idle descendants of Celtic émigrés in Anatolia; bastardized by centuries of Seleucid languor, those "hybrid Gallogrecians" (Liv. 38.17.9: *mixti et Gallograeci*) have mutated from their ancestral vigor since, "whatever grows in its own soil, has greater excellence; grafted into an alien soil its nature changes, and it degenerates towards that in which it is nurtured" (Liv. 38.17.13: *insitum alienae terrae in id, quo alitur, natura vertente se, degenerat*). The biological process of acclimatization is here orientalized into proof of physical weakness and moral inferiority.

What Vulso posits as a ruinous acculturation, Seneca modulates as cosmopolitan resilience. To comfort his mother for his banishment by Claudius, the philosopher contextualizes his predicament within the history of diaspora. His exile in Corsica, he reassures her, is but a footnote in global migrations stretching back into the distant past. She should call to mind displaced peoples such as Macedonians living in India and Persia, Greeks in Scythia, Tuscans in Asia, Tyrians in Africa, Germans in the Pyrenees, and, to wit, "you will scarcely find a land cultivated by its original inhabitants ... all have become intermingled and grafted" (*Dial.* 12.7.10: *ullam terram, quam etiamnunc indigenae colant ... permixta omnia et insiticia sunt*).[23] The overlap between grafting, planting, and migration affords Seneca a kaleidoscopic view of humans and farmlands, with everyone simultaneously at home and abroad.

The ecumenism of the Senecan graftage is reversed by Seneca's contemporary, St. Paul, to address frictions between Israelite and Gentile Christians. In the *Letter to the Romans,* the Apostle likens God's historic people to a cultivated olive tree that has been grafted with feral — that is Gentile — scions (*Rom.* 11.16–24).[24] He sternly warns the newcomers to not feel superior to their Jewish brethren, heeding the power balance between stock and scion: "you, though a wild olive shoot, have been grafted (ἀγριέλαιος ὢν ἐνεκεντρίσθης) among the others, and now share in the nourishing sap from the olive root; do not think yourself superior to those other branches. If you do, consider this: you do not support the root, but the root supports you" (*Rom.* 11.17–18). While the assertion that the stock nourishes the scion is accurate, horticultural practice contradicts

---

22 On Manlius' Galatian campaign in 189 BCE and the Gallic migration a century earlier, see Briscoe 2008, 56–94. The 'orientalist' bias traces to Herodotus' Persians (Munson 2009).

23 Seneca's examples of displaced populations: *Dial.* 12.7.1.3–12.7.2.6. Stoic cosmopolitanism: Sellars 2007; Lavery 1997.

24 A complex passage with ecclesiological implications: Mudge *et al.* 2009, 450–452; Khobnya 2013; ancient olive grafting: Bovey 1999.

the Pauline parable. Grafting takes place between wild stocks and cultivated scions to improve the former, not vice versa; reversing the roles makes *the Gentiles* the civilizing scion grafted into the Jewish oleaster. Aware of the discrepancy, St. Paul restores the hierarchical order with a divine grafter. God, he continues, knowingly inserted the Gentiles into the tree of Israel *despite* their feral state: "you were cut out of an olive tree that is wild by nature, and contrary to nature were grafted into a cultivated olive tree" (*Rom.* 11.24: κατὰ φύσιν ἐξεκόπης ἀγριελαίου καὶ παρὰ φύσιν ἐνεκεντρίσθης εἰς καλλιέλαιον).

An apt model for individual and collective acculturations, grafting also condenses the intellectual outcome of human encounters: novel thinking. Cicero argues that a successful speech embeds new opinions (*Orat.* 98.1: *inserit novas opiniones*), while Quintilian cautions the orator to divert the judge "from some ingrained bias against us" (*Inst.* 4.2.80.7: *contra nos insita opinione*).[25] Lucan's widow conceals him into her very soul (Stat. *Silv.* 2.7.127: *insitum medullis*), while Silius Italicus' Hamilcar sows war into a young Hannibal (*Pun.* 1.80: *sevit puerili in pectore bellum*). When Seneca turns down Lucilius' request to teach one of his acquaintances, he justifies his reasoning with a grafting image: "not all vines can be grafted" (*Ep.* 112.2: *non quaelibet insitionem vitis patitur*). Some stocks, he explains, are too hardened to be reformed, and vices must be excised before virtues can be planted. The rotten vine may yet be saved if it is pruned so deeply that the scion is grafted at the root: "cut off the vine above ground, so that if at first it does not respond, we may try a second venture, and again it is grafted below the ground" (*Ep.* 112.2: *si non respondit ... infra terram inseratur*). Could Lucilius' seedy colleague consent to a drastic such diminishment?

To summarize, grafting envisions the supplementation of existing entities by new ones, their mutual adjustment, and the physical, mental, and moral fault lines of their interaction. Steeped in this rhetoric, Pliny and his audience are primed for the political and ideological connotations of *insitio* in his work. Let us examine two representative instances that form the center of this essay.

---

25 Ciceronian implantations: *persuasum ... insitum* (Verr. 2.4.106.5); *oratio ... insita* (Orat. 133.7); *opinationem ... insitam* (Tusc. 4.26.3, 26.12); *insita et ... percepta* (Top. 31.3); *insita ... virtute* (Mur. 30.7); *libertas insita* (Pis. 15.13).

Imperial Fruits and the Good Grafter

While Pliny's remarks on graftage are scattered throughout his botany (Books 12–19), the books on fruit trees predictably contain several such instances. A third of Book 15 is dedicated to the olive (15.1–34), after which Pliny turns to the daunting task of presenting all other fruits. Before relaunching his narrative, however, he disavows any claims to completeness. The rest of the fruits, he preempts, can be barely itemized because of their great variety, which is due to grafting (15.35: *reliqui ... vix ... permixtis atque insitis enumerari queunt*). Essential to fruit productivity, grafting is an organizing principle in this Book.

One noteworthy example of the formidable diversity created by grafting is the *prunum* or plum (15.41–46).[26] Pliny marvels at the sheer volume of plum varieties (15.41) and he insists that no other fruit has been crossed more ingeniously (15.43). The compatibility of plums with miscellaneous stocks is practically shameless (15.41): "[plums] grafted on nut trees show a remarkable effrontery (*peculiaris inpudentia*), displaying the appearance of the parent tree and the juice of the adopted scion (*parentis ... adoptionis*)". Pliny's arboreal anthropomorphism is as old as Cato, but his preoccupations, as we will see, are eminently Flavian (15.43):

> *nuper in Baetica malina appellari coeperunt malis insita et alia amygdalina amygdalis: his intus in ligno nucleus amygdalae est, nec aliud pomum ingeniosius geminatum est. in peregrinis arboribus dicta sunt Damascena a Syriae Damasco cognominata, iam pridem in Italia nascentia, grandiore quamquam ligno et exiliore carne nec umquam in rugas siccata, quoniam soles sui desunt. simul dici possunt populares eorum myxae, quae et ipsae nunc coeperunt Romae nasci insitae in sorbis.*

> Recently in Baetica the name 'apple-plum' has begun to be given to plums grafted on apple-trees, and 'almond-plum' to others grafted on almonds. The latter have the kernel of an almond inside their stone; and, indeed, no other fruit has been more ingeniously crossed. Among foreign trees, we have already spoken of the damson, named from Damascus in Syria; it has grown in Italy for a long time though it has a larger stone and less flesh here, and here it never dries into wrinkles, because it lacks its native sunshine. With it can be mentioned its compatriots the myxae, which have also now begun to be grown at Rome by being grafted on the sorb tree.

---

26 The genus *prunus* includes subgenera of plums, cherries, peaches, nectarines, apricots, and almonds, all of which are compatible grafts with each other (Burgos *et al.* 2007). Plin. *HN* 15.41–46 applies the name *prunum* to twelve different fruits, some of which have not been identified. *Cf. pruna* in Verg. *G.* 2.34; 4.145; Columella *Rust.* 2.2.20; 3.9.5, 7.9.6; 12.10.2–3.

Plums, apples, almonds, damsons, sebestens, and sorb trees together open a panoramic view of the empire bookended by Spain in the west and Syria in the east. Hispania is ushered on stage through the remark that, in the province of Baetica, plums produced by plum scions grafted on apples or almonds are named after their stock. As often, Pliny's information is vague. "Recently" (*nuper*) is a broad temporal marker, while *malina* and *amygdalina* appear only here. Moreover, his claim that plums fuse with almond stock so fully that their endocarp (*ligno*) encloses an almond seed (*nucleus*) is implausible since grafting is not genetic but only vascular splicing.

Regardless of its accuracy, however, plum graftage in Baetica fits Pliny's larger interests, such as what Aude Doody calls his "aesthetics of naming". In detailing Plinian lists of names (geographical, botanical, mineral, etc.), Doody determines that "names are important within the text as structuring devices and as interesting facts in their own right, and Pliny chooses to list or exclude names for artistic and political as well as practical reasons".[27] *Apple-plums* and *almond-plums* earn Pliny's attention, I believe, both as curiosities and as political indexes. First, those names cleverly submit their grafting pedigree, and they showcase the use of Latinate words in provincial arboriculture.[28] Moreover, apple-plums and almond-plums usher the birthplace of the two Senecas and Lucan (St. Silv. 2.28–30), three prolific Baetican transplants in Rome. Familiar with the region thanks to his procuratorship of the neighboring Hispania Tarraconensis, Pliny highlights Baetica as the most fertile province (3.7: *Baetica ... cunctas provinciarum ... praecedit*).[29] While bearing out Pliny's promise to report names easily pronounced in Latin (3.7: *Latino sermone dictu facilia*), the *malina* and *amygdalina* cue in their greater homeland, Iberia.

In the late 70s, Iberia would be a timely and topical region for Pliny's audience. Shortly before the publication of the *Natural History*, Vespasian had issued proclamations extending Latin Rights (*ius Latii* or *Latinitas*) to the native peoples of all three Iberian provinces.[30] His *edicta* granted the reconstruction of native settlements and veteran outposts (*coloniae*) into *municipia*, as well as the

---

27 Doody 2011, 123.
28 Plinian politics of Latin names and terms: Doody 2011, 121 and 12–125. Doody 2011, 125 points out that Pliny emphasizes Latin as key in the spread of Roman dominance over Italy (*HN* 3.42).
29 Roman Baetica: Keay and Earl 2011; Baetica before Vespasian: Haley 2003, 32–68; Baetica in Pliny: Hoyos 1979.
30 My summary of Vespasian's granting *ius Latii* in Iberia draws from Wiegels 1978; Fear 1996, 131–169; Levick 1999, 138–140; Haley 2003, 70–72. The traditional date for the grant is either 70/71 or (more probably) 73/74 CE.

promulgation of charters for new such communities throughout Baetica, Lusitania, and Tarraconensis.[31]

Without digressing into specifics, we may generalize municipal regulations for our purposes. The defining attribute of a municipium was that its residents became Latins (*cives Latini*), an intermediate status between provincial subjects (*peregrini*) and Roman citizens (*cives Romani*).[32] Latin privileges included the right to business contracts with Roman citizens on equal terms (*commercium*), appeal to laws pertaining to Roman citizens (*ius civile*), and Roman citizenship for former magistrates and their families. The implementation of these and other rights varied across municipia, but the tenor of the promulgation is clear: by elevating peregrine communities and veteran settlements into townships, and by opening a path to Roman citizenship for their office holders, Vespasian promoted a greater symmetry between Rome, Italy, and Iberia.[33]

Pliny's audience does not have to look far to remember those grants. In his geography of Iberia, he commemorates the event, recording that "the emperor Vespasian granted the rights of Latium to the whole Spain when storm-tossed by civil disorders" (3.30: *universae Hispaniae Vespasianus imperator Augustus iactatum procellis rei publicae Latium tribuit*). Despite the ambiguity surrounding the antecedent of "storm-tossed" (*iactatum*), what remains is Vespasian's unifying intervention in Spain after the chaos of 69–70 CE.[34]

Against this recent past, the *malina* and *amygdalina* allude to questions of ethnic identity and imperial membership in Iberia. Neither Roman citizens yet no longer *peregrini*, the Iberian *cives Latini* draw closer from the Atlantic margin to the material, political, and cultural marketplace of Rome. Like their plum counterparts, the Spanish Latins are a composite entity, the outcome of a (Ro-

---

31 Levick 1999, 138–140 and 251 nn. 44–45 for bibliography. On Vespasian's provincial projects in general (*ius Latii* grants, new colonies for veterans, infrastructure, benefactions), see Levick 1999, 136–143.

32 On *cives, Latini, peregrini*, and other legal and hierarchical terms used to distinguish between tiers of privilege in the empire (e.g., *gentes, socii, provinciales, externi*), see Lavan 2013, 25–72; Lavan 2016, 156–157; Lavan 2020.

33 Fear 1996, 166: "[the *ius Latii*] provided a blueprint of a town towards which it was assumed the towns of the province would evolve. Such evolution would be gradual, as the deviation from the law would only come to light, and be corrected, gradually. On the other hand, it would have assuaged conservative opinion in Rome by ensuring that the *cives Romani* and the *cives Latini* of Iberia were living, in theory at least, under the forms of Roman law". Cf. similar points in Healy 2003. Further on Vespasian and Baetica: Levick 1999, 100, 138 and 171–172.

34 Some critics reject the lectio *iactatum* (modifying *ius Latium*) proposing instead *iactatae* (*Hispaniae* or *rei publicae*), or even *iactatus* (Vespasianus). On arguments for each option, see Wiegels 1978, 208–210; Fear 1996, 145; Levick 1999, 139.

man or Iberian) stock and an (Iberian or Roman) scion. I discuss these alternate roles below, but for now it suffices to establish that Baetican graftage offers an expository vehicle for provincial separateness and Roman belonging in Spain.

On the other end of the empire, damsons (*damascena*) and sebestens (*myxae*) reveal a similarly pluralistic vision.[35] Pliny reminds his audience that he has already mentioned the damson, a claim true also for the sebesten. Both fruits appear in the content summary of Book 13, dedicated to foreign trees, in a section titled *syriae arbores* (1.13a.12–20). This context informs our discussion, so let us backtrack for a moment to that earlier book.

There, the plum and the sebesten are preceded by the palm (13.26–50). Pliny introduces the palm as the trademark of Judaea (13.26: *Judaea … incluta est … palmis*), evoking the palm on Vespasian's *Judaea Capta* coinage. He reviews palm varieties from Spain and Italy to Cyprus and Ethiopia, concluding with Syrian types (3.49–50). From there he pivots to other Syrian trees, starting, "Syria has several other trees that are peculiar to it beside this date … the plums born on Mt. Damascus and the myxae, both now acclimatized in Italy" (13.51: *Syria praeter hanc peculiares habet arbores … pruna in Damasco monte nata et myxas, utramque iam familiarem Italiae*).[36] Pliny's cross-reference to his earlier mention of the damson (15.41), which leads to an elaboration of its ethnicity (1.13a.12–20, 13.51), invites readers to consider the two fruits together and in both junctures.

Introduced among *de peregrinis arboribus* (1.13a.1), the two 'compatriots' are verified here as "foreigners" (*peregrinis*, 15.43). It is hard to miss the juridical connotations of *peregrinus*, especially given the specter of *peregrini* turned *Latini* in Iberia. Yet despite their oriental roots, and as Pliny recognizes twice, neither the damson nor the myxa are especially alien. Originally born in Damascus, damsons are being born in Italy for a while (13.51: *nata*; 15.43: *iam pridem nascentia*). A relative chronology emerges in comparison to the Syrian jujube, which came to Italy "not long ago … at the end of Augustus' reign" (15.47: *peregrina … zizipha … ex Syria … non pridem venere in Italiam … Divi Augusti novissimis temporibus*). With 14 CE as a *terminus ante quem*, Pliny defines that past as recent (15.47: *non pridem*). Damsons in Italy must predate Augustus' final years since their cultivation started "long ago" (15.43: *iam pridem*).[37]

---

35 Sebesten (also known as assyrian plum): Al-Ati 2011; Bouby *et al.* 2011.

36 This is the Greek ζίζυφον, *Ziziphus jujube* (12.109; 21.51).

37 Damsons appear in Petronius (31.11), Apicius (4.5.1.6; 6.2.2.2; 6.5.1.2; 7.6.6.2; 8.2.8.2), Statius (*Silv.* 1.6.14) and Martial (5.18.3; 13.29.1).

While damsons have become Italian, sebestens have gone even further, "now" growing in Rome (15.43: *nunc coeperunt*). Unlike the directly planted *damascena*, the *myxae* live off the stock of sorb trees and apparently have not lost their native qualities.[38] Perhaps sebestens were brought to Italy by L. Vitellius, the father of the future emperor, who transplanted Syrian figs into his Alban estate during Tiberius' reign (15.83). Yet enough time has passed since the Roman advent of the sebesten, since Pliny assumes his readers' familiarity with that fruit. For instance, he advises that hawthorns can be grafted with sebestens (17.75), he likens their yellowish color to that of apricots and certain jaspers (15.46; 17.116), he compares them to berries and olives (15.96), and he prescribes gargling with sebesten broth as a sore throat remedy (22.120). Much like the *damascenum*, the *myxa* is foreign only in name.

While apple plums and almond plums awaken Iberia, damsons and sebestens conjure up the province that Barbara Levick calls "the power-house for Vespasian's takeover ... the base from which control was extended eastwards under the Flavians".[39] From his inaugural support by the Syrian legions and his Judaean triumph to his annexation of Syrian client kingdoms and his *adlectio* of Syrian worthies, Vespasian owned Syria in a sense parallel to Augustus' possession of Egypt. Yet the 'Italian conqueror of the East' model did not quite fit Vespasian. Unlike Augustus, the Sabine Flavius was himself a kind of Eastern 'Other', because he had emerged supported by Judaean, Syrian, and Egyptian legions. This perception of Vespasian is evident in the prophecies of his fated arrival from the East, in his consultation with the Serapis oracle, in the tales of his healing miracles in Alexandria, in his imperial *adventus* from Egypt, and even in his keeping among his advisors a Syrian astrologer named Seleucus.[40]

Yet much like its damsons and sebestens, and Vespasian, Syria was less exotic than it appeared. Following its annexation by Pompey in 64 BCE, it had grown into the most vital Asiatic province. Garrisoned by four legions and their auxilia recruited in Italy and locally, on the eve of Vespasian's rise Syria was home to at least forty thousand who considered themselves both Syrian and

---

38 Sebesten (*Cordia myxa*): Meghwal and Singh 2015; sorb tree (*Sorbus domestica*): Majić *et al.* 2015.
39 Levick 1999, 147. Vespasian and Syria: Levick 1999, 147–150; Bowersock 1973; den Hollander 2014, 128–129.
40 Vespasian's eastern support: Nicols 1978; prophecies, consultation with Serapis, miracles, *adventus*: Merkelbach 1979; Luke 2010a; den Hollander 2014, 91–101. Seleucus and Vespasian's interest in eastern mysticism: Levick 1999, 69–70; den Hollander 2014, 104.

Roman.[41] The people of Antioch, Tacitus reports, backed Vespasian because they feared that Vitellius would transfer their legions to Germany. Civilians were outraged at the thought, because "many were bound to the soldiers by ties of friendship and of marriage, and the soldiers from their long service had come to love their familiar camps as their very hearths" (Tac. *Hist.* 2.80).[42] Carried to power by Syrian legionaries, Vespasian brought Syria closer to Rome and forced a reckoning with its putative alterity.[43] Against this background, the damsons and sebestens suggest that Syrian novelties in Italy progressively diminish, and that the Roman naturalization of Syria is as inexorable as the acclimation of its trees in Italy.[44]

Let us bring together the implications of *insitio* in the context of Hispania and Syria. Differently yet in common underwritten by Vespasian, these provinces instantiate his trajectory from the social and geographic margin to Rome, and his reverse outreach from Rome to its periphery. With *Hispania* and *Syria* as examples, grafting configures a dialogue between Vespasianic Rome and the provinces along arboreal lines. In this script, Rome is the tree rooted in armed force, whose military branches reach throughout the Mediterranean. Those limbs receive new territories as scions, and they transmit to them infrastructure, engineering, bureaucracies, and benefactions.[45] Enriched by Rome, the previously vulnerable cultivars grow into productive units, and, in return for reaching their full potential, their output (tribute, crops, minerals etc.) is yielded to the parent tree and exchanged across the empire.[46]

Pliny's colonizing graftage also allows for a role reversal: foreign lands are the feral trees, culturally desolate due to their native poverty. The imperial state is rooted as a civilizing scion into that rough stock, and it harnesses raw resources into material and systemic advancements. Inoculated by Rome, the

---

41 Roman Syria: Kennedy 1996. Syrians recruited in the legions gained citizenship upon conscription; auxiliaries upon retirement (Kennedy 1996, 716–718; Grainger 2018, 15–19, as well as 77–132 for the auxiliaries).

42 Master 2016 well argues that Tacitus' *Histories* links the hybrid ethnicity of provincial soldiers to their volatile loyalties in 69–70 CE. See review by Manolaraki 2017.

43 Syrian influences in Rome culminated in the Syrian emperors of the third century: Grainger 2018, 25–44.

44 Roman acculturation of foreign elements: Dench 2005; Orlin 2010.

45 Pliny's positivist vision of Roman imperium: Fear 2011. Strategies for cultivating provincial loyalty: Ando 2000; Lavan 2013, 156–210.

46 Pliny articulates this point explicitly in botanical contexts: see *HN* 14.1–2; 27.2–3, and 2.118. Cofer 2015, 391–392, 401 discusses *insitio* in Varro as a paradigm of imperialism in the Roman Republic.

badlands bloom into provinces bearing resources fit for consumption across the empire. Whether the mighty stock invigorating flimsy scions or the cultivated scion refining foreign stocks, Rome of course remains the superior partner given its hegemony. The political economy of *insitio* aesthetizes Pliny's "positive imperialism" as an organic exchange with mutual benefits to all partners.[47]

The notion of a mutual engrafting of Rome and its constituencies is raised more explicitly elsewhere. In his preamble to the geography of Italy (3.38–42), Pliny heaps praises on the natural features of the peninsula, extolling his homeland as "the nursling and simultaneously the mother of all other lands" (3.39: *omnium terrarum alumna eadem et parens*). His sententious claim is rightly read as a metonymical (Italy for Rome) justification of the empire, idealized in the language of family.[48] This solid construal can be sharpened in the agrarian context of the *laudes Italiae*.[49] While *parens* and *alumna* do denote parents and children, they also describe stocks and scions in grafting.[50] Italy is not merely a parent and offspring, but also stock and scion of other lands. This arboreal reading sustains Pliny's bucolic tenor, and it even suggests his (positivist) response to the politically dubious *insitio* in Virgil's *Georgics*.

While grafted plums conjure up provincial assimilation, grafted apples evoke social mobility. After listing varieties hailing from Persia, Syria, Africa, and Italy's own Verona (15.47–48), Pliny pauses to deliberate whether he should continue (15.49–50):

> *reliqua cur pigeat nominatim indicare, cum conditoribus suis aeternam propagaverint memoriam, tamquam ob egregium aliquod in vita factum? nisi fallor, apparebit ex eo ingenium inserendi, nihilque tam parvum esse quod non gloriam parere possit. ergo habent originem a Matio Cestioque et Mallio, item Scaudio — quibus cotoneo insito ab Appio e Claudia gente Appiana sunt cognominata; odor est his cotoneorum, magnitudo quae Scaudianis, color rubens. ac ne quis ita ambitu valuisse claritatis et familiae putet, sunt et Sceptiana ab inventore libertino, insignia rotunditate.*

> Why should I hesitate to name the remaining varieties, when they have propagated the memory of those who established them, as though on account of some outstanding achievement in life? Unless I am mistaken, the recital will reveal the ingenuity exercised

---

47 I borrow the idea of Plinian "positive imperialism" from Fear 2011, 34.

48 Bispham 2007, 44; Laehn 2015, 65. Lavan 2013, 208 adds that *alumna* casts all other lands in the role of a servant nurse (*nutrix*), thus implying the power differential between Italy (Rome) and the provinces (similarly Lavan 2016, 158–159).

49 *Laudes Italiae*: Sartori 1995; Harrison 2008; Passavanti 2009.

50 Note *inserit sucos … alieno alumno* (Ov. *Met.* 14.631); *palmis … alumno* (Columella Rust. 4.27.4); cf. Pliny's *ramis … circa parentem* (*HN* 12.22), *ramos … parentem* (15.37), *insitorum … parentis* (15.41).

in grafting, and will show that nothing is so trifling as to be incapable of producing fame. There are kinds of fruit that have their origin from Matius and Cestius, from Mallius, and also from Scaudius; onto which a member of the Claudian family named Appius grafted a quince producing the Appian apple; this has the smell of a quince, the size of a Scaudian, and a ruddy color. And in order that nobody may imagine that it has gained its position by canvassing due to distinction and family, there is also a Sceptian apple named from a freedman who devised it, which is remarkable for its round shape.

Pliny's choice of *insitio* as a site for one of his rare editorials bears scrutiny. Here, his personal voice rises to deliberate whether he should switch from apples named after their place of origin to apples named after their makers. Unlike the apples already mentioned, the ones under consideration are known explicitly as products of grafting. Is that such a noteworthy deed after all? Pliny decides to include those apples, with the rationale that they commemorate the names of their creators. While he affects bemusement that something as mundane as grafting has memorializing power, he concedes that the fact of the grafters' remembrance belies the triviality of their accomplishment.[51]

Pliny's self-created dilemma begs the question of his purpose. After all, he could have omitted his editorial, and instead turn to apples named after grafters without any personal reflections. What his staged conundrum adds, however, is a model for his audience to challenge the notion of *insitio* as commonplace and to wonder at its power to bestow *fama* irrespective to rank and office. To wit, the editorial initiates a socially aware reading of the apples that follow.

Consider Pliny's selections. The Matian, Cestian, and Scaudian apples are known from elsewhere as the adjectival derivatives of their makers, that is as *Scaudiana, Matiana*, and *Cestina*.[52] He, however, chooses to showcase the grafters' *nomina gentilicia,* and hence to draw attention to their social diversity. Within the same sentence he cites four plebeian *gentes* of varied status (Matii, Cestii, Malli, Scaudii), patrician nobility (Claudii), and a freedman (Sceptius). Aside from Appius Claudius, the *nomina* (and *praenomina*) of these individuals are elided, thus occluding the individual grafters. Rather than identify individuals, Pliny's list ascertains the equalizing effect of *insitio* across social ranks and even among members of the same kin.

---

51 Pliny's recognition of 'trivial' accomplishments: *HN* 5.112; 9.129; 11.76; 18.35; 35.115 with Lao 2008, 126–127.

52 *Cf. malorum genera ... Scaudiana, Matiana, orbiculata, Cestina* (Columella *Rust.* 5.10.19); *Ces<t>iana, melimela, Matiana* (12.47.5); *Scaudiana* (Varro, *Rust.* 1.59.1; Celsus, *Med.* 2.24.2, 4.26.6). In the Elder Seneca, a blush is described as *colorem ... Cestianum* (Sen. *Con.* 1.7.17).

A sample of notable Matii, Cestii, and Scaudii communicates this point. The grafter Matius is the individual Pliny mentions elsewhere as an equestrian friend of Augustus and inventor of topiary (12.13); Columella cites cookbooks written by that Matius, but he criticizes his recipes for their expensive ingredients.[53] Three members of the gens *Cestia* stand out in our sources as potential grafters. One is Gaius Cestius Epulo (of the pyramid fame), tribune of the plebs and one of the seven priests in charge of religious banquets under Augustus.[54] Another is Gaius Cestius Gallus, consul under Tiberius, a spendthrift old man who entertained the emperor with sumptuous feasts (Suet. *Tib.* 42). A more principled character is the consul's son by the same name, governor of Syria from 65 to 67 CE and succeeded by Mucianus.[55] No other author mentions Mallian apples, but we do know several members of the gens Mallia.[56] A notable figure is Gnaeus Mallius Maximus, elected to the consulship in 105 BCE. Sent to Transalpine Gaul against the Cimbri, Mallius was rebuffed by the proconsul Quintus Servilius Caepio, because Mallius was a *novus homo*.[57] On the other end of the spectrum is the penniless freedman Mallius Glaucia, a go-between implicated in the murder of Sextus Roscius Amerinus (Cic. *Rosc.* 19, 96).[58] The grafter could be either man, or Glaucia's patron, or any other Mallius. Pliny's lack of specifics exposes the wide social (let alone chronological) range within the same gens, a range narrowed by grafting *fama*.

The next two families, the unattested Scaudii and the patrician Claudii offer a stark contrast.[59] Whether Appius Claudius Caecus, Appius Claudius Caudex, or any of the Claudii Pulchri, the Plinian Appius Claudius relies on Scaudius' graft to produce his own. Named after him, the Appian is both quince and apple, exhibiting properties from both its parents. The commoner and the noble acquire kinship due to their common offspring.

---

53 The G. Matius of our sources is probably two persons, a father and son. The former appears in Cicero (*Fam.* 11.27.28) as a friend of Caesar and Octavian; the latter is the friend of Augustus. On the Elder Matius, see Hall 2005; on the latter, see Columella *Rust.* 12.4.2 and 12.46.1; Matian apples are mentioned in Suetonius (*Dom.* 21) and Apicius (4.3.4).

54 Cestius' pyramid: Neudecker 2005.

55 Udoh 2005, 211 nn. 28 and 30.

56 Manuscripts often confuse *Manlius* and *Mallius* (Wiseman 1965). The third-century horticulturalist and Plinian compiler Quintus Gargilius Martialis refers to *malis manlianis* (Garg. Mart. 42), probably the Plinian apples from Mallius.

57 Caepius' obstinacy led to the defeat of two Roman armies at Arausio and to his punishment at Rome (Kerremans 2016, 823–824, 829–832). Social and electoral disadvantages of "new men": Wiseman 1971, 65–77 and 95–116.

58 Mallius Glaucia: Dyck 2003, 329 and 244.

59 Pliny also mentions Scaudian pears (*HN* 15.58).

Pliny's social sensibilities peak in his last item, the Sceptian. The obscurity of this apple is highlighted by its very existence (*sunt et Sceptiana*), and indeed Sceptius and his apple appear only here. For Pliny, however, the unknown Sceptian is noteworthy for correcting the notion that only the well-heeled may gain fame from grafting. That apple, he jests, has not earned its status though electoral corruption (*ambitus*), since its maker is only a freedman (and therefore ineligible for office). Despite its lack of lineage and connections, the Sceptian boasts a perfectly round shape, thus holding its own among its more glamorous rivals. The joke recapitulates the idea expressed in the editorial, that anyone (from the patrician Claudius to the freedman Sceptius) can earn recognition by their talent for *insitio*.

The following anecdote similarly suggests Pliny's emphasis on grafting as an uncanny equalizer of class and privilege (17.122):

> *Corellius eques Romanus Ateste genitus insevit castaneam suomet ipsam surculo in Neapoli-tano agro; sic facta est castanea quae ab eo nomen accepit inter laudatas. postea Tereus ei-usdem libertus Corellianam iterum insevit. haec est inter eas differentia: illa copiosior, haec Tereiana melior.*

> In the territory of Naples, a Roman Equestrian named Corellius, a native of Este, grafted a chestnut with a slip cut from the tree itself, and this is how the celebrated variety of chest-nut tree named after him was produced. Subsequently, his freedman Tereus grafted a Co-rellius chestnut again. The difference between the two varieties is this: the former is more prolific but the latter, the Tereus chestnut, better.

The method elaborated here is 'double working', the successive grafting of new scions on previously engrafted ones.[60] The Tereian is the combined product of the original chestnut stock, of Corellius' (intermediate) scion, and of Tereius' (upper) scion implanted on the former.

Because the stock, intermediate scion, and upper scion belong to the same tree, the Corellian chestnut should not be different from its stock, and the Tereian should not be distinct from the Corellian. What makes this instance remarkable for Pliny is the self-diversification of the original nut, combined with the relationship of the two grafters.[61] The freedman's double working of his patron's graft is presented as a playful competition, in which (Tereian) quality

---

60 Double working is used when the scion and stock are incompatible, but the intermediate scion is compatible with both the upper scion and the stock (Talbert 1938, 10–11; Hottes 1950, 159–160; Mudge *et al.* 2009, 439–440 and fig. 9.1).

61 Neapolitan chestnuts: Mart. 5.78.14–15. Syme 1991, 508–509 believes that Pliny was famil-iar with this Corellius from Ateste (modern Este in Venetia).

outdoes (Corellian) quantity. The apposition *Tereiana* after *haec* aims to assure readers that the superior chestnut is indeed the freedman's, as if Pliny expects them to disbelieve Tereius' success over his former master. Corellius and Tereius complement each other (like Scaudius and Appius Claudius do) with Tereius' social inferiority leveled out by his grafting victory. Taken together, the apples named after their makers extend *insitio* beyond its agronomic context. Grafting emerges as an exercise in aptitude and collaboration, and as a meritocratic arena open to all.

The ideal of grafting *ingenium* (15.49) as a path to distinction strikes a chord with Pliny's audience not unlike his references to Baetica and Syria. The unpredictable succession of the modest gens Flavia, the ascendancy of Italian and provincial *adlecti,* and the imperial fosterage of urban talent (Suet. *Vesp.* 17: *ingenia … maxime fovit*), all suggest the idea of talent and skill rewarded by upward mobility.[62] Within the cultural framework of his agronomy, Pliny could imagine the imperial prime mover of those developments both as a graft on the Palatine and as a master gardener grafting diverse constituents in an imperial orchard of bounteous peace.

The above has argued that Pliny's *insitio* transcends agronomic utilitarianism to become one narrative thread in his botanical politics. Technical instruction blends with the history, geography, and politics of grafting, prompting reflection on the practice along socio-cultural lines. For Pliny's contemporaries, that socio-cultural framework is inevitably pervaded by the imperial ascension, persona, and policies. Catalyzed by Vespasian, ideas about *novitas*, selection, supplementation, change, and integration, are captured by the rich paradigm of grafting. As image and process, *insitio* conceptualizes diverse Vespasianic enterprises as rapprochements between margins and center, assimilating imperial fiats to natural processes. Pliny's grafting of arboreal pragmatics with Vespasian's inclusionary ethics makes ideology out of trees.

---

62 Woodside 1942 discusses the sources (chiefly Suetonius) for Vespasian's patronage of letters and arts.

Jonathan Master
In the Realm of the Senses: Simulus' Experience in the *Moretum*

Abstract: This chapter examines the *Moretum* of the Appendix Vergiliana and the marginalized figures contained within that poem: Simulus, making the dish that gives the *Moretum* its name, and Scybale, who helps him in his labors. Eschewing the questions of tone and metapoetics traditionally asked of the text, this chapter argues that analyzing Simulus' physicality and senses within the poem reveals a convincing portrait of the man's humanity; this humanity in turn elicits from the reader recognition of their own sense-experiences. If the poem is at times comedic, it is not parodic. The intertextual implications of this argument are compelling, for they reveal much about the anonymous poet's treatment of *the* epic exemplar of ekphrastic physicality to which the *Moretum* owes so much: Hephaestus' crafting of the shield of Achilles.

Introduction: Simulus' Sensory World

The anonymous *Moretum* is a short 122–verse poem that describes a few hours in the life of a poor farmer named Simulus ("Snubnosed").[1] He wakes up, bakes some bread with assistance from a woman called Scybale ("Dung") with whom he lives, makes the herb and cheese spread for which the poem is named, yokes his oxen, and heads out to the fields. Over eighty years ago, Heinze made a number of insightful observations about the poem.[2] He first noted the detailed description of the physical person of Simulus.[3] The lasting legacy of that article in scholarship, however, has been Heinze's remark that the characterization of

---

I am grateful to the editors for inviting me to contribute a chapter to this volume.

---

1 More specifically modern scholarship would term it an "epyllion," a short poem in hexameters that usually features mythological heroes. The poem is of uncertain date with mid-first century CE most likely. See Kenney 1984, xxi–xxv.

2 Heinze 1960, originally published in 1939, "Das Kräuterkäsgericht (Moretum)".

3 Heinze 1960, 412: "Auf das Sichtbare richtet er sein Augenmerk beim Menschen, auf das, was seine Füße und Finger tun, und wenn er vom üblen Geruch spricht, den Simylus unangenehm empfindet, so setzt er das sofort in Mienen und Gesten um".

https://doi.org/10.1515/9783111063942-004

Simulus is realistic.[4] Literary scholars over the last half century have reasonably attacked that view and focused exclusively on the poem's engagement with earlier literature. The learned texture of the *Moretum*, with antecedents in Virgil, Ovid, Alexandrian poetry, and Homeric episodes[5] is undeniable, even if the tone cannot be agreed upon (parodic?).[6] This scholarship has focused most intensively on the things Simulus makes in the poem, bread and the *moretum*, and his garden, all of them rich in metaliterary significance. But the frame of the poem, the narrative such as it is, is a morning in the life of Simulus.[7] Everything that follows his waking up before sunrise derives from his first anxious thought of the day: how to fend off the hunger that the passing hours will bring (4): *tristia venturae metuens ieiunia lucis* ("fearing grim hunger in the approaching day").[8] The poem thus begins its characterization of Simulus with attention to his interrelated physical and emotional states. While the poem might end up with Simulus feeling secure for the day — and it certainly shows him making the most of his extremely slender resources[9] — it foregrounds the vulnerability and fragility of his existence. It would not be productive to characterize the poem as realistic, but what scholars have largely passed over since Heinze is the energy the poet devotes to creating Simulus' physical and sensory existence.

In fact, the poem already subtly begins to emphasize Simulus' sensory experience with its grandiloquent opening statement of the season and the time of

---

4 Heinze 1960, 412: "dieser Simylus ist eben einfach, wie er ist — und damit gut". Ross 1975, 255 n. 52 and Kenney 1984, xix–xx detail the realist case only to reject it by noting the literary texture of the poem. Kenney 1984, xx calls the anonymous poet *"doctus,* master of his craft". Gowers 1993, 46, Fitzgerald 1996, 390, and Hellmann 2004 carry on the fight against the realist scholars from the first half of the twentieth century.

5 Perutelli 1983, 18–35; Kenney 1984, xxvii–xl; Gowers 1993, 46–48. Cf. Thomas 1992 on the literary tradition behind Virgil's old Corycian man (*G.* 4.116–148).

6 Ross 1975, Perutelli 1983, 35, and Gowers 1993, 48 see parodic intent. Fitzgerald 1996, 398 has a more nuanced perspective: "... the detailed attention to this subject matter takes on its own weight and may unsettle the parodic intention". Kenney 1984, lii sees the attitude of urban readers that fantasizes about country life as the object of the satire.

7 What is Simulus' status? Kenney 1984, l and 41 n. 80 sees suggestions that Simulus was a slave building his *peculium*; Perutelli 1983, 75 n. 3 sees a freedman; Fitzgerald 1996, 390 n. 6 sees ambiguity but emphasizes the master-slave relationship between Simulus and the only other person to appear in the poem, Scybale.

8 All translations of the *Moretum* taken from Kenney 1984 with only an occasional revision.

9 Much of the produce Simulus grows in his garden is reserved for sale on market days and even when he has earned a profit on his sales, he resists the temptation to squander any of it on discretionary purchases (77–81). Kenney 1984, 41 suggests the money may be for Simulus' *peculium*, so he is not just a frugal Roman farmer, but a slave accumulating some savings of his own.

day (1): *iam nox hibernas bis quinque peregerat horas* ("Already the winter's night had completed its tenth hour ...").[10] The epic language should not distract us from the content of the verse: Simulus will wake up to the cold and dark. And sure enough, his first movements are to feel tentatively, again anxiously, for the few embers remaining from the previous night's fire (6–7):

sollicitaque manu tenebras explorat inertes
vestigatque focum, laesus quem denique sensit.

... with cautious hand groped in the blank darkness in search
of the hearth, which at length, painfully, he found.

Simulus knows he has found those embers in his dark room only when he experiences pain from burning himself. The latent comic frustration generated by Simulus' jerking his hand back from the fire should not overshadow the anxiety which the poet ascribes to Simulus with *sollicitaque manu* as he reaches blindly through the dark in search of that ember. This is not going to be an easy morning for Simulus.

Simulus' physical interaction with his environment remains the focus in the following verses when his next purposeful action is lighting his lamp (8–12):

parvulus exusto remanebat stipite fomes
et cinis obductae celabat lumina prunae;
admovet his pronam summissa fronte lucernam
et producit acu stuppas umore carentis,
excitat et crebris languentem flatibus ignem.

There remained a little piece of kindling in the shape
of a charred log, and the ash hid the glow of the hot
coals beneath. With his forehead bowed down low he
brought his lamp forward to the embers, teasing out
with a needle the wick, dry of oil, and awoke the
sluggish fire with repeated breaths.

The poet focuses his lens tightly on the process of lighting the lamp, a process which entails a nearly full body effort from Simulus, with his forehead close to the lamp, the movements (with hand and arm) directing the tool he uses to draw out the wick, and the vividly conveyed action of blowing to coax the fire to life.

---

10 Dehon 2018 on the winter's seasonal frame to the narrative, esp. 347: "En résumé, le poète qui nous a laissé le *Moretum* a lu les Géorgiques et les développements relatifs à la saison froide ont retenu toute son attention".

The image expands upon one in the *Fasti*, where Ovid's poor farmer Hyrieus bends down to revive the previous day's fire (5.507–508):[11]

> *ipse genu nixus flammas exsuscitat aura*
> *et promit quassas comminuitque faces.*

> He himself, on his knees,
> brings the flames to life with his breath, and brings out battered
> torches and chops them up.[12]

Perhaps we might see Simulus' existence differentiated from Hyrieus' in the emphasis on the number of breaths required to revive the former's fire.[13] Rather than just the humble detail of the poor man reviving his fire, the vivid image of the Simulus' repeated blowing, with cheeks puffed out, connotes struggle even with the smallest actions of his life. Simulus' careful physical efforts do not end with lighting the fire, because he then must keep lamp's halting flame from blowing out. As he moves through his room he shields the flickering light with his hand (13–15): *oppositaque manu lumen defendit ab aura* ("and he drew back, shielding the draughts with his hand ..." [14]). Thus we see that the poem named for the cheese and herb dish Simulus makes toward the end is in fact entirely derived from the experience of Simulus on what we might conclude is an average difficult morning in his life.

The following verses which narrate baking the bread, the produce in his garden, and creating the *moretum* are all a part of Simulus' experience, they serve to define him and his existence. And Simulus' experience in the world of the *Moretum* is more than anything else sensory. Beginning with the pain and anxiety over hunger in the opening ten verses, the poem abounds in descriptions of the stimulation of Simulus' senses as well as suggestions of the physical toll Simulus' work takes on his body: Simulus wakes up sore, he puts tools in various places, he sings and yells, he constantly does repetitive actions with his hands and arms, he carries heavy burdens, prefers certain flavors over others, he reacts to strong odors. The poem even alludes to impotence. While the *Moretum* does refer to vocal sounds Simulus makes, it features no direct speech. It is

---

11 The ember carefully buried so as to be available to light a new fire the following day derives from Hom. *Od.* 5.488–490.

12 Translation is taken from Wiseman and Wiseman 2011, 99.

13 Hyrieus' is a hospitality scene, like that of Baucis and Philemon, in which a mortal at first unknowingly hosts divinities. Readers also encounter the Corycian old man and Hecale through scenes of hospitality.

Simlulus' physical and more specifically "lower", non-verbal sensory interaction with his environment around which the poem builds its narrative.

Relying on any part of one's body to earn a living in Rome marked a person as low status. Elite Romans directed others to do physical labor; they did not do it themselves.[14] An occupation that involved a lot of physical contact through touch indicated a person of low status.[15] While *coloni* — the small-scale farmers so mythologized in Roman discourse — might be an exception, their highly physical occupation was not so much the focus of serious elite effort as the object of a fantasy of self-sufficiency and contented simplicity.[16] Status was not only encoded in visible physical activities; it could be detected by the nose too.[17] Having pronounced, untreated body odor, whatever the source, was a guarantee of a person's lowly station. The work and workers in industries like tanning or butchering were shunned.[18] Conversely, redolence of aromatic scents was a sign of wealth and power. Control of one's senses, especially the "lower senses" of odor and touch — both in terms of shielding oneself from unpleasant sensory experiences and covering up unpleasant odors from one's own body — were aspects of elite status. Writing about later European history, Classen has shown that self-defined "high" culture scorned the lower senses: "To achieve respectability, societies needed to be seen to have risen above the 'animal' life of the body".[19] Research into the sensory world of antiquity and the later eras in which scholarship of this type was first developed has focused on lived experience and the intimately related issue of the social construction of the senses.[20]

The *Moretum* certainly reflects the culturally contingent ideologies built around the senses, but what makes the poem unique is its intensive and sustained emphasis on Simulus' sensory experience. Reading the poem we can conclude from the exiguous resources available to him that Simulus is not wealthy and may in fact be enslaved,[21] but the *Moretum* most vividly dramatizes

---

14 Potter 1999, 171: "No members of the ruling classes could soil their bodies with the performance of banausic tasks: the ruling classes were those that oversaw the bodily labors of others". See also Fitzgerald 1996, 392–393 with nn. 12 and 13.

15 Lennon 2018, 128–130. On later European history, cf. Howes 2003, xi.

16 Garnsey 1980, 35.

17 Toner 2009, 129–133.

18 Toner 2009, 130.

19 Classen 2012, xii.

20 Corbin 1986 is groundbreaking in the field.

21 Unlike the poor Baucis and Philemon in *Metamorphoses* 8, a key touchstone for the *Moretum*, the poet makes explicit that Simulus does not have any meat hanging by the fireplace at

Simulus' poverty through the representation of his sensory world. The picture of Simulus the poem presents demonstrates in a more thoroughgoing fashion a "show don't tell" quality that the Ovidian and Virgilian antecedents do not.[22] The anonymous author not only refrains from providing direct speech, but also uses a light touch when it comes to providing descriptions of Simulus. The poem largely resists explicitly defining Simulus, offering only that he is an *exigui cultor ... rusticus agri* and a *pauper* (63 and 64). Simulus is not described as contented or happy.[23] It is his movements, actions, and reactions in the world that define him.

I have already touched upon some of the sensations the poet creates for Simulus in the opening verses, but a few more illustrations of the lower senses are to be made. It has been noted that in contrast to the idealizing images of the peasant farmer in Ovid and Virgil, Simulus is not contented with his lot in life.[24] But rather than providing an assessment of Simulus' life, the poet shows readers the effects of the unceasing demands of his survival. The description of his getting out of bed draws attention to the soreness he feels that morning (5): *membra levat vili sensim demissa grabato ...* ([he] rose and slowly lowering himself from his poor bed ...).[25] The adverb *sensim* adds crucial physical detail. Kenney translates it as "slowly", which is fine as it goes and in line with the primary definition in the *OLD*, but the word implies quite a bit, perhaps something more like "gingerly", because we are to imagine a person who is stiff (perhaps from that cheap straw mattress) and/or sore (perhaps from yesterday's labors) getting out of bed. The poet pushes on the root of *sensim, sentio*, to highlight again the challenging physical and sensory experience of Simulus at the start of his day.

Readers should not be surprised that Simulus's body may already be aching when he rises from bed, since the rest of the poem shows us him in constant often quite careful motion. As Simulus works the millstone to grind the grain for

---

all: *non illi suspensa focuum carnaria iuxta | durati sale terga suis †trunci vacabant ...* (55–56). See Kenney 1984, xxvii and 32–33. Cf. n. 9.

22 The Corycian old man (Virg. *G.* 116–148), Hyrieus (Ov. *Fast.* 5), and Baucis and Philemon (Ov. *Met.* 8.618–724) stand out in the background of the *Moretum* but see n. 5 for references to the deeper literary antecedents.

23 Cf. Virgil's Corycian old man (*G.* 4.132): *regum aequabat opes animis ...* and Ovid's Baucis and Philemon (*Met.* 8.633–634): *paupertatemque fatendo | effecere levem nec iniqua mente ferendo.*

24 Hellmann 2004, 12–13.

25 The exact meaning of *membra levat ... demissa* is "slightly ambiguous": Kenney 1984, 15, though the overall action of getting out of bed is clear. See also Perutelli 1983, 77.

his bread, the poet emphasizes the repetitiveness of the process and its effects on the farmer (26–29):

> *haec rotat adsiduum gyris et concitat orbem*
> *(tunsa Ceres silicum rapido decurrit ab ictu),*
> *interdum fessae succedit laeva sorori*
> *alternatque vices.*

> The right hand turned the round
> stone and kept it in swift incessant circular motion (the
> grain, crushed, ran from the rapid strokes of the
> millstones), and from time to time the left took over
> from her wearied sister and changed places.

This repetitive physical labor comes directly after another detailed description of Simulus as he moves his small heap of grain to the table on which he places his lamp, frees his arms from his clothing, and sweeps bits of stone off the millstone (19–23). Again, for much of the action the diction is elevated (*advocat inde manus operi, partitus utroque:* | *laeua ministerio, dextra est intenta labori* [24–25]), but that high register of the language contains precise descriptions of physical movement, which clearly takes a toll on Simulus' body.

Bodily exhaustion and even the possibility of a failure of at least some part of the body is suggested in the catalogue of vegetables in Simulus' garden. Amidst onions, chives, watercress, and endive is arugula, to which the poet adds an amusing bit of information (84): "or arugula which calls back flagging potency" (*et Venerem revocans eruca morantem*). The poet does not explicitly write that Simulus grows the arugula for himself. We should at least be open to the possibility that he grows it to sell to the enervated rich man who comes over in search of food (63). Still, Kenney, calling the inclusion of this verse as "a little unexpected", takes it to imply that Simulus may need chemical assistance for relations with Scybale, while other commentators take it to show that he is old.[26] But one other possible interpretation that follows from the interest the poem takes in Simulus' physicality makes this verse sit more comfortably with the portrait of this hard-working and worn-out farmer. The poet may be hinting that Simulus requires a boost from arugula because he has so thoroughly exhausted himself with his incessant labors that the physical component of sex does not match his desire. The detail about arugula should not surprise, since the poem includes so many other details about Simulus' exertions and the toll they take.

---

26 Perutelli 1983, 126 mentions but does not endorse either interpretation. Kenney 1984, 42 on Simulus' possible lack of attraction to Scybale.

Simulus' physicality and tactile experience remain present throughout the poem. Indeed, *manus* is the most frequently used noun in the entire work,[27] and passages such as the one where Simulus uses two fingers to wipe the edges of the bowl in which he mixes the *moretum* to form the concoction into a ball (114–115) show that precise description of bodily motion continues throughout the poem till the end. As Simulus grinds his bread, two of the very few references to the human voice[28] occur in the poem: Simulus sings a rustic tune (*rustica carmina cantat*) and shouts (*clamat*) to Scybale.[29] These references to Simulus' voice, which do not quote what was actually uttered, reinforce that it is the body at work and the use of the lower senses, not the vocal and sonic worlds, that are the greatest interest of the poem.

The fact that Similus' name means "snubnosed" should alert us to the significance of the sense of smell in the poem. A snubnose has strong associations throughout antiquity with satyrs, Socrates, and generally unsightly appearance.[30] Surely we can take for granted that Simulus is not meant to be a handsome specimen — though we are only inferring that Simulus' name refers to his appearance — but the example of Socrates' resemblance to snubnosed Satyrs, discussed at length in the *Symposium* and elsewhere, reminds readers that a snubnosed person's interior may be far more beautiful and productive than his exterior. The poem also explicitly shows Simulus' nose at work in his impoverished lifestyle. As he is mixing all the ingredients of the *moretum* together in a bowl, the odor is overwhelming (105–108):

> *saepe viri nares acer iaculatur apertas*
> *spiritus et simo damnat sua pandia vultu,*
> *saepe manu summa lacrimantia lumina terget*
> *immeritoque furens dicit convicia fumo.*

> Often the sharp smell went
> right up the man's spreading nostrils and with uptilted
> nose he passed judgment on his dinner; often with the

---

27 Évrard 1982, 562. Cf. Gowers 1993, 47. There are additionally two references to Simulus' fingers (*digiti*) at 86 and 114, and one reference to his palms at 47.

28 The cock's crow before dawn is the first sound within the poem. As first observed by Heinze 1960, 412–413, there is not a single word of direct or reported speech within the poem.

29 vv. 29 and 31. The two other references to the human voice are Simulus calling out to Skybale again at 91 and cursing at the pungent odor of his *moretum*, 108.

30 Socrates's snubnose: Plato, *Tht.* 143e; Socrates as snubnosed Silenus or Satyr: *Symp.* 215a-e, 216c-d, 221d-e, 222d. See Bradley 2015, 4 n. 12 with further references to importance attached to snubbed noses versus hooked noses.

back of his hand he wiped his streaming eyes and in a
fury cursed the offending reek.

Simulus puts a comically large number of heads of garlic into his *moretum* (87). The odor would be overwhelming as he mixed that amount of garlic into the dish. This must be a comic touch by the anonymous poet to exaggerate the topos of the idealized farmer's humble fare so beloved by Roman writers.[31] According to a topos, the poor ate more strong-smelling foodstuffs like garlic, the ingredient that dominates Simulus' *moretum*, so we should assume that in addition to emphasizing Simulus' sense of smell, the poem implies that he was malodorous too.[32] But the topos should not overshadow other aspects of the poet's technique and the coherence of the portrait of Simulus' life. He offers the humble farmer preparing a garlic dish, but with an unprecedented anatomical emphasis on the man's nostrils. The olfactory world of Simulus is not pleasing even to him. The further detail of Simulus' wiping his eyes with the back of his hand, presumably because it is the part of his hand that is not covered in the *moretum*, adds still more vivid detail to the sensory dimension.

Alongside odor, the poet briefly refers to Simulus' sense of taste too. While Simulus' *moretum* with its endive, onions, and rue would surely have a rather intense flavor profile — and would also render his breath overpowering — the poet does not linger on the sense of taste very long. We never see Simulus or Scybale consuming the bread or the *moretum*, let alone enjoying them, perhaps because the poem is more interested in showing Simulus relieve himself of anxiety about hunger rather than actually sating it. Nevertheless, he takes time to concoct something that will enliven the taste of his bread (52–54):

> *Simulus interea vacua non cessat in hora,*
> *verum aliam sibi quaerit opem, neu sola palato*
> *sit non grata Ceres, quas iungat comparat escas.*

> Simulus did not idly leave the time
> unoccupied, but went in search of another resource for
> himself, and so that bread alone should not be displeasing
> to his palate, he gathered food to add to it.

The poet creates the image of Simulus himself through detailed depiction of the farmer's physical and sensory experience. Simulus' existence is characterized by movement, frugality, aches, and pains. Some of those moments like Simulus

---

31 Horsfall 2001, 304. Cf. Höschele 2005, 249–251.
32 Gowers 1993, 290–298 and Horsfall 2001, 303–304 and 306.

burning himself are played for gentle laughs but we should see sympathy for Simulus in the portrayal of his frustrations. It may be impossible for a poem to be "realistic" but the humane tone behind the narrative draws readers into seeing themselves reflected in the poem.

Hephaestus at Work

While the poet sustains a level of detail that is unusual, at least in Latin literature, the image of a hardworking laborer whose body shows signs of that labor is an old topos. Unsurprisingly, the detailed image of the laborer hard at work, moving quickly between tasks, with specific focus on his limbs and his body's visible signs of exertion goes all the way back to the *Iliad*. When Thetis visits Hephaestus in Book 18, she discovers him hard at work (*Il.* 18.372–374):

> τὸν δ' εὗρ' ἱδρώοντα ἑλισσόμενον περὶ φύσας
> σπεύδοντα: τρίποδας γὰρ ἐείκοσι πάντας ἔτευχεν
> ἑστάμεναι περὶ τοῖχον ἐϋσταθέος μεγάροιο.

> She found him sweating as he turned here and there to his bellows
> busily, since he was working on twenty tripods
> which were to stand against the wall of his strong-founded dwelling.[33]

In this depiction of Hephaestus at work we see programmatic features that will recur in the *Moretum*. The god of fire is working on a project at the bellows, but more than any specific action, the language makes clear that he is exerting himself: sweating (ἱδρώοντα), bustling back and forth (ἑλισσόμενον), and hurrying to carry out a sequence of tasks (σπεύδοντα). The god's effort is as conspicuous as the wondrous products of his labor. Later when we see Hephaestus start to make the shield (472), Homer uses the active participle of σπεύδω again to show that rapid action is characteristic of the god's process of working.

All that hurrying between tasks produces visible physical effects, and the detail of Hephaestus sweating adds an earthy, perhaps even undignified, note to his characterization that is seen with only one other god.[34] While Homer does not repeat ἱδρύω, he returns the audience's attention to the god's sweaty exertions when Hephaestus prepares to greet Thetis (*Il.* 18.414–417):

---

33 All translations from the *Iliad* are taken from Lattimore 2011.
34 Only Hera when she is marshalling Greek forces in Book 4. On the role this image plays within the broader context of conceptions of Hephaestus, see Bremmer 2010.

σπόγγῳ δ' ἀμφὶ πρόσωπα καὶ ἄμφω χεῖρ' ἀπομόργνυ
αὐχένα τε στιβαρὸν καὶ στήθεα λαχνήεντα,
δῦ δὲ χιτῶν', ἕλε δὲ σκῆπτρον παχύ, βῆ δὲ θύραζε
χωλεύων.

Then with a sponge he wiped clean his forehead, and both hands,
and his massive neck and hairy chest, and put on a tunic,
and took up a heavy stick in his hand, and went to the doorway
limping.

To make himself presentable Hephaestus wipes away the visible effects of his work. Homer emphasizes the god's physicality, not just listing the grimy parts of his body that require cleaning, but adding adjectives that reinforce the theme: *massive* neck and *hairy* chest. Homer uses λαχνήεις only a few times in the *Iliad*, including his description of the Calydonian boar (*Il.* 9.548), implying that the god's physicality, perhaps impressive but certainly not beautiful, places him closer than his fellow Olympian gods to animals. Thetis' visit to his workshop reveals the wondrous things he can create, even if that effort produces some sweat and grime. Being a god, the effects of his labor are temporary, but visible nonetheless.

The passage of Hephaestus at work establishes at least one other paradigmatic aspect of representing the laborer at work that the *Moretum* reflects. The laborer's hands receive special attention. We already saw Hephaestus wipe his hands clean just above, but later in Book 18, again when he starts to work on the shield, Homer draws attention to Hephaestus' coordinated use of them (*Il.* 18.475–477):

αὐτὰρ ἔπειτα
θῆκεν ἐν ἀκμοθέτῳ μέγαν ἄκμονα, γέντο δὲ χειρὶ
ῥαιστῆρα κρατερήν, ἑτέρηφι δὲ γέντο πυράγρην.

And thereafter set forth
upon its standard the great anvil, and gripped in one hand
the ponderous hammer, while in the other he grasped the pincers.

In addition to the passage discussed above (26–29), the poet of the *Moretum* shows Simulus using both hands in concert again as he makes the *moretum* (98–100):

et laeva †vestem† saetosa sub inguina fulcit,
dextera pistillo primum fragrantia mollit
alia, tum pariter mixto terit omnia suco.

... and with his left hand
[he] wedged *the mortar* into his shaggy groin; his right
had first mashed the pungent garlic with the pestle,
then pounded everything so as to mix the juices evenly.

We see in both the *Iliad* and *Moretum* that it is the laborer's arms and his hands, used in concert, that are the fundamental instruments of his craft.

The Homeric template for a laborer at work might bear on the issue of tone in the *Moretum* too. The incongruity between the epic language and the seemingly trivial context of Simulus' life and deeds may also be a legacy of Homer's depiction of Hephaestus. Hephaestus was an anomalous divinity because of his disability and his day job as smith for his fellow gods, and Homer frequently includes an element of humor and mocking in his portrayal of the god. In Book 1 of the *Iliad* Hephaestus diffuses tension lingering from a quarrel between Zeus and Hera that ended with the king of gods threatening his wife with violence by drawing attention to himself as he takes on the role of cupbearer (1.571–600). The other Olympians burst out laughing at the sight of him serving their wine and then relax and enjoy the party. Homer adds a significant coda to the story (*Il.* 1.605–608):

αὐτὰρ ἐπεὶ κατέδυ λαμπρὸν φάος ἠελίοιο,
οἱ μὲν κακκείοντες ἔβαν οἰκόνδε ἕκαστος,
ἧχι ἑκάστῳ δῶμα περικλυτὸς ἀμφιγυήεις
Ἥφαιστος ποίησεν ἰδυίῃσι πραπίδεσσι.

Afterward when the light of the flaming sun went under
they went away each one to sleep in his home where
for each one the far renowned strong-handed Hephaistos
had built a house by means of his craftsmanship and cunning.

The image of Hephaestus contains the tension between his unusual appearance and his tremendous skill. The worker may not be pretty, in fact he may be downright ugly, and the process of his work might be dirty, but the product is meaningful and deadly serious. Homer's tone mirrors this by becoming outright comical but also by reminding his audience of who these laborers that appear out of place in epic are. So when the *Moretum* calls Simulus a *providus heros* (59) we should not insist on finding a single, parodic valence to the epithet. The context may be his breakfast, but the poem is about survival. Laughing too hard at the apparent incongruity between the epithet and the context of the farmer's life, we make the same mistake the Olympian gods do: of missing the talent underneath the exterior. The author of the *Moretum* can exploit the exemplum of Hephaestus in the *Iliad* to tell a seemingly minor story in an epic setting without turning the laborer who is the subject of the poem into a joke.[35]

Hephaestus' Roman equivalent makes a very brief, symbolic appearance in the *Moretum*. When Simulus bakes the bread, we see the god of fire at work (51–52):

> *dumque suas peragit Vulcanus Vestaque partes,*
> *Simulus interea vacua non cessat in hora ...*
>
> Meanwhile as heat and hearth were performing
> their functions, Simlulus did not idly leave the time
> unoccupied ...

Not quite Vulcan sweating at the forge, but a suggestive passing reference none-theless. The poet uses the epic register to elevate the process of baking the bread once again to create an apparent incongruity between language and con-tent. But what is being described? It is the very substance that will keep Simulus and Scybale alive for another day.

Scybale: The Ethnographic Gaze of the *Moretum*

Thinking in terms of Homeric epic's pattern-setting conventions may shed some additional light on the infamously anatomical description of Simulus' compan-ion Scybale and the poem as a whole.[36] The poet does not offer much context for Scybale or her relationship with Simulus. She appears to live with him, since she responds to his call as he works at the millstone, but where she was before that is not mentioned; perhaps she was sleeping in. Her legal status, like that of Simulus, is not something the poet dwells upon — scholars usually assume she is enslaved.[37] An allusion to the episode in the *Metamorphoses* that features the loving and pious couple Baucis and Philemon implies that Scybale and Simulus

---

35 Here a straight parodic reading of the poem like that of Ross or even Gowers fails to capture the breadth of the portrait of Simulus. It is not just the sustained attention of the poem that undermines the parodic reading as Fitzgerald 1996, 398 (cf. n. 6) points out, it is that represent-ing the craftsman with the inevitable physicality of his work often has a comic edge.
36 McCoskey 2012, 137–138.
37 Kenney 1984, xix; Fitzgerald 1996, 390 n. 6 and 402–403; Kennedy *et al.* 2013, 193, though Kenney 1984, li and McCoskey 2012, 137 are more cautious about determining her precise sta-tus.

are also a pair, though again the precise nature of the relationship is unclear.[38] However Scybale ended up with Simulus on that chilly morning, the poet uses four verses of the short poem to portray her as exotic. She is of African origin and in his description, the poet offers the most detailed portrait of an African from all antiquity (30–35):[39]

> *interdum clamat Scybalen. erat unica custos,*
> *Afra genus, tota patriam testante figura,*
> *torta comam labroque tumens et fusca colore,*
> *pectore lata, iacens mammis, compressior alvo,*
> *cruribus exilis, spatiosa prodiga planta.*

> ... from time to time calling for Scybale. She was
> sole caretaker, African by race, her whole appearance
> bearing witness to her native land, with tightly curled hair, swollen
> of lip and dark of complexion, broad chested, with breasts
> hanging slackly and flat belly, thin-shanked, with prodigiously
> large feet.

The detailed description of Scybale's appearance, the exoticizing objectivity of which is so distasteful today, extends the poem's already established technique of sustained graphic description of some aspect of its subject. The poet does not tell us anything explicitly about how Simulus looks, though very much about what he does.[40] But it is precisely the clinical description of Scybale that reinforces the connections between the Homeric epic tradition and the *Moretum*.[41] The passage reflects in miniature epic poetry's convention of ethnographic de-

---

38 *Moretum: erat unica custos* (30) and Ov. *Met.* 8.684: *unicus anser erat, minimae custodia villae*. The connection to Baucis and Philemon's goose is dehumanizing and may suggest her enslavement, but that is in keeping with the harsh gaze of the passage. See McCoskey 2012, 137–138. Horsfall 2001, 307 denies that their relationship is sexual, since the text makes no reference to it. Sex need not be referred to in a scenario in which an economically vulnerable or outright enslaved woman is living with a man; the ancient audience would simply assume it.
39 Snowden 1983, 10 with n. 37. Cf. Aubert 1999, 166. Haley 1993, 30–31 offers a translation of lines 30–35 that avoids stereotypes of African women.
40 Perutelli 1983, 75 and Laudani 2004, 12–13 offer the possibility that Simulus may also be of African origin, noting that his name recalls an ancient stereotypical feature of Africans (Xenophanes, D-K 16) and may even allude to the Ethiopian tribe of Simi mentioned by Diodorus Siculus (3.28.6).
41 Kenney 1984, 23 identifies literary descriptions of statues behind the portrait of Scybale. Aubert 1999, 166 sees an ethnographic perspective.

scription, beginning with the *Iliad* but developed most fully in the *Odyssey*.[42] Homer's ethnographic passages focus on difference from the narrator's expectations (*Od.* 9.105–112):[43]

ἔνθεν δὲ προτέρω πλέομεν ἀκαχήμενοι ἦτορ:
Κυκλώπων δ' ἐς γαῖαν ὑπερφιάλων ἀθεμίστων
ἱκόμεθ', οἵ ῥα θεοῖσι πεποιθότες ἀθανάτοισιν
οὔτε φυτεύουσιν χερσὶν φυτὸν οὔτ' ἀρόωσιν,
ἀλλὰ τά γ' ἄσπαρτα καὶ ἀνήροτα πάντα φύονται,
πυροὶ καὶ κριθαὶ ἠδ' ἄμπελοι, αἵ τε φέρουσιν
οἶνον ἐρισταφυλον, καί σφιν Διὸς ὄμβρος ἀέξει.

From there, grieving still at heart, we sailed on further
along, and reached the country of the lawless outrageous
Cyclopes who, putting all their trust in the immortal
gods, neither plow with their hands nor plant anything,
but all grows for them without seed planting, without cultivation
wheat and barley and also the grapevines, which yield for them
wine of strength, and it is Zeus' rain that waters it for them.

The negation in the passage makes clear not only what the Cyclopes do not do but also that the narrator understands their opposites as normal: mortals do hard agricultural labor for their food. Herodotus picks up on this tradition and extends the element of confounded expectations to wonders of all sorts.[44] Ancient ethnography tells us more about the narrator than the subject.

One additional feature of ethnographic passages especially in the historiographical tradition: they are often digressive, breaking up the primary narrative with interesting information about far-off or otherwise unusual peoples and places.[45] The pause in the narrative of making the bread to describe Scybale

---

42 *Iliad* 13.1–9 is often recognized as the first example of ethnographic writing in Homer. Haubold 2014 disputes the value of such a claim, arguing that the *Iliad* is already responding to an existing ethnographic discourse and is anyway far more interested in the difference between mortals and immortals than between individual human communities.

43 Malkin 1987; Dougherty 2001, esp. 6–11; Hartog 2001. Skinner 2012 pushes beyond the literary to show how ethnographic representation and its role in inventing and defining identity was omnipresent in Greek culture.

44 Munson 2001.

45 Caes. *BGall.* 5.12–16 and 6.11–28; Sall. *Iug.* 17–19; Tac. *Hist.* 5.2–10. Herodotus structured his entire narrative around the advance of the Persian empire through Egypt, north into Scythia, and then west into Greece. Herodotus provided ethnographic information about each people the Persians encountered, e.g., Cambyses attacks Egypt so Book 2 is filled with a description of

reflects the digressive aspect of the tradition. The description of an African woman with such emphasis on her visible appearance signals that the author of the *Moretum* is engaging with the tradition of ethnographic digression. While this miniaturized epic motif may not carry the humor that the incorporation of the topos of the frenzied laborer does, it offers insight into how to read the poem's emphasis on visible activity rather than speech, beginning with the principle that the poet is interested in describing difference. Scybale receives such a detailed description because she is deemed exotic. The poet focuses not on the familiar but on what his observer and expected readership would find unusual and worthy of comment. If we interpret the description of Scybale as a *mise en abyme* that offers a way to read the rest of the poem, we can put the unique focus on Simulus' sensory world into a new context. The world of the individual farmer that is worth literary commemoration is not the supposed contented and pious poverty of the Ovidian, Virgilian, and other earlier versions, but a non-stop, muscle-aching effort to provide for oneself: survival takes a toll on one's body.

Conclusion

> *eruit interea Scybale quoque sedula panem,*
> *quem laetus recipit manibus, pulsoque timore*
> *iam famis inque diem securus Simulus...* (*Mor.* 117–119)

> Meanwhile, Scybale, also active,
> dug out the bread, which Simulus joyfully received in his
> hands, and with the fear of hunger banished, and
> free from care for that day.

These verses coming just three lines from the end of the poem and bringing relief to Simulus' mind close the ring that was opened with Simulus' anxiety about his hunger back in the fourth verse (*tristia venturae metuens ieiunia lucis*). The language, especially *pulso timore* and *securus*, has strong philosophical resonance.[46] Simulus has defeated the emotion of fear and achieved an enviable

---

the geography and culture of Egypt. As Hartog 2001, 17 notes, even in the *Odyssey* it is precisely when Odysseus' nostos is delayed that he encounters other peoples.

46 E.g., Sen. *Ep.* 53.12–13: *Est aliquid quo sapiens antecedat deum: ille naturae beneficio non timet, suo sapiens. Ecce res magna, habere inbecillitatem hominis, securitatem dei* ("There is one thing in which the sage has an advantage over the god; for a god is freed from terrors by the

and elusive freedom from care for one day. This may not be the permanent equanimity of the *sapiens*, the Stoic wise man, but the poet is alluding to that idea. The physical sensation of hunger, the daily, unrelenting need to eat, and the burden this need exerts on Simulus' psychology are not trifles. This highly literary and learned poet builds the poem around that universal, basic aspect of human existence. The *Moretum* ultimately offers a triumph of human persistence and discipline that one might almost characterize as philosophical. Simulus remains at the mercy of forces outside his very limited control but he makes the most of what he can control.

A focus on the physical sensory experience of poor farmer Simulus enables us to interpret the poem from a fresh perspective. By defining so clearly Simulus' physical interactions with his environment we can see how the poet of the *Moretum* innovated within the tradition of the impoverished but honorable farmer so dear to earlier Latin and Greek poets. The graphic description of Simulus does not render the poem more realistic; in fact, it just further connects the poem to a literary tradition of the hard-working, frenetically moving laborer that goes all the way back to Homer's Hephaestus. That character also reflects the inherently comic nature of the laborer. His work may be divine, but it is still sweaty and undignified. We should not minimize the humanity of the *Moretum* because of the incongruity between the epic tone and the apparently mundane activity of Simulus on the morning depicted. The poem is about life and death, and the all-consuming work for survival. The focus on Scybale introduces a way of reading the entire poem that is centered on difference. Simulus, Scybale, and their incessant activity earn a place in this epyllion because their characterization is different from Baucis and Philemon, Hyrieus, the Corycian old man, Hecale, and the others. Simulus and Scybale's lives are hard and their only reward is living to struggle another day.

---

bounty of nature, the wise man by his own. What a wonderful privilege, to have the weaknesses of a man and the tranquillity of a god!"); cf. Graver 2007.

Paul Roche
Satire from the Margins: The Periphery in Persius' *Satires*

Abstract: This chapter examines the speaker's voice and identity in Persius' *Satires*; it seeks to illuminate the decentralized and marginal persona of the author. Persius often presents himself at the margins of society in terms of morality and taste, even terming himself *semipaganus*, a half-member of the *pagus* ("country community"), and thus belonging, at least in part, to the rustic community outside of Rome. However, by focusing on recurrent images of displacement in the *Satires*, this chapter highlights the fictive nature of much of this claimed social marginality. The precise nature of Persius' isolation can be seen as resulting from the poet's intellectual and aesthetic choices rather than his performed social status.

Introduction

In this article I consider the way in which the speaker's voice and identity are decentralized in the *Satires* of Persius. This position at the margins is intrinsic to Persius' satiric *persona* and is related to satire's normative dynamic of mocking elevated subjects from below. In her taxonomy of this phenomenon, Maria Plaza has argued that Persius idiosyncratically participates in the tradition of mocking from below in figurative terms, by variously inflating the objects of his satirical gaze, "seen in the absurdly big men, fat bodies and big poems" that attract his ire. She reads the speaker of these poems as defined by a flipside of the same image: as "things which will cure swelling and dissolve fat: decoctions, vapor, and acid".[1] Presently I revisit the manner in which Persius claims not so much a subordinate, but rather a peripheral position from which to make satirical attacks via the notion of his own poetic and social status, made visible to the reader despite his "autobiographical reticence".[2] I first argue that the marginal position claimed by the poet — his poetic, aesthetic and intellectual alienation from society's mainstream — is matched by a performed social isolation. This appears initially to be a consequence of the speaker's relatively lower-ranking social status, but it is grad-

---

1 Plaza 2005, 53–57 and 90–104; I quote Plaza from pp. 91 and 103.
2 See, e.g., Coffey 1989, 109–113.

https://doi.org/10.1515/9783111063942-005

ually revealed that he is an aristocrat, albeit one with limited power in society, whose bigotry and conservative anxieties regarding newly enfranchised citizens and morally corrosive foreign influences have placed him on society's fringes. I then argue that a recurrent suite of images suggesting temporal displacement and interiority help constitute the world of the *Satires*, and that these same images abstract and reflect the speaker's marginal position. In my discussion of the latter of these two suites of images, an important predecessor is Victoria Rimell's wide-ranging study of the inward turn in early imperial literature; I hope to show that Persius' attention to interiority pervades his collection and contextualizes his withdrawn viewpoint.[3] I shall often situate Persius' various claims and imagery against those of Horace's *Satires*.[4] This point of comparison, which is made striking by the strong continuities linking the two collections, consistently serves to clarify the more isolated position, the more extreme forms of deferral and displacement, and the more inwardly-turned stance that is characteristic of Persius.

Social Marginality

At the outset of the *libellus*, the speaker lays claim to a peripheral position which is expressed in images pertaining to two distinct groups: a tradition of celebrated poets, from which he excludes himself altogether, and an assemblage of villagers, a civic community, of which he claims only half-membership. In this way the prologue programmatically combines a poetic and social position at the margins; and this issue of the poet's alienation is one that will recur and develop throughout the collection (*Prol.* 1–7):[5]

> *Nec fonte labra prolui caballino*
> *nec in bicipiti somniasse Parnaso*
> *memini, ut repente sic poeta prodirem.*
> *Heliconidasque pallidamque Pirenen*
> *illis remitto quorum imagines lambunt*
> *hederae sequaces; ipse semipaganus*
> *ad sacra vatum carmen adfero nostrum.*

---

3 Rimell 2015.
4 On the importance of Horace for Persius, see Pers. 1.114–120 and for aspects this relationship, see, e.g., Rudd 1976, 54–83; Hooley 1997; Freudenburg 2001; and many of the essays in Braund and Osgood 2012.
5 The translations of Persius are adapted from and occasionally use Braund 2004. All other translations are my own.

I neither washed my lips in the nag's spring, nor do I remember sleeping on Parnassus' twin peaks, to come forth (hey presto!) a poet. I leave the Helicons and pale Pirene to those whose busts are licked by running ivy; it is as half-countryman that I bring my song to the rites of the poets.

Persius' opening claim of semi-isolation may be contextualized by various moments of programmatic self-fashioning in Horace, his most important poetic influence. Most directly, at *Sat.* 1.4.39–42 Horace had disavowed his inclusion among the poets on the criterion of his (and the satiric genre's) relatively prosaic hexameters.[6] Both Persius and Horace are positioning themselves against the higher genres, but Persius' more critical stance is clear from the comparison. Horace — however firmly his tongue is in his cheek — excludes himself from a category, "poet", that he presents as something good: *ingenium cui sit, cui mens divinior atque os | magna sonaturum, des nominis huius honorem* (1.4.43–44: "you may give the honor of this name to someone who has talent, an inspired mind and a voice suited to resound"). Furthermore, the issue of Horace's exclusion from this group had already been undercut by his counting himself as a poet earlier at 1.4.33, when he notes that all potential targets of satire hate "the poets", and it is flatly and plainly contradicted at the conclusion of the same poem, when Horace is again in the company of poets (*Sat.* 1.4.140–142):[7]

... cui si concedere nolis,
multa poetarum veniat manus, auxilio quae
sit mihi — nam multo plures sumus.

If you should refuse to concede this, a great band of poets will come to my assistance — because we're very much in the majority.

In contrast to Horace, Persius actively denigrates the poets by mocking their pretensions. He nowhere corrects or undercuts the opening image of his estrangement from a poetic community, and whenever else he uses the term *poeta* or *vates* in his collection, it is used of others, and in a disparaging context.[8] Persius' rejection of poetic traditions and his distancing of himself from "those whose busts are licked by running ivy" — that is, busts of celebrated poets that

---

6 See Gowers 2012, 162–163 for discussion.
7 Cf. Gowers 2012, 181 "as if from nowhere, the recluse mobilizes a multitude of poets, claiming solidarity with the group from whose number he had previously excluded himself [sc. at 1.4.40]".
8 Cf. *Prol.* 13; 1.34, 36, 68, 75; 6.1.

are set up in libraries[9] — can also be contrasted with Horace's programmatic lyric ambition to be added to — to be considered among — a canonical community of poets at *Carm.* 1.1.29–36. There the ivy of learned poets separates Horace from the *populus*, but it puts him in company with the gods (*dis miscent superis*), and his final wish is to be included within a community of former poets: *quod si me lyricis vatibus inseres,* | *sublimi feriam sidera vertice* (*Carm.* 1.1.35–36: "but if you'll insert me into the canon of lyric poets, I'll strike the stars with my uplifted head").[10]

Persius eschews full social inclusion by identifying as a *semipaganus*, a half-member of the *pagus* ("country community"): a term that may place him in the reader's mind at the margins of Rome's boundaries with its rural surroundings or at the margins of civic membership of a rustic community.[11] This pretence sits in contrast to Horace's projection of his gradual admission and inclusion in the *Satires*. This contrast is felt particularly clearly in the finale of *Satires* 1 (1.10.78–91). There Horace proclaims himself to be immune from the carping of four critics provided that his verses find acceptance from a large suite of discerning and appreciative friends, many of whom are of course also eminent literary figures: Plotius, Varius, Maecenas, Virgil, Valgius, Octavius, Fuscus, the Visci brothers, Pollio, Messalla and his brother, Bibulus Servius, Furnius, and "many other learned and wise friends whom I deliberately pass over". Persius in fact defines friendship as an essential element of Horatian satire (1.116–117): *omne vafer vitium ridenti Flacco amico* | *tangit* ("cunning Flaccus touches every vice in his laughing friend") and friendship is, of course, a major concern of both books of Horatian satire: *amicus, comes,* and their cognates appear 53 times in the *Satires*, and the poet's gradual integration into a community of friends within the circle of Maecenas is thematized as a kind of quasi-plot of

---

9 As is clear from Plin. *HN* 35.9–10; see Harvey 1981, 11; Barr and Lee 1987, 65; Kißel 1990, 83–85.

10 As commentators note, the keynote is struck by *inseres* (*OLD* s.v. 3c "to insert") as the equivalent of ἐγκρίνειν, "to admit/accept someone into a group": see Pfeiffer 1968, 206; Nisbet and Hubbard 1970, 15; Mayer 2012, 61. The imagery of the final sentence of Hor. *Carm.* 1.1 has been interpreted in different ways. Farrell 2007, 189–190 has argued that the image is of Maecenas inserting the book of Horace's odes "on a particular shelf or in a particular *capsa*, the one that hold the lyric poets": an image that would align closely with the image of Persius' prologue. Leigh 2010, 269–271 has suggested rather that the image is of Maecenas weaving the lyric poetry of Horace into a "garland" of poetry similar to that of Meleager.

11 See esp. *TLL* x/1.79.20–80.14 and cf. *OLD* s.v. *paganus* 1a "an inhabitant of a *pagus*, peasant, countryman" and 1b "the inhabitants of the low-lying districts of Rome"; on *semipaganus* see Harvey 1981, 11; Kenney 2012, 122; Roche 2012, 194–195.

Satires 1.[12] This emphasis upon social integration is much more muted in Persius, as we will see, but to make a preliminary point, friendship as a concept is much less visible in Persius: *amicus*, *comes*, and their cognates appear only eight times, and only four times are used in reference to Persius' friends. Although individual friends are intermittently visible in the collection — Macrinus, the unnamed and highly critical friend of *Satire 3*, his old tutor Cornutus, Bassus — there is nothing to compare with the social circle that admits Horace, who emerges as positively gregarious by contrast.

The notion of the speaker's social and poetic marginalization recurs throughout the collection of satires and is constructed out of different, often interrelated poses and aspects. Morality, taste, diction, and rhetoric are all frequently intertwined in the collection, and variously feed into Persius' claim upon a peripheral social position. In order to illustrate this, I shall consider Persius' claim to marginal status from four angles. Fundamental to Persius' social alienation is his poetic position at the periphery of contemporary tastes, where he is both rejected by and highly critical of the contemporary mainstream. Secondly, the speaker's social status, the position from which he speaks, is gradually revealed as a pretense: it develops from an unelaborated position as an outsider into a portrait of a conservative aristocrat whose intellectual inclinations have alienated him from a philistine mainstream. A third issue is the relative powerlessness of the speaker. Finally, we will consider his chauvinism which, as much as any socially-determined position, locates him at the margins of his world.

The poetic marginalization of Persius is fundamental to his self-representation in the *Satires*; it is both a cause and effect of his social marginalization. Throughout the collection, Persius develops an oppositional stance in relation to *vates*, a term reserved for high genre poets: their pretentions of poetic initiation, as we have seen above (*Prol.* 7), the dismal heroines who feature in their poetry (1.34),[13] and their grandiose diction (5.1–13). Although Horace does not use the term *vates* of poets, the same satirical target is carried over from Horatian satire, where elevated diction defines satire's *musa pedestris* by con-

---

12 Zetzel 1980; cf. Gowers 2012, 78: "*Satires* 1 is a paean to friendship and the desirability of acquiring and keeping non-related friends".

13 Bramble 1974, 104 called the two characters named by Persius, Phyllis and Hypsipyle, "professionally inconsolable heroines"; Persius' adjective *plorabile* ("dismal, lugubrious") describes both the inconsolability of these characters, as well as the sentimentality of the poems in which they appear: see Kißel 1990, 160.

trast.[14] It is characteristically Persianic to set this generic opposition in a more combative context and against the backdrop of his rejection by contemporary tastes. *Satire* 1 develops from this notion: Polydamas and the Trojan dames — Roman critics of Persius — prefer Labeo, a translator of Homer's *Iliad* (1.4–5).[15] Persius in turn is highly critical of contemporary taste: he labels Rome *turbida* (1.5), a term suggesting both her confusion (*OLD* s.v. 4) and her turgid excess in opposition to the refinement of Callimachean aesthetic ideals (*OLD* s.v. 2);[16] he laughs at her for her folly (1.12); and he mocks the kinds of effete, sentimental and tragic subject matter she favors (1.32–40). The mainstream taste celebrates smooth rhythm and stock material of the kind that Persius despises (1.63–90); he imagines a warm reception for poets writing *grande aliquid* ("something grand"), which is cast as social acceptance: a public recitation to a spellbound audience (1.15–21). This acceptance is withheld from him, since his own recitation is interrupted and derailed by hostile interlocutors (1.1–3), and he can only write satire for consumption by no contemporary audience, works that are to be buried in a hole (1.119–120).

Persius' position at the margins is a result of the conviction of his poetic principles: he claims not to fear praise but will not value it above all else (1.41–43, 44–49), he wants genuine rather than contrived material (1.90–91), and he despises poetry composed without effort and angst (1.106). In contrast to mainstream acceptance, Persius claims to desire a limited but discerning audience (1.120–126). This stance is distinct from and more extreme than the one we find in Horace's *Satires*. Horace claims that no-one reads his work and that he is afraid to read it in public (1.4.22–23), but this is because of a general hostility to the genre of satire that stems from a public who rightly fears being censured by it (1.4.24–25).[17] Likewise, Horace claims not to recite in public but, importantly, concedes that he is asked to give readings by his friends and that they press him hard to do so (1.4.73–74).

The poetic and aesthetic isolation that finds full expression throughout Persius' work is at first matched by the impression of a lesser if not lower ranking social status at Rome. In *Satire* 1 the speaker repeatedly refers to, or places him-

---

14 Cf. the characteristics described at Hor. *Sat.* 1.4.43–44 with Gowers 2012, 163 "H. contrasts his pedestrian, lowly writings ... with the inspired boomings of the epic or tragic *vates*".

15 The ancient scholiast (*ad* 1.4) claims that Labeo was an overly literal translator of Homer: see Clausen and Zetzel 2004, 5.

16 Cf. Hor. *Sat.* 1.1.60, 1.4.11 with Gowers 2012; Callim. *Hymn* 2.108; Wimmel 1960; Freudenburg 1993, 158–160; Stephens 2015, 98–99.

17 And as Gowers 2012, 159 notes, "the denial of readership is belied by [1.4.]91–3, where H. cites imagined criticisms of an earlier poem".

self in opposition to, the Roman elite without any indication of his own possible inclusion within that group. His observations at 1.30–40 of the *Romulidae*, the "descendants of Romulus", later labelled the *viri* ("the [great] men", in contrast to their guests 1.36, 38), are made firmly from the perspective of an outsider. Likewise, a lower social viewpoint is suggested by his critique of the *crudi proceres* (1.51–52: "engorged leaders") and stingy patrons (1.54) as much as in his apostrophe of oblivious patrons "of patrician blood" (*o patricius sanguis*) to tell them that they are mocked by their clients behind their back (1.61–62). At 1.81–82 the speaker seems to be alienated from the equestrians as well when he speaks of the ecstatic reactions of the *trossuli* to bad poetry: the word can describe young men of fashion (*OLD* s.v.), but it was also known as an archaic synonym for *equites*.[18] These details, in combination with the threat that the thresholds of the great (the *maiores*) may grow chilly towards Persius if he "scrapes delicate ears with biting truth" (1.107–110), are suggestive of a lower social position, dependent upon the patronage of the great families but nevertheless "punching up" against their vices.[19] This impression carries over in some detail in *Satire* 2: his observations of *bona pars procerum* ("a good number of our leaders") and the contrast struck between his authentic values and those of the descendant of great Messalla (2.71–72: *magni Messalae propago*) seem likewise to be views from below.

This first impression of the speaker's social status is transformed as the collection progresses. The speaker's offer to make sacrifice on behalf of the community of Rome at the conclusion of *Satire* 2 at least imagines a position for him at the center of Rome's religious community (2.71–75).[20] In *Satire* 3 it is revealed that he has a family estate and a richly stocked larder; his family has a stemma tracing their long genealogy back to its Etruscan origins and they enjoy equestrian status (3.24–29, 27–29, 74; cf. 6.57–60). In the same poem his friend reveals that Persius has studied philosophy, one hallmark of an aristocratic education (3.52–57),[21] and later teases him with the prospect of eating plebeian beet (3.113–114).[22] At the end of *Satires* 3 and 5 he is mocked for his philosophical

---

18 See e.g., Plin. *Nat.* 33.35–36; Kißel 1990, 220 with further references.
19 Cf. McNelis 2012, 252: "Persius, the self-characterized *semipaganus* who does not fully belong to his community, justifies (and perhaps even explains) the intense ferocity that characterizes his satire".
20 Roche 2012, 194–195.
21 See e.g., Bonner 1977, 85–87, 90–91 and 110; Morgan 2011, 504 and 509–510.
22 Bartsch 2015, 76–78 well explores the connotations and symbolism of the beet, although I take it that the friend is addressing Persius (following, e.g., Braund 2004; Barr and Lee 1987), not the *aegrotus* who dies in the bathhouse.

inclinations by a philistine majority, represented in both poems by a Roman centurion (3.77–87; 5.189–191). In *Satire* 5 more details accrete: he wore the *toga praetexta* and *bulla* as a youth, and his tutor was L. Annaeus Cornutus, a renowned Stoic philosopher who moved in the highest social circles of Neronian Rome.[23] As the collection closes, Persius is revealed as withdrawn on his Ligurian estate, protesting his equanimity regarding the *vulgus* ("the common people", 6.12) and those of inferior social origin (6.15: *orti peioribus*) and anxiously eyeing his own grasping heir, to whom Persius is a personal god of wealth (6.41–80). In fact, Persius has the money to produce a show of one hundred pairs of gladiators with gifts for the audience (6.48–51). In short, the speaker's marginalized position is revealed as a cultural and intellectual alienation from the mainstream, felt by a speaker who in social and financial terms sits comfortably within the upper echelons of society.

The financial power that Persius enjoys over his heir sits in contrast to a limited social power beyond his own family. As alluded to above, in *Satire* 1, immediately following on from his lambasting of effete tastes, Persius is warned that his satire will bring with it the possibility of rejection by the great at Rome (1.107–110): *vide sis ne maiorum tibi forte | limina frigescant* ("take care that the thresholds of the great don't grow cold to you").[24] Persius' response is an immediate capitulation (1.110–111): *per me equidem sint omnia protinus alba; | nil moror. euge omnes, omnes bene, mirae eritis res. | hoc iuvat?* ("Well then, as far as I am concerned, from now on, everything's fine. I won't stop you. Bravo all of you! Well done all, you're marvelous"). The petulance of the speaker's response — in which he acts as if a child warned off from defiling a shopfront (1.112–114) — does little to mask the position of social powerlessness that prompts it. It is in this context that Persius disowns the notion of outspoken invective against powerful contemporaries in the tradition of Lucilius, and makes clear that he will even avoid the more limited contemporary licence of Horatian satire (1.114–120):

---

23 On Cornutus, see *Vita Persi* 10–14.

24 Cf. Freudenburg 2021, 71 on Hor. *Sat.* 2.1.62: "The idea [is] that the poet's friendships will turn icy and that he will be socially frozen out". A key difference between Horace and Persius in these lines is that Horace risks being frozen out by a social group whose intimacy he has long enjoyed: cf. esp. 2.1.75–76, where envy will have to confess that Horace has "lived with the great" ("in the sense of being an intimate friend", Muecke 1993, 112). No such sense of social intimacy with the great is conveyed in Persius' version.

secuit Lucilius urbem,
te Lupe, te Muci, et genuinum fregit in illis.
omne vafer vitium ridenti Flaccus amico
tangit et admissus circum praecordia ludit,
callidus excusso populum suspendere naso.
me muttire nefas? nec clam? nec cum scrobe? nusquam?
hic tamen infodiam.

Lucilius ripped inot Rome — you Lupus, you, Mucius — and broke a molar on them. While his friend is laughing, the rascal Horace touches every fault in him and, once he's got in, he frolics around his heart, clever at dangling the public from his cleaned out nose. Am I forbidden a mutter? Not even in secret? Not even in a hole? Nowhere? Never mind: I'll dig a hole for it here.

It is not the case that Persius is "pretending momentarily to accept the warning to refrain from satire",[25] but that he positions himself as writing secretly, as adopting an even less publicly engaged form of satire than Horace, and he does this in the face of the potential social consequences of a more vigorous satirical attack. Persius' disavowal is made clear by Hor. *Sat.* 2.1.60–86, where Horace is similarly warned but resolves to continue to write satire against the powerful.

Persius' marginal position and relative powerlessness are partially shaped and sharpened for the reader by the chauvinism and bigotry of the speaker, which define him as clinging to Roman traditions perceived as being under threat from foreign influences and newly enfranchised citizens. In *Satire* 1, the speaker claims that the modern effete diction so favored by the mainstream of contemporary critics is a betrayal of paternal *mores*. The speaker quotes four lines of highly mannered contemporary poetry, which he introduces as *tenerum et laxa cervice legendum* (1.98: "[something] delicate and to be read with a lolling neck"); he immediately after observes (1.103–106):

haec fierent si testiculi vena ulla paterni
viveret in nobis? summa delumbe saliva
hoc natat in labris et in udo est Maenas et Attis
nec pluteum caedit nec demorsos sapit unguis.

Would these things happen if any vein of our fathers' testicle still lived in us? This emasculated stuff swims on the lips, on the surface of our saliva, and "Maenas" and "Attis" dribble out; it doesn't bash the desk or taste of chewed nails.

---

25 Barr and Lee 1987, 184.

Testicle does not merely convey a sense of normatively manly verve;[26] the nuance "witness" is also operative here:[27] modern speech takes place as if freed from the critical observation of one's ancestors. In contrast, Persius offers a number of models of praiseworthy styles of speech. In *Satire* 5.1–24, Cornutus celebrates Persius' diction in contrast to the empty bombast of tragic diction (5.14–16):

> *verba togae sequeris iunctura callidus acri,*
> *ore teres modico, pallentis radere mores*
> *doctus et ingenuo culpam defigere ludo.*

> You follow the language of the toga, an expert at the pointed juxtaposition, smooth with moderate utterance, wise at scraping pallid morals and transfixing fault with freeborn wit.

Ingenuus strikes at the same point as *testiculus patris*: Persius preserves a morally upright, native Italian mode of speech which is being marginalized by contemporary poetry and criticism. When Persius confirms Cornutus' description in the same poem, he says that he speaks *hortante Camena* ("with the Camena encouraging me", 5.21): that is, with the encouragement of a precisely identified *Roman* muse.[28] The explicit point is reprised in *Satire* 6 where Bassus is positively commended (6.3–4):

> *mire opifex numeris veterum primordia vocum*
> *atque marem strepitum fidis intendisse Latinae ...*

> Extraordinary craftsman at setting in verse the ancient elements of our speech and intensifying the male sound of the Latin harp ...

Here, as at 1.103–104, a claim on normative Latin masculinity reinforces the claim on the paternal tradition. Further aspects of Persius' back-footed chauvinism reveal themselves in his comments about luxury in which Italian products are corrupted by eastern additions (2.64–65):

> *haec sibi corrupto casiam dissoluit olivo,*
> *haec Calabrum coxit vitiato murice vellus ...*

> This [our own sinful human flesh] has polluted our olive oil by mixing in cassia, this that has misused Tyrian purple for dyeing Calabrian fleeces ...

---

26 Kißel 1990, 248: "männliche Ehre".
27 Cf. *OLD* s.v. *testis*[1] and *testis*[2]; Adams 1982, 67 "when used as an anatomical term, *testis* never wholly lost its literal sense [sc. "witness"] in the classical period".
28 Cf. Verg. *Ecl.* 3.59 with Cucchiarelli 2012, 222 *ad loc.*; Hor. *Sat.* 1.10.45.

The moral geography as well as the sentiment is brought over from Virgil's celebration of the simple blessings of country life; in each case a "pure" Italian product is corrupted by the admixture of foreign, eastern influences (*G.* 2.465–466):

> *alba neque Assyrio fucatur lana veneno,*
> *nec casia liquidi corrumpitur usus olivi*

White wool is neither stained by Assyrian dye nor is the use of clear olive oil corrupted by cassia.

The motif reaches its conclusion in Bestius' reported complaints about Greek intellectuals at Rome in Persius' *Satire* 6 (38–40):

> *"ita fit; postquam sapere urbi*
> *cum pipere et palmis venit nostrum hoc maris expers,*
> *fenisecae crasso vitiarunt unguine pultes."*

"That's how it is: since this emasculated know-how of ours arrived in Rome along with pepper and dates, the haycutters have spoiled their porridge with thick sauces".

Finally, Persius' defensive position at the margins of society is felt in his hostile comments regarding newly enfranchised citizens and in a more general social snobbery. The detail of the heart-attack victim's newly manumitted slaves — disdainfully labelled "yesterday's new citizens" — carrying his body out for burial is saved up for the punchline of the satirical sketch at 3.105–106.[29] *Satire* 5 contains an extended rant against the same social group: newly manumitted slaves have no sense of true freedom (5.73–75, 82–84) and they are themselves untruthful (*mendax*, 5.77). The Greek name given to the newly minted citizen, Dama (Δάμας, 5.76), though a common slave name, also reprises Persius' hostility to foreign influences under a novel heading: (cf. Hor. *Sat.* 1.6.38: *Syri, Damae aut Dionysi filius* "a son of Syrius, Dama or Dionysus"; on magistrate sons of freedmen from foreign backgrounds).[30] Indeed, when Persius coins the new citizen "Marcus Dama" he is in two words restating the contrast between native traditions and corrosive foreign influences familiar from his earlier satires.

---

29 Kißel 1990, 481–482 suggests that since these slaves are imagined as being manumitted by his will, they are brought to our attention as a party who stand to gain from the death
30 With Gowers 2012, 229 *ad loc.*; cf. Freudenburg 2021, 207 on Hor. *Sat.* 2.5.18: "The name was often used as a slur (in the sense "some lowlife") by persons of high birth in contemptuous dismissals of persons of servile origin".

Deferral and Imminence

Throughout the *libellus*, Persius' position at the margins of contemporary tastes and society is abstracted and reflected through a recurrent pattern whereby the present moment and fully realised states of being are continually deferred or displaced. He and a number of his characters are not just out of place, but out of time: alienated from the present moment, encumbered by the past or obsessed with the near future. We see this in an attention to liminal and deferred moments of time, in a speaker and characters who are unable to fully emerge from the recent past, in the potentially infinite deferral of self-interrogation and in delayed resolutions pertaining to the future.

The very beginning of the collection proper is displaced. Where does *Satire* 1 begin? The opening line, a quotation from Lucilius or a pastiche of Lucretius, is immediately interrupted by an unnamed, hostile interlocutor and the performance shudders to a halt (1.1–3):[31]

> O curas hominum, o quantum est in rebus inane!
> "quis leget haec?" min tu istud ais? nemo hercule. "nemo?"
> vel duo vel nemo. "turpe et miserabile!" quare?

> O the anxieties of humanity! How insubstantial are our affairs!
> "Who'll read that?"
> Are you talking to me? No-one for god's sake.
> "No-one?"
> Well one or two.
> "It's disgraceful and pitiful!"
> Why?

In the performative fiction of the poem (to whomever we attribute the quoted material), Persius is set to recite *someone else's poetry* and is baited by another voice into a diatribe on contemporary poetic tastes. We may compare this strategy with the immediacy of Horace's first satire, where the speaker launches into his diatribe on *mempsimoiria* at once, in his own voice, in direct address to a named interlocutor and with "no context or preamble" (*Sat.* 1.1.1–3):[32]

> Qui fit, Maecenas, ut nemo, quam sibi sortem
> seu ratio dederit seu fors obiecerit, illa
> contentus vivat, laudet diversa sequentes?

---

31 See Zetzel 1977; Sosin 1999.
32 Gowers 2012, 62.

> How is it the case, Maecenas, that no-one lives content with that lot that design granted or fortune cast in his way, and rather praises those pursuing different courses of life?

Persius' false start sits in even starker comparison with the conversational opening of Horace *Satires* 2. Here the speaker is addressing an interlocutor by name and openly inviting their comment (*Sat.* 2.1.4–5): *Trebati | quid faciam? praescribe,* ("Trebatius what am I to do? Tell me what to do").[33] Horace's rhetorical move in *Sat.* 2.1 is programmatic for his collection, since dialogue is the main narratological strategy of *Satires* 2.[34] This is not the case in Persius, who will have dialogue as a structuring principle only again in *Satire* 3, and even the pretense of a real interlocutor in *Satire* 1 is destroyed at line 44 when the speaker admits he has invented the other voice. Moreover, the opening remarks of both Horace's *Satires* 1.1 and 2.1 directly announce the subject matter of their poems: discontent with one's lot, and the decision to write satire. In Persius, *o curas hominum! o quantum in rebus inane* does not declare the topic of its poem, however much morality and aesthetics are intertwined in the diatribe, and however appropriate the allusion proves ultimately to be.[35] The lines which follow swerve away from contemporary morality, and the exchange at the poem's outset defers Persius' monologue until line 3, his diatribe against contemporary poetry until line 5, and the beginning of his exposition until line 13.

A similar sense of deferral is revisited at the beginning of *Satire* 3. There the speaker is berated by a friend for sleeping off a hangover well past the new day's dawn. The poem begins with Persius remarking upon his own behavior (3.1–3):

> *Nempe haec assidue: iam clarum mane fenestras*
> *intrat et angustas extendit lumine rimas.*
> *stertimus, indomitum quod despumare Falernum*
> *sufficiat, quinta dum linea tangitur umbra.*

> So I guess this is how it is now: already the clear morning enters through the shutters and lengthens the slender cracks with light. We're snoring enough to stop unmixed Falernum foaming, while the shadow touches the fifth line.

---

33 *OLD* s.v. *praescribo* 5 "prescribe", i.e., a course to be followed: see Muecke 1993, 102; Freudenburg 2021, 56.

34 Muecke 1993, 99: "the predominant structural mode"; Freudenburg 2021, 49: "the main new tactical approach of the book".

35 See Sosin 1999.

This sleeping-in is quickly cast as a deferral of literary activity, since Persius' panicked response to his friend's reminder of the hour is to attempt to write. He calls out for slaves but finds no-one present; he then collects his book, parchment, paper, and pen before the attempt is foiled by his own whining about the quality of his ink (3.7–14). That we should associate Persius at his desk with the composition of satire (3.19: *tali studeam calamo?* "how can I study with such a pen?") is suggested by the black cuttle ink (*sepia*) he uses, since it is made a metaphor in Horace of satirical malice (*Sat.* 1.4.100–101: *hic nigrae sucus lolliginis, haec est | aerugo mera* "this is the ink of the black cuttle fish, this is unadulterated poison").[36] The lecture on his dissolute lifestyle and the madness of not availing oneself of philosophy's help — the core subject matter of the poem (19–106) — is delivered to Persius in this imminent state of composition. The setting decisively swerves away from the model of Hor. *Ep.* 2.1.112: *prius orto | sole vigil calamum et chartas et scrinia posco*, ("awake before sunrise I demand a pen, paper and holders"). That Persius is out of step with the present moment is pointedly reprised when his friend tells him at 3.58–59, in a richly allusive accusation: *stertis adhuc laxumque caput compage solute | oscitat hesternum dissutis undique malis* ("you are still snoring and your head, lolling on its loose hinge, yawns yesterday's yawn with your jaws open wide"). Here Persius' sleeping-in revisits the criticism of Hor. *Sat.* 1.3.18 where the inconsistency of Tigellius is illustrated by similar behavior: *noctes vigilabat ad ipsum | mane, diem totum stertebat* ("each night he would stay awake until dawn, he would snore the whole day through").[37] The context further suggests Persius as an ersatz version of Virgil's Silenus — another learned poet figure sleeping off a hangover and needing to be coaxed into producing verse — at *Ecl.* 6.14–15: *iacentem, | inflatum hesterno venas, ut semper, Iaccho* ("lying, his veins, as always, inflated with yesterday's wine").[38] Perhaps most plainly, the moral danger of being loaded down by yesterday had already been made clear in Horace's second book of *Satires* (2.2.77–79):

---

36 Cf. the appearance in Hipponax's iambics of the cuttle fish's ὑπόσφαγμα, a word that scholiasts understood as referring to its ink (Ath. 7.324a).

37 One positive contrast of Persius' indolence as expressed in *stertis* is that it contrasts him with the victims of *avaritia*, who are roused from their snoring to pursue financial gain at 5.132.

38 The ancient scholiast (*ad* 3.59) had already made the connection: see Clausen and Zetzel 2004, 83. On Virgil's Silenus as a poet figure, see Clausen 1994, 175–177. The implicit comparison of Persius and Virgil's Silenus had been foreshadowed in the pastoral details of 3.6 and in the comparison of his splitting headache and the braying of Arcadian sheep at 3.9.

corpus onustum
hesternis vitiis animum quoque praegravat una
atque adfigit humo divinae particulam aurae.

The body loaded with yesterday's vices drags down with it the mind and nails to earth a small bit of its divine spirit.[39]

The theme of temporal displacement is developed further in more general terms in Persius' *Satire* 5 in the potentially infinite deferral of self-interrogation (5.64–72):

petite hinc, puerique senesque,
finem animo certum miserisque viatica canis.
"cras hoc fiet." idem cras fiet! "quid? quasi magnum,
nempe diem donas?" sed cum lux altera venit,
iam cras hesternum consumpsimus: ecce aliud cras
egerit hos annos et semper paulum erit ultra.

Seek from here [Cleanthes], boys and old men alike, a fixed goal for your mind and resources for your wretched grey hair. "I will tomorrow." It will be the same thing tomorrow! "What? I suppose you are granting a day as if it is a great thing?" But when that next day's light comes, we have already used up yesterday's tomorrow: look, another tomorrow spends these years and will always be just out of reach.

The collection as a whole is prone to more radical disruptions and dislocations of time as well, as when *Satire* 4 presents itself as occurring in fifth century Athens, or *Satire* 6 belatedly reveals its temporal setting as 40 CE, and the immediate aftermath of Caligula's German campaigns.

This notion of time's deferral, displacement and dislocation is part of a larger thematic attention to imminent states of being in which the speaker's position is often implicated. Persius' world often exists in anticipation or sits on the threshold of existence. We can see this in its imagery of eternal expectation, such as the never-ending projections of the sheep-farmer (2.50–52):

"iam crescit ager, iam crescit ovile,
iam dabitur, iam iam"; donec deceptus et exspes
nequiquam fundo suspiret nummus in imo.

---

39 See Freudenburg 2021, 97 *ad loc.* for the philosophical contexts. Seneca revisits the theme at *Ep.* 122: cf. esp. the opening scene at 1–2 and the moral at 3: *hos tu existimas scire quemadmodum vivendum sit, qui nesciunt quando?* ("Do you think these men know how to live who don't know when to live?").

"Now the estate is increasing, now the sheepfold is increasing, now my prayer will be granted, any time now ..."; until deceived and hopeless, a single coin sighs in vain at the bottom of his coffers.

We can see it in the notion of life moving without direction, as when Persius' friend asks him: *est aliquid quo tendis et in quod derigis arcum?* ("Is there something you are aiming at and at which you are stretching your bow?" 3.60). This last accusation may pull against the notion that Cornutus' instruction gave Persius direction when he found him at life's crossroads (5.34–35):

cumque iter ambiguum est et vitae nescius error
diducit trepidas ramosa in compita mentes.

When the path was uncertain, and inexperienced ignorance of life splits trembling minds at the branching crossroads.

There are clearly two points of view on Cornutus' influence, even within *Satire* 5. Persius himself will claim that Cornutus had straightened him out at this formative moment in his life (5.37–40), but the friend has already cast the adult Persius as soft wet mud that is *still* (*nunc nunc*, "now, now") urgently in need of being shaped on the wheel (3.23–24).

The reader encounters the same phenomenon in the imminence of speech, as when *Satire* 5's interlocutor, Cornutus, reprises *Satire* 1's false start by interjecting (5.5–9): *quorsum haec? aut quantas robusti carminis offas | ingeris, ut par sit centeno gutture niti?* ("Where is this heading? Or what great lumps of solid song are you heaping up that need a hundred-fold throat to struggle with?"). The interjection develops into a lecture on appropriate speech which elicits a response from Persius (5.19–29) that further delays the poem's interrupted beginning.

Interiority

An abiding attention to interiority also contextualizes the peripheral position of the poet. Throughout the collection, inner spaces — inner rooms, places inside the human body, locations that are hidden or submerged under the surface — are made to be indicative of good and bad moral qualities, and this provides a backdrop against which Persius intimates an exceptional status for himself by comparison with a general moral corruption. We will see that these are not in themselves loaded positively and negatively but as arenas of moral competition in which Persius can prove or disprove exemplary behavior.[40]

A negatively loaded group of images associates inner spaces with hidden vice and hypocrisy. In *Satire* 2, the speaker describes the morally reprehensible desires for which many people secretly pray while hidden from view and out of earshot within temples. Macrinus is exceptional because he does not entreat the gods with prayers that can only be uttered in private: disgraceful prayers which can only be offered to the gods in confidence from a secretive censer (*seductis ... divis | tacita ... acerra*), as is the practice of the majority (2.4–5). The poet develops the image by describing nefarious prayers as muttering and low whispering that takes place inside temples; the true moral challenge is to live *aperto ... voto* (2.6–7: "with one's prayers on display"). Inner guilt is described at various points in the collection. When his friend upbraids the dissolute Persius in *Satire* 3, he offers the negative example of Natta, whose vices have so overwhelmed him that a rich layer of fat has encased his liver and his guilt is described metaphorically as a body of water into which he has sunk so deeply that he can no longer make bubbles on the surface (3.32–34). At 3.42–43 a paradigm of abandoned *virtus* turns pale inside (*intus | palleat*) at the thought of a transgression that is unknown to his wife beside him (3.42–43). Inner spaces can also act as the locus for vices' consequence, as at 3.98–106 where a gourmand who repeatedly demands to be examined medically but ignores both his doctor's advice and the bodily symptoms of his malaise withdraws to the baths where he suffers his heart attack.

It is against these negatively loaded images that Persius claims an interiority pointing to authenticity and inner virtue. As *Satire* 2 ends, true values are marked as residing within, and they are claimed by the speaker as his own sacrifice (74–76):

> *compositum ius fasque animo sanctosque recessus*
> *mentis et incoctum generoso pectus honesto.*
> *haec cedo ut admoveam templis et farre litabo.*

> A sense of justice and morality arranged within the spirit, the mind's recesses blameless, and the heart steeped in noble honor. Come now let me bring these forth to the temples and I shall make a worthy sacrifice with grits.

---

40 A related suite of images links the interior of the human body to poetic production, a well-studied aspect of the *libellus*: see e.g., Reckford 1962; Bramble 1974; Bellandi 1996; Barchiesi and Cucchiarelli 2005, 216–219; Bartsch 2012 and 2015, 17–25; Dinter 2012.

This imagery of the acceptable sacrifice further chimes with Persius' claim to be a priest bringing his poetry as an offering to the Paganalia at *Prol.* 7 (*ad sacra vatum carmen adfero nostrum*). In *Satires* 3 and 5, the image of ringing truly or falsely repeatedly features as a measure of authenticity: his friend critiques Persius for ringing falsely at 3.21–22, but Persius trusts Cornutus to tap his soul, like a mason would a wall, in order to determine whether it rings "solid" or not at 5.24–25. A key question for new citizens is whether they have the skill to distinguish appearance from reality, with the former cast as the false ring of gold overlaid on copper (5.105–106). A novel take on the imagery of inner-authenticity is the Stoic convert who still holds on to his former beliefs, cast as keeping his old skin, and hiding a cunning fox within his vapid heart (5.114–115). The image of a morally-positive interiority finds prominence in *Satire* 4, when Socrates castigates society because no-one attempts the decent into one's self (4.23), a sentiment that is reprised at the end of his speech in the Delphic travesty "spit out what isn't you" (4.51), a notion revisited at 5.129–130 when we are told that masters are born inside (*intus ... | nascuntur domini*). In *Satire* 5 the true friendship between Persius and Cornutus is guaranteed by their private communication and the genuine feeling that reside within the poet (5.21–29):

> secrete loquimur. tibi nunc hortante Camena
> excutienda damus praecordia, quantaque nostrae
> pars tua sit, Cornute, animae, tibi, dulcis amice,
> ostendisse iuvat. pulsa, dinoscere cautus
> quid solidum crepet et pictae tectoria linguae.
> hic ego centenas ausim deposcere fauces,
> ut quantum mihi te sinuoso in pectore fixi
> voce traham pura, totumque hoc verba resignent
> quod latet arcana non enarrabile fibra.

> We are speaking privately. Now with the Camenae encouraging, we offer you our heart to be scrutinized and it pleases me to show you how great a part of my soul is yours. Tap it: you are wise at discerning what rings solidly from the plaster of a painted tongue. Now I would dare to demand one hundred throats so that with pure voice I may draw out how much of you I have fixed within the recesses of my heart, and so that my words might unseal everything that lies, unable to be spoken, in the hidden fiber of my organs.

Here morality and poetry are mixed. Cornutus has just corrected the poet for the turgid and overblown expressions of higher genres with which he opened the poem, and instead recommends to Persius "the language of the toga," figured as consisting in sharp juxtapositions and moderate register (*modico ... ore*) and given an explicitly moral function (5.15–16): *pallentes radere mores | doctus et ingenuo culpam defigere ludo* ("expert at scraping pallid morals and skewering guilt with freeborn wit").

To end at the beginning, in *Satire* 1 Persius two dominant modes of interiority, moral and poetic, are established in quick succession, when the speaker links poor contemporary tastes with an aversion to introspection (1.5–7):

> *non, si quid turbida Roma*
> *elevet, accedas examenve improbum in illa*
> *castiges trutina nec te quaesiveris extra.*

> If deranged Rome should diminish something, don't draw near or chastise the inferior balance in those scales, and don't search outside yourself!

Whether we take the final command as "take outside opinion on the matter", "search for yourself outside", or as translated above, as an exhortation to self-examination,[41] the fundamental message is that aesthetic judgment should flow from an inner conviction, not from the consensus of a corrupted peer group. Soon after, Persius offers us a generalized image of poetic composition at Rome 1.13: *scribimus inclusi, numeros ille, hic pede liber* ("we write, shut away from view, some in verse others in prose"). The first-person plural is inclusive: Persius and all authors write like this.[42] The distinction between the marginalized position of the satirist and the warm critical reception of his foils lies in the manner of distributing their compositions. His target will declaim their works to the public from a high seat (1.15–17). The satirist himself — in contrast to both contemporary public recitation and to the outwardly-turned practices of Lucilius and Horace — will famously write satire to be hidden away (1.119–120):

> *me muttire nefas? nec clam? nec cum scrobe? nusquam?*
> *hic tamen infodiam.*

> Is it forbidden for me to mutter? Not even secretly? Not even in a hole in the ground? Nowhere? And yet I shall bury it here.

---

41 Cf. Barr and Lee 1987, 68; Kißel 1990, 120–121.
42 See Rimell 2015, 4 and 188–189.

Conclusion

Persius' claim upon a defensive position at the fringe of society is basic to his *persona* and the project of his *Satires*. The gradual revelation that his estrangement from society results from cultural and intellectual choices, prejudices, and anxieties rather than his social status and resources, sharpens both the conservative moralizing contours of his *libellus* and his professed commitment to an Italian tradition of speech, appropriate for satire and driven to the periphery, in his view, by decadent contemporary tastes and foreign cultural influences. The speaker's position at the social and cultural margins of the world he observes is reflected variously in other images of displacement and liminality: he and the objects of his gaze are variously out of step with the moment, and authentic arenas of evaluation are figured as being physically hidden away from sight. These decentralising pretences are in many ways a perfect match for the difficult idiolect of his *Satires*, for its dense concoction of language and the mutable, associative, evasive imagery that so often estranges his reader from its precise meaning. Language, image, and *persona* all work together in complimentary ways to create the distinctive experience of coming to grips with Persius' *Satires*, in which a speaker at the margins, out of step with time and inwardly-turned, gives voice to the obscure and inexpressible secrets hidden deep within him in a decoction of language to be buried in a hole in the ground.[43]

---

43 Cf. Pers. 5.28–29; 1.125; 1.120; 1.2–3.

Christopher Star
Crime and Punishment: Law and Marginality in Petronius' *Satyrica*

Abstract: This chapter examines the role of law in the surviving fragments and possibly in the lost opening sections of the *Satyrica* as a means of shaping the chaotic world of Petronius' novel. The text functions around Encolpius' status as a criminal, who has broken both human and divine laws, and one who, from time to time, shows awareness that his crimes require him to flee from respectable society as well as the various marginal settings in which he finds himself. However, the role of law in the *Satyrica* is not limited to Encolpius' crimes as the surviving text is also concerned with legal education, the law of slaves, and the law of testamentary bequests. Despite the often exaggerated and subverted descriptions of these practices, their presentation in the text may also lead the reader to consider their function in their world.

Introduction

Petronius' *Satyrica* is a uniquely chaotic text. Throughout the surviving fragments, chaos does not risk intruding upon order. Rather, it is just the opposite: order exists on the margins and threatens to burst in upon the chaos. In this work marginalized characters are not minor figures who threaten the stability of the world of text. The *Satyrica* is set in a provincial demimonde populated by slaves, freedmen, rogues, and legacy hunters.[1] The narrator, Encolpius, has committed several crimes, and admits that he is living "outside of the laws" (125.4). Other characters do not view the law as an objective site of authority but claim that justice is for sale (14.1–2, 137.9). The law can also be misused to undermine family connections and get rich quick, as demonstrated by the legacy hunters in Croton. The text's focus on outlaws and the characters' negative view of the law goes against the typical Roman self-aggrandizing view of bringing law and order to the world.[2] Nevertheless, the law, in various forms, plays a central and complex role throughout the *Satyrica*.

---

1 As Slater 1990, 2 notes, the *Satyrica* "plays itself out in a marginal world".
2 E.g., referring to Octavian/Augustus: Virg. *G.* 4.562 (*per populos dat iura viamque adfectat Olympo*, "he bestows laws on nations and pursues the path to Olympus"), and Ovid *Met.* 15.832–833 (*pace data terris animum ad civilia vertet | iura suum legesque ferret iustissimus*

https://doi.org/10.1515/9783111063942-006

The goal of this chapter is to demonstrate some of the ways in which law shapes the chaotic world of the *Satyrica*, both in the fragments that survive, and possibly in the lost opening sections. It appears that Encolpius has committed several criminal acts against human and divine law. The text functions around Encolpius' status as a criminal in need of expiation and one who is, at least occasionally, conscious that his crimes require him to flee from respectable society and into the various marginal settings in which he finds himself. Yet Encolpius' crimes, which likely include theft, murder, and profanation of a temple and/or divine rites, do not represent the limits of the roles given to law in the *Satyrica*. The surviving text is concerned with legal education, the law of slaves, and the law of testamentary bequests. These practices are often subverted and portrayed in an exaggerated and surreal way, but their presentation in the text may also encourage readers to consider how these forms of law work in their world.[3]

The study of law and literature is particularly helpful for investigating marginality in texts for the simple fact that law is a key force in creating social margins.[4] The law determines the lines between slave and free, as well as those between respectable citizens, who seem to make up the core of a society, and the outcast criminals who exist outside of it. The power of law to cast people into the margins is central to the surviving portions of the *Satyrica*.[5] On a more general level, questions of law are also particularly relevant if we ascribe this text to Tacitus' Petronius, who likely was well-versed in law and forensic rhetoric as part of his early education. Law would also play a key role in Petronius' position as proconsul in Bithynia, consul in Rome, and finally as Nero's "judge

---

auctor, "when peace has been bestowed upon all lands, he shall turn his mind to the rights of citizens and as a most righteous jurist will promote the laws"). See also Abdy and Harling 2005 on coins of Octavian/Augustus dating to 28–27 BCE with the inscription, "He restored to the Roman people their laws and rights". Seneca grants Nero a similar role at the start of his principate (*Clem* 1.1.5).

3 As Bakhtin 1981, 58 notes, "Laughter proved to be just as profoundly productive and deathless a creation of Rome as Roman law". The *Satyrica* brings laughter and law together.

4 See Nussbaum 1995 and Posner 2009 on law and contemporary literature. On law in Greek and Roman life, see Crook 1967; Schiavone 2012. For examples of explorations of law and literature in classical texts, see, e.g., Scafuro 1997 on comedy; Hall 2014 on Cicero and legal drama; Ziogas 2021 on Ovid.

5 Another avenue for the study of the *Satyrica* and the law is via the censorship that has been part of its reception. See Onelli 2014 on early modern Italy, and Briggs 1999 and Glass 2017 on the obscenity trail in the early 1920s.

of good taste" (Tac. *Ann.* 16.18: *elegantiae arbiter*).[6] In addition, Petronius' contemporary, Seneca the Younger was also interested in re-evaluating the role of law in relation to the self (*De ira* 3.36) and the emperor. Claudius' abuses of the law are a key theme of the *Apocolocyntosis*. Seneca discusses Nero's relationship to the law throughout *De clementia*. While Seneca considers the role of law with respect to philosophers and emperors, Petronius by contrast uses the law as a force to shape the marginal world of the *Satyrica*.[7] The novel demonstrates how various avatars of law both construct the lives of its characters and are often manipulated by them.

Lost Chapters: Encolpius' Original Status and Crimes

As is well known, only a small portion of the original text has survived. Although the surviving fragments, and possibly the entire novel, function around Encolpius' status as a fugitive from human and divine law, we do not know the specific nature of Encolpius' crimes that are alluded to in the extant fragments. We will treat the references to Encolpius' transgressions below, but first it is necessary to consider the ancient testimonia on how the *Satyrica* may have begun and concluded.

Using ruses and resorting to crime to avoid poverty seems to be part of Encolpius' mode of living. The *Satyrica* may have begun with Encolpius engaging in an elaborate means to live off the largess of others. We must leave the fragmented world of the extant text and briefly consider two late antique reports that may offer clues to the beginning and ending of the novel. The surviving portions of the *Satyrica* likely contain parts of books fourteen through sixteen. The *Cena* likely represents the bulk of Book 15. These portions relate Encolpius' stay in the Bay of Naples, his travels down the coast of Italy, eventual shipwreck, and journey by land to Croton in southern Italy. It is conjectured that the entire novel may have extended to twenty or twenty-four books, if it was ever completed. Scholars also conjecture that the story began in Massilia (modern Marseille) and related Encolpius' journey southeast through Italy and concluded in Lampascus (in modern Turkey), the cultic home of Priapus. Presumably,

---

6 The *OLD* (*arbiter* 2) notes that an *arbiter* is typically granted more sway in deciding cases and making decisions than a *iudex*.

7 On the links between Seneca and Petronius, see Star 2012.

the book concluded with Encolpius finally expiating the wrath of Priapus once and for all. This narrative trajectory is based on a passage from the mid-fifth century poet Sidonius Apollinaris in which he praises the eloquence of Cicero, Livy, Vergil (*Carm.* 23.145–146) and "you, Arbiter, worshipper of the sacred stump in the gardens of Massilia, equal to Priapus of the Hellespont" (23.155–157 = Petron. fr. 4: *et te Massiliensium per hortos | sacri stipitis, Arbiter, colonum | Hellespontiaco parem Priapo*).[8] Another ancient witness provides more information about what may have happened in Massilia.

In his commentary on *Aeneid* 3.57 (*auri sacra fames* "accursed hunger for gold"), Servius provides the following explanation (Petron. fr. 1):

> *sacra id est execrabilis. tractus est autem sermo ex more Gallorum. nam Massilienses quotiens pestilentia laborabant, unus se ex pauperibus offerebat alendus anno integro publicis <sumptibus> et purioribus cibis. hic postea ornatus verbenis et vestibus sacris circumducebatur per totam civitatem cum execrationibus, ut in ipsum reciderent mala totius civitatis, et sic proiciebatur. hoc autem in Petronio lectum est.*

> *sacra*, that is accursed. The word is taken from the custom of the Gauls. For whenever the people of Massilia are suffering from a plague, one of their poor folk offers himself to be nourished for a full year at public expense and with very pure food. Afterwards this man is decorated with branches and sacred clothes and carried around the entire city with curses, so that the evils of the entire citizenry might fall upon him, and thus he is thrown out. This also can be read in Petronius.

Based on this evidence, scholars conjecture that the *Satyrica* began with Encolpius taking on the role of the *pharmakos*, the scapegoat whose ostracism serves to as a form of ritual purification.[9] If Encolpius' wanderings began after his year living at public expense as a *pharmakos*, his position as one living outside the law becomes more complex and ambiguous. This ritual takes a person from the margins of society, brings them into the center for a prescribed period during a time of crisis and then expels them from the out of the city's boundary.[10] Yet this act of integration and expulsion is also central to the life of the collective group. As Walter Burkert notes, "the outcast is also the savior to

---

8 Sidonius seems to believe that the events in the text actually happened to Petronius, rather than being a fictional narrative about Encolpius. See Schmeling and Setaioli 2011, 419. The text of the *Satyrica* and fragments is Müller 2009. All translations are my own.

9 If the text did begin with Encolpius taking part in a *pharmakos* ritual to cure a plague, his reference to divine oracles on how to cure a plague in the opening fragment would take on a deeper meaning in relation to the novel as a whole.

10 The *pharmakos* may also have been killed. For an overview of this ritual, see Burkert 1985, 82–84.

whom all are most deeply indebted".[11] If Servius is correct about the opening of the *Satyrica*, Encolpius' role as *pharmakos* sets him up as one who is both sacred and accursed.[12] In this context, Enclopius might also be understood as a parody of the *homo sacer*, the sacred and accursed outlaw who is both inside and outside of human and divine law.[13] Thus, from the very opening of the text, the *Satyrica* could have used Encolpius' legal and ritual status to explore the boundaries between outside and inside, sacred and profane, center and margins.

Encolpius and the Law in the Surviving Fragments

The extant text of the *Satyrica* opens with Encolpius' speech against the current craze for declamation and how it has ruined the contemporary program of education. One of the specific points of Encolpius' critique is that the current training in rhetoric does not prepare students for a career in public life. Rather, once students leave school and enter the forum, they feel as if they have entered into another world (1.2: *cum in forum venerint, putent se in alium orbem terrarum delatos*). This focus on forensic rhetoric implies that, at least in part, the contemporary system does not prepare students for the practice of law.[14] Encolpius also provides an example of the types of exercises that students have to speak: "pirates with chains standing on the shore, tyrants writing edicts that order sons to cut off the heads of their fathers, oracles given to cure a plague in which three or more virgins must be sacrificed" (1.3: *sed piratas cum catenis in litore stantes, sed tyrannos edicta scribentes quibus imperent filiis ut patrum suorum capita praecidant, sed responsa in pestilentiam data ut virgines tres aut plures immolentur*). On the surface these do seem like outlandish exercises which grant no practical help for a forensic career. Yet on another level, these prompts are all concerned with testing the limits of different aspects of law. All three stand

---

11 Burkert 1985, 84.

12 There may be a reference to Encolpius' ritual status as scapegoat in the surviving text. Lichas insultingly addresses Encolpius as *pharmace* (107.15). On the uncertainties and ambiguities of this word, which only appears here in classical Latin, see Schmeling and Setaioli 2011, 419.

13 See the work of Giorgio Agamben on this topic: Agamben 1998, 71–74; Agamben 1998, 104–111 also connects the *homo sacer* with the werewolf. The story of the werewolf during the Cena (61–62) may thus have deeper connections to Encolpius' status.

14 Quintilian mentions the importance of preparing students for the practice of law in the opening of his *Inst.*; cf. 1.*proem*.10 and 22. The English word "forensic" captures this connection between the forum and the practice of law.

outside of traditional civic law and represent independent laws unto themselves. Pirates are the prototypical outlaws; the chains they hold symbolize their power to immediately turn free citizens into slaves. Tyrants are also extralegal actors who can invert the proper functioning of familial duty. Similarly, divine law exists outside the normal order of things and can overturn the established ritual of animal sacrifice. While each of these events lie outside the world of the quotidian practice of law, they are disruptive events that could happen in the real world as well as in the world of fiction.[15] Such extreme events do not happen in the surviving text of the *Satyrica*. Yet, as we will see, what remains of the text explores legal questions about slave and free, as well as duty to members of one's household via testamentary law. The focus on cannibalism throughout the text suggests a link with human sacrifice.[16] Encolpius' example of the murderous edicts written by tyrants suggests a connection to Petronius' own world under an autocrat. The opening of the surviving text also picks up on the image of the forum as "another world". Soon after Encolpius' condemnation of training in forensic rhetoric, he and his companions enter the forum (12.1: *veniebamus in forum deficiente iam die*). They do not find it to be a place of pirates, tyrants, and oracles; nor is it a place of light and law. Rather, it is a twilight world of rogues and stolen goods. It also contains some of the text's most explicit references to law and the courts, as well as the threat of being called before the bar on the following morning.

Over the course of his early wanderings, Encolpius appears to have committed crimes in violation of human and divine law. In the opening fragments, it is clear that Encolpius, Ascyltos, and Giton have come into possession of gold coins, which they have sewn into an old cloak. The cloak and coins have been lost, possibly through the negligence of Encolpius. At some point, they also have stolen a more valuable cloak, usually described as a Greek cloak, or *pallium*. On what may be the evening of the first day of the surviving narrative, Encolpius, Ascyltos, and Giton set off for the town's forum to try and sell their valuable stolen cloak only to find that someone is also trying to fence their lost gold-coin-containing cloak.[17] The illegal origins of both of these articles pre-

---

15 Capture by pirates or brigands is a key theme of several other ancient novels; see Knapp 2011, 307–309. This event does not happen in the surviving fragments of the *Satyrica*, a fact that is perhaps alluded to by Eumolpus' ironic claim that Lichas is an "archpirate" (101.5: *archipirata*).

16 On cannibalism as a central trope in the *Satyrica*, see Rimell 2002.

17 The account of what happens in the forum at dusk (sections 12–15) may be misplaced and could have come earlier than the opening section with Encolpius and Agamemnon critiquing the current state of education.

sumably were recounted in an earlier, now lost portion of the text. Some clues do survive as to the origins of their first cloak with its hidden gold coins. In an elliptical and possibly misplaced comment during the planning of their testamentary deception in Croton, a character, presumably Encolpius states, "whatever he should want, provided that the cloak, our companion in crime, were pleasing and whatever the villa of Lycurgus had offered to the thieves" (117.3: *quicquid exigeret, dummodo placeret vestis, rapinae comes, et quicquid Lycurgi villa grassantibus praebuisset*). These lines suggest that in a lost portion of the text Encolpius, and possibly Ascyltos and Giton, murdered and robbed the villa of their host, Lycurgus. This mysterious event may help explain the origin of the cloak and gold coins from the opening fragment.

Nevertheless, Encolpius' legal backstory remains uncertain. Indeed, if he had recently killed Lycurgus and stolen his money, Encolpius surprisingly wants to use legal procedures to get back his lost cloak. This desire to use the law to continue to break the law reveals Encolpius' foolish naïveté, his ultimate lack of concern for the law, as well as his feelings of intellectual superiority. At first Ascyltos seems to be more conscious of their guilt and to "fear the laws" (14.1: *leges timebat*). Nevertheless, his fear is not grounded in their status as criminals, but rather is due to the corruption of the laws themselves. Giving his argument in both prose and verse, Ascyltos states the following (14.1–2):

> 'quis' ... 'hoc loco nos novit aut quis habebit dicentibus fidem? Mihi plane placet emere, quamvis nostrum sit, quod agnoscimus, et parvo aere recuperare potius thesaurum quam in ambiguam litem descendere:
> quid faciunt leges, ubi sola pecunia regnat
> aut ubi paupertas vincere nulla potest?
> ipsi qui Cynica traducunt tempora pera
> non numquam nummis vendere verba solent.
> ergo iudicium nihil est nisi publica merces,
> atque eques in causa qui sedet empta probat.'

"Who knows us in this place, or who will believe us when we speak? Although it is ours, I strongly suggest that we should buy it, now that we've seen it. And I think that it is better to get back our treasure by spending a small amount of money than to bring about a court case, which could go either way:
What can the laws do, where only money rules, or where poverty has no chance to win? Even those who follow the Cynics and live in poverty sometimes sell their words for coins. Therefore, justice is nothing but a public auction and the judge who presides over the case approves the sale."

Ascyltos' fears are almost realized, however, and the case of the two stolen cloaks nearly comes before the magistrate. The clamor caused by the two accusations of theft attracts to the scene some other dealers (*cociones*), who marvel that this case is being argued over such disparately valuable articles of clothing. Encolpius' tunic appears worthless; but the *pallium* of the farmer and his wife is valuable. Ascyltos proposes an exchange, which is agreed upon by both parties. Despite this seemingly equitable solution, some of the night watchmen appear and demand that they take possession of both articles to be held in evidence and brought before a judge in the morning (15.2). Encolpius states that no such court case will in fact happen; the night watchmen simply want the *pallium* for their own profit. One of the dealers, who occasionally also argues in court, is appointed to watch over the cloak and swears to bring it as evidence the next day. Yet again, the court proceeding is only a threat. Encolpius believes that the dealers and the night watchmen are counting on the fact that the thieves will not risk appearing in court (15.5). The appeal to law is only a means to steal the cloak again. Miraculously, these threats of legal action work in Encolpius' favor. The farmer is incredulous that such a tattered old tunic will be brought into court as evidence and indignantly throws it back in Ascyltos' face. In turn, Ascyltos gladly deposits the valuable *pallium*, which is now the only item in dispute for court the next day.

As expected, Encolpius and Ascyltos have no intention of appearing in court on the following day. They return to their lodging, believing that they have regained their money and ridiculing the lack of intellectual acumen of the dealers and their accuser. They soon are laughing out of the other side of their mouths, however. In the next scene Quartilla and her handmaiden reveal that our heroes have violated divine law. Here again, these crimes have taken place in a lost part of the text. Although she declares that their theft and disturbance of the rites of Priapus are crimes never before imagined, Quartilla nevertheless excuses them.[18] She states that there was no real criminal intent behind their actions, and attributes them to the folly of youth. She is also glad that such handsome young men have come into the area. The ensuing sexual events are not a punishment for their crimes, but rather a means to cure Quartilla of her fever.

Near the end of the surviving fragments, Encolpius again commits a crime against Priapus. Here we learn the specific act, which is once again described in

---

18 Encolpius' crimes against Priapus are described in hyperbolic terms. Quartilla's first words are: "What is the boldness? Or where have you learned this thievery that goes even beyond stories" (17.4: *quaenam est inquit haec audacia, aut ubi fabulas etiam antecessura latrocinia didicistis?*).

hyperbolic terms. After Encolpius heroically, but unknowingly, kills the scared goose of Priapus, Oenothea cannot believe the magnitude of the crime (137.1–3):

> 'scelerate' inquit 'etiam loqueris? nescis quam magnum flagitium admiseris ... itaque ne te putes nihil egisse, si magistratus hoc scierint, ibis in crucem. polluisti sanguine domicilium meum ante hunc diem inviolatum, fecistique ut me quisquis voluerit inimicus sacerdotio pellat.'

> "Criminal, you're still speaking? You do not know the magnitude of the crime you have committed ... And so, lest you think that you have done nothing, if the magistrate were to know about this, you would go on the cross. You have polluted with blood my little house, which has never been violated before this day, you have brought it about that one of my enemies could drive me from my role as priestess".

When Proselenos returns she acts as if Encolpius has killed his own father, rather than a goose (137.5).[19] In both cases these crimes are easily atoned for. Encolpius simply promises Quartilla that he will not reveal the secret rites of Priapus and that he will help to cure her fever. Encolpius buys off the goose and the gods with two gold coins (137.6), and the women happily cook and feast upon the goose.[20]

In these final portions of the text to survive, Encolpius succinctly sums up his position on the wrong side of justice: "Gods and goddesses, how terrible it is for those living outside the law: they are always expecting whatever they deserve" (125.4: *dii deaeque, quam male est extra legem viventibus: quicquid meruerunt, semper expectant*). In its immediate context, Encolpius' worries about crime and punishment refer to his fears that his role play as a slave and Eumolpus' pretending to be a childless millionaire among the legacy hunters in Croton will be discovered, and he will again have to flee and return to a life of poverty.

During his time in Croton, Encolpius offers other hints about the crimes he has committed, yet these are elusive and contradictory. As part of his explanation for his failure to perform sexually with Circe, Encolpius obliquely refers to his guilt. In an exchange of letters with Circe to help cure his impotence, Encolpius provides this written confession (130.1–4):

---

19 See also 137.6: *si vos provocassem, etiam si homicidium fecissem* ("If I had insulted you, or even if I had murdered someone").
20 These ultimately bathetic crimes may relate to the crimes of Senecan tragedy, which also are described as being previously unheard of violations of human and divine law. See, for example, *Tro.* 1104–1110; *Pha.* 165–170; *Med.* 45–50; *Oed.* 936–938; *Ag.* 28–30; *Thy.* 753–754.

Polyaenos Circae salutem. fateor me, domina, saepe pecassae; nam et homo sum et adiuc iuvenis. numquam tamen ante hunc diem usque ad mortem deliqui. habes confitentem reum: quicquid iusseris, merui. proditionem feci, hominem occidi, templum violavi: in haec facino-ra quaere suppplicium. sive occidere placet, <cum> ferro meo venio, sive verberibus contenta es, curro nudus ad dominam. illud unum memento, non me sed instrumenta peccasse.

Polyaenos to Circe, Greetings. I admit, my lady, that I have often done wrong; for I am human and still young. Nevertheless, never before this day have I committed a crime worthy of death. You have the confession of your defendant: I have committed treachery, I have killed a man, I have violated a temple: seek punishment for these crimes. If you wish to kill me, I will come with my sword; or if you are content with beating me, I run naked to my lady. Remember this one thing, not I but my instrument has done wrong.

When this epistolary defense and confession of crimes does not cure his impotence, Encolpius goes to a temple of Priapus and begs to be cured in seventeen lines of verse. In apparent contraction to his letter to Circe, Encolpius presents himself as ritually pure (133.3.6–10):

non sanguine tristi
perfusus venio, non templis impius hostis
admovi dextram, sed inops et rebus egenis
attritus facinus non toto corpore feci.
quisquis peccat inops, minor est reus.

I do not come here covered in guilty blood, I have not robbed temples as an impious ene-my, but poor and worn down by my destitute situation I committed a crime not with my whole body. Whoever does wrong due to poverty, is a defendant for misdemeanors.

Scholars have long puzzled over Encolpius' apparent about-face declaration of innocence. Is he lying? Is he simply referring to his present status, and leaving out his earlier, now lost, crimes? Is he adjusting his performance to offer up the typical language of prayer?[21] As the text now stands we cannot be sure. From what survives of the text, it is clear that Encolpius is much more willing to submit to divine law and punishment, especially when it involves impotence. Violation of human law, such as theft and murder, is less of a concern.

---

21 For an overview of the scholarly debate on this passage and Encolpius' sincerity, see Schmeling and Setaioli 2011, 516–517.

Outlaws and Bandits

In his book, *Invisible Romans*, Robert Knapp devotes a chapter to outlaws. He focuses on pirates and groups of bandits and argues that these criminal collectives offer an alternative, egalitarian society. He states that these groups develop their own codes of law and provide a critique of the rigidly hierarchical society of the Roman empire.[22] Knapp further argues that people turned to piracy and brigandage as a means to escape domination and poverty.[23] Much of his evidence comes from ancient novels. Significantly, however, Petronius' *Satyrica* is omitted. Indeed, the portrayal of the outlaw Encolpius differs considerably from Knapp's portrait of large groups of brigands and pirates forming an egalitarian counterculture in the Greek novels and Apuleius' *Metamorphoses*. Encolpius certainly resorts to crime to avoid poverty, but here is where the commonalities with the other extant ancient novels end.

Encolpius is not part of a large band of outlaws. Moving from Ascyltos in the first half of the surviving fragments, to Eumolpius in the latter half, Encolpius appears to prefer to work with a single partner, in addition to his lover, Giton. In contrast, as Knapp notes, boys and women were excluded from bands of outlaws, because they risk destroying the unity of the group, which is made up solely of adult male desperados.[24] Giton is in fact a continual source of problems between Encolpius and his two criminal companions. Rather than being egalitarian, Encolpius does not wish to share Giton with his partners (e.g., 100.1–2). The only times Encolpius adopts a spirit of egalitarianism with Ascyltos is when he realizes that they cannot continue together due to their competing desires for Giton. After learning from Giton that Ascyltos tried to rape him, Encolpius demands that the two divide their goods and separate (10.4). They agree not to effect this division immediately because of their invitation to Trimalchio's dinner on the following day. After the dinner, Ascyltos surreptitiously "shares" Giton with Encolpius. When he learns about this crime (80.9: *iniuria*), Encolpius demands that the two immediately divide their possessions and separate. Ascyltos then takes the concept of egalitarianism to the extreme. In a possible mockery of the Biblical Judgment of Solomon, Ascyltos states that they must also divide the boy (79.12).[25]

---

22 Knapp 2011, 313–314.

23 Knapp 2011, 297–300.

24 Knapp 2011, 305–306, 310–311.

25 It remains a possibility that Petronius was aware of Jewish and Christian texts and culture. The three crucified criminals in the story of the Matron of Ephesus may allude to Christ's cruci-

After parting with Ascyltos and joining up with Eumolpus, the ruse to dupe the legacy hunters in Croton is not based on egalitarianism. The plot reproduces the hierarchies of society, as Encolpius, Giton, and Eumolpus' hired-hand, Corax, agree to serve as Eumolpus' slaves. In hopes of having their deception succeed, the three swear an oath that casts them as slaves and gladiators. Thus, as they symbolically cross the margin from free to gladiator-slaves they lose the right to avoid corporal punishment (117.5: *in verba Eumolpi sacramentum iuravimus: uri, vinciri, verberari ferroque necari, et quicquid aliud Eumolpus iussisset*, "we swore an oath dictated by Eumolpus, that we would be burned, chained, flogged, put to the sword, or whatever else Eumolpus had ordered").

This oath is likely hyperbolic. Nevertheless, it shows how in the *Satyrica*, this band of criminals uses social hierarchy in order to carry out their long con on the legacy hunters. By crossing the line from free to slave this oath also demonstrates a crucial difference that separates the two in Greek and Roman culture. Encolpius and his companions renounce the bodily integrity and inviolability that is part of the legal privileges of a free citizen. Now they can be beaten and tortured at their master's whim for any offence.

Law of Slavery

Encolpius and Giton have already learned how dangerous it can be to pretend to be a slave. While on Lichas' boat they disguise themselves as runaway slaves and also shave their heads to avoid recognition. They are witnessed performing this ill-omened act by one of the passengers, who reports it to Lichas. As the text makes clear, sailors shave their heads as an offering to the gods to avoid shipwreck during a storm. As the faux slaves shaved their heads during calm weather, Lichas must avert this potentially ill-omened act. He orders the still-disguised Encolpius and Giton to be whipped (105.4–5). Their play acting and writing of false brands on their faces leads to real servile marks upon their backs.

While Encolpius and Giton willingly cross the boundary from free to slave, there are no examples in the surviving fragments that offer accounts of illegiti-

---

fixion. Eumolpus' "new testament" demanding that his heirs consume his body may mock the Eucharist. Several characters in the text have Semitic names, most notably, Trimalchio. Scholars have found references to Jewish dietary laws as well as Hebrew or Aramaic turns of phrase in the *Cena*; see Bauer 1983. These examples suggest yet another way Petronius may have brought marginalized groups into his text.

mate movements in the other direction. In what remains of the *Satyrica*, slaves are freed via testamentary law. On one occasion, a slave is freed by Trimalchio's fiat (54.5), but it remains unclear whether this sudden and unexpected manumission is genuine or part of the staged drama that makes up Trimalchio's dinner party. Despite the topsy-turvy world that characterizes the *Satyrica*, in the extant fragments, there are no accounts of actual runaway slaves. The legal status of slaves remains firmly in place throughout. Fugitive slaves are only part of the play acting and disguises of Encolpius and Giton while on Lichas' ship. Here the threat of corporal punishment of slaves is central, as it is throughout the text.

One of the first things we learn about Trimalchio's household is that its doorway bears the inscription threatening that any slave who leaves without his master's permission will receive one hundred lashes (28.7). Trimalchio's power to punish and grant remission from penalty is highlighted during the dinner. When a cook apparently forgets to gut a pig before cooking it, Trimalchio orders him to be stripped bare for a beating (49.6: *despolia*). When a slave accidentally drops a cup, Trimalchio orders him to kill himself (52.4–6). The threat of violence is averted, however; in both instances Trimalchio also grants clemency to the offending slaves. These acts of mercy are foreshadowed by the pardoning of a slave set to be beaten for losing his master's clothes in the bath. The master here is not Trimalchio, but rather another slave, the accountant, Cinnamus (30.5–11). Punishment and clemency are based on the whim of the master. Yet during the Cena, Trimalchio's verdicts are part of the role playing and acting that characterize his dinner party. The cook plays the worthless and forgetful slave, while Trimalchio plays the cruel and then merciful master.[26]

Trimalchio also demonstrates his final act of legal power over his slaves. He will free all of them in his will (71.1). This act reproduces Trimalchio's own progress from slave to free (76.2), as well as, presumably, that of the other freedmen at his party.[27] While the *Cena* sets out an idealized display of the power of testamentary law to free slaves and perpetuate the master's power even after his death, the legacy hunters in Croton explore a key fault line in the workings of testamentary law.[28]

---

26 Trimalchio also pretends to render judgment in an apparent quarrel among two slaves carrying water jugs. One of the slaves pretends not to like Trimalchio's judgment and breaks one of the vessels. Oysters spill out to the surprise and delight of the guests (70.4–6).
27 See 57.10.
28 Already the possibility of a person not leaving their estate to their family is briefly hinted at in the *Cena*, see 43.5.

Testamentary Law

The possible disruption of testamentary law by legacy hunters points to the anxiety Romans felt about the transmission of family wealth to the next generation. It is unknown how widespread this practice actually was, but in the literary tradition there is widespread concern that legacy hunting corrupts the proper functioning of kinship, friendship and the laws of inheritance. As Seneca notes, it is difficult to tell whether someone visits you on your sickbed as a friend, or simply in hopes of getting written into your will (*Ep.* 95.43).[29] Keith Hopkins draws attention to the problematic status of legacy hunters: "They lived at the margins of the rules of polite society. Their success violated overt ideals that status was ascribed by birth, not achieved ... Legacy-hunters had hit upon a transmission fault in the passage of wealth from one generation to the next. They were pilloried for their success in exploiting it".[30]

Eumolpus and Encolpius' time in Croton reveals a problem with legacy hunting itself: deceit and deception can flow in the opposite direction. Just as one can pretend to be a friend in order to receive a testamentary bequest, so one can pretend to be wealthy and live off the competitive largess of legacy hunters. In the final surviving fragment, the legacy hunters are starting to realize that Eumolpus may only be pretending to be wealthy (141.1). He appears to attempt to solve this problem by a reading of his will. It is unclear, however, if Eumolpus has died or is only pretending. Like Trimalchio, Eumolpus also frees his "slaves" in his final testament. He also states that those included in his final testament will only receive their bequests if they publicly eat his body (141.2). Perhaps Eumolpus thought that this requirement for inheritance would cause the legacy hunters to reject his bequest, and they might be able to escape. If this was their hope, the final surviving passage proves it likely was illusory. The end of the text states that all were blinded by the prospect of receiving money and that a certain Gorgias was prepared to carry out the cannibalistic requirement (141.5).

We have no way of knowing if Eumolpus' body was in fact eaten and how Encolpius, at least, escapes from Croton. The final lines of the surviving text are a speech, perhaps given by Gorgias, explaining how one can become a cannibal and offering examples from Roman history.[31] This gruesomely outlandish piece

---

29 See also Sen. *Ben.* 4.20.3 and 6.38.4.
30 Hopkins 1983, 238–239. See also Champlin 1991, 24–25 who cautions against accepting the historical reality of legacy hunting being as widespread as the sources would lead us to believe.
31 Albeit false examples; see Courtney 2001, 212–213.

of testamentary law, which destroys the norms of animal sacrifice and consumption, is naturalized by rhetoric. This point brings the closing words of the text back to the opening ones. As we have seen, at the start of the surviving text Encolpius complains that contemporary forensic education is based on seemingly otherworldly examples and exercises, such as divine oracles demanding the sacrifice of virgins to avert a plague. On what practical grounds would one need training in forensic rhetoric in order to argue for or against this norm-breaking example of the divine will? Nevertheless, at the end of the surviving text, rhetoric serves the purpose of convincing people to follow the norm-breaking legal requirement of Eumolpus' will.[32] Similarly, Ascyltos noted in the opening fragments that the law has become subservient to money and greed (14.1–2). At the end of the surviving text Eumolpus' will is a travesty of testamentary law. The faux slaves are freed. The legal requirement for inheritance requires a corruption of sacrifice and demands that the legacy hunters cross the line from human to animal in order to inherit. The final irony is that Eumolpus in fact has no money to bequeath, and it is unclear whether he has actually died.

Conclusion

Despite the topsy-turvy, chaotic world of the *Satyrica*, law is central to the text. Law functions in various ways: as pressure to keep Encolpius traveling on the margins of society throughout the Mediterranean, as part of rhetorical, forensic training, as a means to keep slaves in their place, and as a means to enforce one's power after death via testamentary law. By using law to shape the margins, the *Satyrica* manipulates an institution that was central to Roman culture and identity in order to explore the "other world" that exists outside of the boundaries of elite society.

---

32 There's a further connection. The oracle is given to help avert a plague (1.3: *in pestilentiam*). Croton is described as a town in the grips of a plague (116.9: *oppidum tamquam in pestilentia campos*).

Konstantinos Arampapaslis
Much to Do with Priapus: From Religious Margins to the Center of Petronius' *Satyrica*

Abstract: This chapter examines how Petronius elevates Priapus, a marginal deity of the Graeco-Roman pantheon, to the status of a major god in the *Satyrica*: from the reason that led Encolpius to depart Massilia to the rituals and festivals he witnesses or participates in, everything falls under the auspices of Priapus, thus underscoring the god's central position and the religious character of the hero's travels. The feature of 'marginality' which permeates every aspect of the novel also characterizes the protagonist, whose adventures might have been modelled after the mythological life of the deity. This is perhaps the result of the author's effort to reflect contemporary anxieties, when people would become 'marginalized' through their wanderings in search of better life conditions.

Introduction

Neronian literature shows a peculiar interest for the 'marginal' as a thematic source for literary creation. Its focus on accurate representations of witchcraft (Seneca's *Medea*, Lucan's Erichtho), popular superstitions (Persius' *Satire* 2, Petronius), as well as depictions of low-class life and characters (Petronius) aptly illustrates this point. What the Augustan poets considered unworthy, unfit, or even inappropriate for extensive literary treatment became the source of inspiration for Neronian authors, and concurrently a way to differentiate themselves from their predecessors.[1]

In the *Satyrica*, the obsession with the 'marginal' primarily manifests in Petronius' choice of elevating Priapus, a minor deity of the Graeco-Roman pantheon, to the status of a major god who is the sole divine agent responsible for everything that happens in the narrative. This development, combined with the salacious character of the deity, produces a parodic effect which has long been

---

[1] The ways in which Lucan, Seneca, and Petronius interact with earlier literature, and especially their Augustan predecessors has been discussed in earlier scholarship. For a general assessment on the transformation of Augustan models in Neronian literature, see Littlewood 2017, 79–92.

https://doi.org/10.1515/9783111063942-007

recognized by scholars.[2] This chapter expands further the offshoots of parody in the novel by arguing that Encolpius' adventures can be read as a mock-version of religious travels: from the reason that led him to depart Massilia to the rituals and festivals he witnesses or participates in, everything falls under the auspices of Priapus, whose presence greatly impacts every aspect of the novel. This becomes evident in the dominant feature of 'marginality' which characterizes not only the religious events in the narrative, but also the protagonist, thus bringing his figure closer to that of the deity by means of a persuasive analogy.

The *Satyrica*: A Religious Journey

The characterization of a journey as religious depends essentially on the reason that leads an individual or group to embark on it: travelling for the purpose of attending festivals or initiation rituals, healing, consulting oracles, spreading the cult and worship of a deity as well as religious tourism were some of the most common instances throughout the Graeco-Roman antiquity.[3] The destination does play some role, but only insofar as the cause of the trip is not clearly religious such as in cases of sightseeing sacred places.[4] Even though the reason that led Encolpius to begin his wanderings does not fall in one of these categories, his journey evidently has strong religious overtones as it seems to have been the direct consequence of a purificatory ritual.

Based on frs. 1 and 4, scholars assume that Encolpius' adventures began in Massilia where he served as a scapegoat (Serv. ad Virg. *Aen.* 3.57):[5]

---

2 Klebs 1889 read the *Satyrica* as a parody of wandering epics (e.g., the *Odyssey* and the *Aeneid*) and paralleled the central position of Priapus to that of the Odyssean Poseidon. Heinze 1899 suggested that Petronius parodies certain features of the ideal novel. However, these interpretations seemingly overestimate the importance of 'Priapus' wrath' based on Encolpius' explanation for his impotence which, even if it holds true, arguably concerns only a small part of a fragmentary narrative (Jensson 2004, 105).

3 The different types of religious travel in antiquity are discussed in Harland 2011, 5–17, and Elsner and Rutherford 2005, 12–27. The latter use the term 'pilgrimage' after they have it redefined in the context of Graeco-Roman polytheism.

4 The destination should be considered differently when individuals travel to specific locations of great religious significance (e.g., the temple of Apollo at Delphi) where the divine presence was thought to be stronger (Petsalis-Diomidis 2005, 186–187).

5 Sullivan 1968, 40–41; Walsh 1970, 73–74 (emphasis on the notes), and more recently Jensson 2004, 96–103. Most scholars appropriately examine frs. 1 and 4 together when attempting to reconstruct the beginning of Petronius' novel.

auri sacra fames] sacra id est execrabilis. Tractus est autem sermo ex more Gallorum. Nam Massilienses quotiens pestilentia laborabant, unus se ex pauperibus offerebat alendus anno integro publicis <sumptibus> et purioribus cibis. Hic postea ornatus verbenis et vestibus sacris circumducebatur per totam civitatem cum exsecrationibus, ut in ipsum reciderent mala totius civitatis, et sic proiciebatur. Hoc autem in Petronio lectum est.

auri sacra fames: *sacra* means accursed. The expression derives from a custom of the Gauls. Whenever the inhabitants of Massilia suffer from a plague, one of their poor people offers himself to be fed at the public expense for a whole year on special religious foods. Afterwards he is dressed in sprigs of sacred foliage and certain ritually prescribed clothing and led round the whole city with curses, so that the ills of the whole city will fall upon him. He is then cast out. This is found in Petronius.[6]

In this comment Servius describes the rite of the *pharmakos* which subjected a usually marginalized individual to ritual humiliation with the purpose of transferring the communal pollution to a single member of the community. The religious procedure concluded with the banishment of the person who offered themselves for this role, thus purifying the city from the *miasma*.[7] This was, as Servius claims, part of the narrative of the *Satyrica*. But was indeed Encolpius the *pharmakos* in Massilia? Fr. 4 allows for the identification of the scapegoat with the protagonist (Sid. Apoll. *Carm.* 23.145–157):

> *quid vos eloquii canam Latini,*
> *Arpinas, Patavine, Mantuane, ...*
> *et te Massiliensium per hortos*
> *sacri stipitis, Arbiter, colonum*
> *Hellespontiaco parem Priapo?*

> What shall I say to you, glories of Latin eloquence,
> Cicero of Arpinum, Livy of Padua, and Mantuan Virgil ...
> And you, Arbiter, worshipper of the sacred stump
> Amid the gardens of Massilia,
> A match for Priapus of the Hellespont.

In these lines, Sidonius refers to Petronius as a Massilian, probably convoluting the character of Encolpius with the author.[8] This suggestion points to the right direction, i.e., that of the hero being the *pharmakos* of fr. 1, and is sufficiently

---

6 The Latin text of the *Satyrica* and its fragments is cited from Müller 2009; the translations are taken from Sullivan 2011.

7 For the ritual of the *pharmakos*, see Burkert 1979, 64–72.

8 The confusion over the identity has been noted early on in Petronian scholarship: Walsh 1970, 73 n. 3; Jensson 2004, 100–102, citing Bücheler's 1862 edition on n. 223; Courtney 2001, 44.

confirmed by Lichas' address to Encolpius as such in 107.15 (*cui deo crinem vovisti? Pharmace, responde*) as well as the protagonist's self-reference as an *exul* (81.3).[9]

Frs. 1 and 4 might also provide the general context for fr. 31, which has been considered part of an oracle or dream experienced by Encolpius while in Massilia:[10]

> *Linque tuas sedes alienaque litora quaere,*
> *<o> iuvenis: maior rerum tibi nascitur ordo.*
> *Ne succumbe malis; te noverit ultimus Hister,*
> *te Boreas gelidus securaque regna Canopi,*
> *quique renascentem Phoebum cernuntque cadentem:*
> *maior in externas Ithacus descendat harenas.*

> Youth, leave your home for alien shores.
> For you now dawns a mightier day;
> Be strong, and the Danube, that last boundary,
> The icy North and the safe Egyptian realms,
> The nations of the morn and setting sun,
> Will learn of you: a great Odysseus
> Might descend on distant sands.

Since Priapus is the sole or at least the central deity in the narrative as far as we know, it is only reasonable to identify the speaker of these lines with the god or one of his priests, advising the protagonist to leave his hometown in search for a better and greater future.[11] Contrary to Sullivan who argues that Encolpius had committed some sacrilege against the god in Massilia, and subsequently was instructed to depart, there is no need to infer a personal offence against Priapus.[12] The instructions could have been given to Encolpius before the ritual of expulsion described in fr. 1. Or again, as it seems more plausible, he might have offered himself as a scapegoat exactly because the god asked him to do so in

---

9 Jensson 2007, 108 has already made this observation; see also Star in this volume.
10 Heinze 1899, 502; Walsh 1970, 73–74.
11 Priapus also appears in a dream to Lichas (104.1), and most probably to Quartilla (17.7). These epiphanies are in line with the convention of ancient novels which does not allow the active interference of gods in mortal lives; see the discussion in Dowden 2010, 368–369 and Jensson 2004, 106–107.
12 Sullivan 1968, 41; see also Jensson 2004, 108.

order to leave Massilia. In either case, it seems certain that Encolpius travelled on the god's command.[13]

The *pharmakos* ritual which triggered the hero's departure, as well as the possible involvement of Priapus in his decision to become a scapegoat can adequately support the reading of the *Satyrica* as a narrative of religious travels. This was recognized early on, specifically by Sidonius Apollinaris (fr. 4), who characterizes Petronius' protagonist as *colonus*, which in late Latin might be also translated as "worshipper".[14] Thus, Sidonius' verses, in conjunction with fr. 1, allude not only to Massilia as the starting point of the journey, but also to its strongly religious, albeit parodic, character.

Encolpius and Priapus: Outcasts Walking Hand in Hand

But in what sense is Encolpius a *colonus par* (fr. 4) to Priapus? There are several parallels, in different levels, that one can draw between the god and the protagonist. The obvious, physical similarity is the supposedly large size of Encolpius' genitals as well as his sexual promiscuity — at least before being afflicted with impotence —, which were also the proverbial characteristics of Priapus.[15] The phrase could also allude to the analogy between the god's mythological life and his 'sufferings' as a literary figure, and the adventures of Petronius' protagonist. A euhemeristic version of Priapus' myth which is found in Arnulf Aurelianensis'

---

13 Divine message dreams and oracles were not uncommon in ancient literature, including novels, for which Jensson 2004, 107 points out that "god-sent dreams, as well as divine oracles and utterances by priests in trance, conform to normal ancient religious experience and practice". The idea that gods can provide guidance in real-life religious travels through dreams and oracles is clearly exemplified in Aelius Aristides' *Sacred Tales*. In this diary of his travels to the healing sanctuaries of Asclepius, Aristides recounts the instructions he receives from the god in his dreams in order to both commence and continue his trip.
14 This meaning of the word *colonus* in the context of fr. 4 is noted in Courtney 2001, 44 and Jensson 2004, 100.
15 Courtney 2001, 44; Jensson 2004, 108: "... Encolpius was his [Priapus'] equal with respect to the size of his *mentula* and may have inadvertently entered into competition with the god for the attention of worshippers. Nothing provokes divine anger like the impersonation of a god by a mortal, which is really what is implied by Sidonius, when he apostrophizes Petronius and calls him, or rather Encolpius, *Hellespontiaco parem Priapo*".

scholion on Ovid's *Fasti* 1.400 and expands Servius' on *Georgics* 4.111,[16] provides the following account:

> *Priapus quidam iuvenis fuit, qui virilis membri magnitudine multas interfecit mulieres et ob membri magnitudinem in tantam venit gratiam inter mulieres etiam, ut pro deo haberetur. Ad cuius imaginem in ortis factam cum mulieres ad colligenda olera accederent, iuvenes eas opprimebant. Iuvenis ille de Hellesponto eiectus est. Pro magnitudine virilis membri mariti enim ab uxoribus contemnebantur.*[17]

> Priapus was some young fellow who, due to the size of his genitals, had intercourse with many women, and for the same reason gained so much favor among them to the point that he was considered a god. When women would go to collect vegetables, the young men caught them by surprise next to his effigies which stood in the gardens. That young man was expelled from the Hellespont. Because of the size of his genitals, husbands were scorned by their wives.

The description of Priapus as a well-endowed *iuvenis* echoes that of Encolpius in the *Satyrica* (e.g., 16.4: *iuvenes*; 17.8: *iuvenili impulsi*; 140.13). This physical characteristic makes both the god and Petronius' protagonist the women's favorite, the former among the female population of a city in Hellespont, the latter of Circe (126.5) as well as Lichas' wife (106.2; 113.3). But it also turns out to be a cause for their troubles: Priapus is expelled from the city by the cheated husbands as the text implies, while Encolpius is pursued by an enraged Lichas due to the affair he had with his wife, and later gets beaten by Circe for his impotence (132.2–5). Jensson has also pointed out that the large size of Encolpius' *phallus* renders the hero an ideal candidate for the role of *pharmakos* since the ritual appears to have also included the abuse of the scapegoat's genitals.[18]

Apart from these superficial resemblances, the two figures share a quintessential similarity: their marginality. According to most myths about Priapus, the god is born with deformities due to Hera's *mala manus* which leads his mother,

---

16 *HELLESPONTIACI SERVET TUTELA PRIAPI non dicit Priapum illic esse debere, sed praecipit tales esse hortos, ut mereantur deum habere custodem. hic autem Priapus fuit de Lampsaco civitate Hellesponti, de qua pulsus est propter virilis membri magnitudinem. post in numerum deorum receptus, meruit esse numen hortorum ...* "'Let Priapus of Hellespont hold [them] in tutelage'· he does not claim that Priapus ought to be there but informs us that the gardens were such that they were considered worthy of having a protective deity. So this was Priapus of the city of Lampsacus in Hellespont, from where he was expelled because of the size of his genitals. After he was received among the gods, he deserved to be a deity of gardens ...".

17 The text is from Rieker's edition.

18 Jensson 2004, 98–99.

often identified with Aphrodite, to abandon him in the wild.[19] Therefore, Priapus is a marginal figure among the divine community by birth. Similarly, Encolpius lives in the margins of society as a *pauper*, and perhaps the encouraging words (fr. 31: *ne succumbe malis*) refer to the sufferings of the hero caused by his social status. Finally, both are further marginalized by being expelled from their respective communities.

The abandoned Priapus is saved and nurtured by a local shepherd, who in his belief that the enlarged phallus will bring fertility to the crops, creates a statue and reveres him as a god (Migne, *PG* 36, 1053 B). Priapus' rescue and worship by the shepherd might be interpreted as the god's beginning of a new life in a different community, with a partial reclaim of his earlier status within the world. The marginal (among the divine community) god has now become a deity among the rural people.

Priapus' resettlement after his initial excommunication might have offered the model for the *Satyrica*'s ending. Perhaps Petronius' aspiration was to create a fictive narrative of a marginalized individual's wanderings and subsequent reestablishment of a new life, in a new world, that of the Roman empire, in which people travel more frequently, leaving behind their communities in search of a better future for themselves and their families.[20] Besides, fr. 31 in which Priapus prophesies to Encolpius that he will gain importance and fame after he is cut off from his community and wander around the world, could support such a reading. The role of Priapus as a protector of travelers, attested in the epigrams of the *Anthologia Palatina* (16.261: παρ' ὁδοῖσι φύλαξ ἕστηκα Πρίηπος; 6.102: φιλοδίτης) and the writings of ps.-Nonnus, might add to the argument (Migne, *PG* 36, 1053 B):

καὶ ὠνόμασε Πρίαπον, δηλῶν κατὰ τὴν τῶν Ἰταλῶν γλῶσσαν τὸν ἐκ πλάνης τοὺς ἐν πλάνῃ καὶ ἐρημίᾳ σώζοντα.

And he named [the child] Priapus, denoting in the language of the Italian peoples the one who was saved from his wanderings to save those who roam alone.

If there is a lone wanderer in need of Priapus' succor, that is nobody else than our scapegoat, Encolpius.

---

19 E.g., Schol. Apoll. 1.932–933a; Hdn. *Pros.* p. 96.31–35 Lentz; *Suda* s.v. Πρίαπος.
20 Whether Greek novels reflect these anxieties is a topic of scholarly debate (Montiglio 2005, 224 cites the relevant bibliography).

The Hitchhiker's Guide to Becoming a Priapus Worshipper

Encolpius' wanderings and sufferings are only a step in the process of him becoming a *colonus* of Priapus. Like anyone who settles in a new community must adapt to a different lifestyle, the hero also needs to undergo a transformation, which is effectuated gradually through his participation in various religious events. All the festivals and rituals which are either attested or alluded to in the narrative are, one way or the other, related to Priapus. This connection establishes their marginal character, especially in the case of Quartilla's, Proselenos', and Oenothea's rituals, because as priapic rites they are in complete accord with the marginal character of the deity supervising them. The marginality of these rites is underscored further by their close resemblance with witchcraft, the simplicity of the space where they take place, as well as their highly sexualized nature, reflecting the common elitist prejudice for low-class religion in general.[21]

Before his arrival in the bay of Naples, however, Encolpius had probably made a stop at Rome where he witnessed the celebration of the Saturnalia as 69.9 suggests (*vidi Romae Saturnalibus eiusmodi cenarum imaginem fieri*).[22] The Saturnalia, along with the *ludi triumphales* and the Floralia, belonged to a peculiar category of festivals which centered around the inversion of social and/or moral norms and as such it is possible to view them as a religious event during which the unusual became the norm or, as one might say, the mainstream was replaced by what was considered marginal (e.g., the treatment of slaves as masters, and vice-versa). Their purpose was to ward off the Evil Eye, a function further affirmed by the prominent use of obscenities in many of them.[23] Even though our knowledge on the Saturnalia is limited, it is quite possible that Priapus, who did not have his own festival, but was worshipped during those of other deities, would be honored in the Saturnalia as the main apotropaic deity

---

21 Šterbenc Erker 2013, 130 (referring to the rituals of Quartilla): "Customarily, however, propagating the stereotype of sexual debauchery during nocturnal religious festivals is a way of proclaiming upper-class morality ... In the *Satyrica*, we thus find not only parodic versions of 'correct' ritual, but also the misconceptions of the Roman elite about the superstitious beliefs of lower social strata".

22 For the presence of Encolpius in the Saturnalia before his arrival in the *Graeca urbs*, see Schmeling and Setaioli 2011, 286.

23 My discussion on these festivals is greatly indebted to the discussion in Richlin 1992, 10 who cites the relevant bibliography on pp. 228–229.

of Roman religion.[24] In addition, since these festivals required the annulment of boundaries, the participants would ask for divine permission from the deity who was charged with their protection. Therefore, we can assume that the narrative of Encolpius' adventures in Rome would have included a 'priapic' episode during the Saturnalia, in which everyone was allowed to join, unlike the mysteries of Quartilla.

The journey continues to the south, and at some point, Encolpius arrives in Pozzuoli.[25] While roaming in the city, the company came across a shrine of Priapus, and somehow disturbed the god's mysteries (16.3: *vos sacrum ante cryptam turbastis* ...). Quartilla appears soon after to reveal her distress because the uninitiated fellows witnessed the *nocturnas religiones* (17.8), further claiming that she fell ill because of their actions. She also states that she sought a cure and was given specific instructions for a remedy in her dream (17.7). Even though she does not reveal who gave the instructions, Quartilla's role as priestess of Priapus, the lewd character of the ritual in 20–26, as well as the epiphanies of the god to Lichas (104.1) and possibly to Encolpius in fr. 31 suggest that it would have been the god who appeared in her dream and advised her on the proper course of action.[26]

The ritual described in 20–26 is odd, and the sole consensus among scholars concerns its parodic character.[27] Its exact purpose is unclear, but it has been argued that it serves as Encolpius' initiation rite to the priapic cult, based on the statements of Quartilla as well as certain elements of the scene.[28] Instead of a temple, the whole ritual takes place in a brothel (16.4: *stabulum*), which seems an appropriate venue for the worship of a salacious deity like Priapus, who was also the patron god of Roman sexuality. The priestess orders no one to enter the

---

24 Juv. 6.314–317 mentions that the Maenads of Priapus participated in the festivals of the *Bona Dea*; Saint Augustine (*De civ. D.* 7.21), citing Varro, informs us that the priapic phallus was worshipped in the Dionysiac festivals around the countryside; the *fascinum* played an apotropaic role in the *ludi triumphales* as a talisman worn by the victorious general during the triumphal procession (Macrob. *Sat.* 1.6.9). Perhaps Priapus was also venerated in the *ludi Florales* considering the role of prostitutes in the festival, and the position of Priapus as the patron god of Roman sexuality. Mart. 10.92 draws a mythological connection between Flora and Priapus, and maybe *CP* 34 refers to the festivities of the Floralia.

25 For the identification of the *Graeca urbs* with Pozzuoli (Puteoli) see Sullivan 1968, 46–47.

26 Schmeling and Setaioli 2011, 51: the appearance of Priapus in Quartilla's dream is further supported by Encolpius' indirect statement in 18.3 (*si quod praeterea aliud remedium ad tertianam deus illi monstrasset*).

27 Walsh 1970, 89: Quartilla is a comic version of Virgil's Sibyl; Šterbenc Erker 2013, 130; Pinna 1978, 223–236 (parody of dionysiac and oriental mysteries).

28 Cosci 1980, 199–201; Panoussi 2019, 68–69 (parody of initiation or mystery rites).

building (19.2), thus turning the place into an *abaton* or *telestērion*. Like other mysteries such as the Greater Eleusinians, it was in this isolated space where the initiates along with the priests would witness the *legomena*, the *drōmena*, and the *deiknymena*, and later reenact parts of the deity's life. In the framework of an initiation ritual the *satyrion* (20.7) can be viewed as the communion drink shared among the participants, with its role being similar to that of the *kykeon*.[29] The procedural similarities with the Eleusinian mysteries might confirm the role of Quartilla's rites as a ritual of initiation, while the transformation of the *stabulum* in a sacred space underscores the marginality of the whole process.

The subsequent rapes of Encolpius and Ascyltus by the *cinaedi* as well as Giton's defloration of Pannychis also fit the parodic and ritualistic character of the scene. The sexual penetration of Petronius' heroes (21.2) might be viewed as an exaggerated mock-version of the practice of διαμηρισμός, which appears to have been part of maturation rites.[30] But it also reminds us of the usual punishment the god inflicts on thieves (*CP* 28; 35; 38) which, in some sense, is justified on the grounds of the company having 'stolen' the secrets of the god's cult (17.4). The phrase used to describe the change of active partners during the scene with the second catamite (24.4: *equum cinaedus mutavit*) is a metaphor for intercourse, but it is also a verbal replication of ritualistic imagery from the festivals of Dionysus (Florence Cup).[31] The culmination of the parodic ritual is the defloration of Pannychis by Giton which occurs during a mock ritual of wedding in 25.2:[32]

> *'ita, ita' inquit Quartilla 'bene admonuisti. cur non, quia bellissima occasio est, devirginatur Pannychis nostra?' ... plaudentibus ergo universis et postulantibus nuptias [fecerunt].*

> 'Yes, yes,' said Quartilla, 'thanks for reminding me. It's such an excellent opportunity, why shouldn't our little Pannychis lose her virginity?' ... Everyone applauded and called for a wedding.

---

29 A brief but enlightening discussion on the Eleusinian mysteries, and what they entailed can be found in Keller 2009. For my comparison with the rituals of Quartilla I rely on her discussion on page 35.

30 Barringer 2001, 72, 75 and 113 with relevant bibliography.

31 In his discussion of the Florence Cup, Csapo 1997, 269 observes that "on Side A there is another figure in addition... He rides the satyr like a horse and hits the satyr's flanks with a riding crop that he carries in his left hand". The satyr, in turn, is depicted riding an oversized phallus. For the meaning of the expression *equum ... mutavit* see Adams 1982, 165–166.

32 Panoussi 2019, 75–78 interprets the wedding as a parody of an *hieros gamos* in the context of an initiation ritual.

The custom of the bride's defloration on the first night of marriage was partially under Priapus' authority, as Christian authors attest, claiming that the bride should 'sit on a statue' of Priapus before her sexual union with her husband.[33] Of course this testimony is probably an invention of the conservative Christian writers or an exaggeration of the role of Priapus in the first night of marriage, and it is more reasonable to assume that Priapus was among those gods who were summoned to attend the defloration.[34]

From another aspect, these sexual encounters also exemplify the motif of inversion which characterized the festivals of the Saturnalia and the Floralia: Encolpius and Ascyltus who were the active partners in their respective relationships with Giton, assume a submissive role in their sexual encounter with the *cinaedi*, while Giton becomes the active partner for the mock wedding with Pannychis.[35] This might be the result of Petronius' attempt to apply the inversion model on the mysteries of Priapus. The presence of the motif also points to the marginality of the ritual through the transgression of sexual boundaries.

Unorthodox Healing at Croton

After leaving Pozzuoli for Tarentum and while on board of Lichas' ship, Encolpius gets shipwrecked, and is saved by some sailors (114.14). He then arrives to the city of Croton (116.2). There he becomes the lover of Circe, a wealthy *matrona* who uses him as her boy-toy. However, the hero is afflicted by impotence and is unable to please her, thus recalling the literary figure of Priapus in the *Carmina Priapea* who admits or alludes to his temporary impotence and inability to please the *pathicas puellas*.[36] Thus, Encolpius' illness reenacts the sufferings endured by the god not in the mythological framework, but in the literary context.

Encolpius' assumption that the cause of his impotence is some type of magic (128.2: *veneficio contactus sum*) as well as the sexual nature of his problem prefigure his subsequent resorting to the shrine of Priapus for healing since the

---

33 Arn. *Adv. Nat.* 4.7 (referring to Tutunus who was assimilated with Priapus [Aug. *De civ. D.* 4.11]); Lactant. *Div. Inst.* 1.20.36; Aug. *De civ. D.* 6.9; 7.24.

34 For the role of Priapus in Roman weddings, see Hersch 2010, 270.

35 Panoussi 2019, 68 discusses the reversal of sexual roles between men and women in the scene but applies it also to the union of Giton and Pannychis.

36 *CP* 73 is the most conspicuous example. The motif of Priapus' impotence in the *Priapea* is explored in Holzberg 2005, 368–381.

god was considered the divine protector against magic, and the patron of Roman sexuality. Before that, however, Proselenos, the assistant of the god's priestess attempts a healing ritual in a grove (131.4–7), the space which was often guarded by the god through his effigies:[37]

> *Illa de sinu licium prolulit varii coloris filis intortum, cervicemque vinxit meam. Mox turbatum sputo pulverem medio sustulit digito, frontemque repugnantis signavit ... Hoc peracto carmine ter me iussit expuere terque lapillos conicere in sinum, quos ipsa praecantatos purpura involuerat, admotisque manibus temptare coepit inguinum vires. Dicto citius nervi paruerunt imperio, manusque aniculae ingenti motu repleverunt. At illa gaudio exultans: 'Vides, inquit, Chrysis mea, vides, quod aliis leporem excitavi?'*

> The old woman brought out of her dress a string of variously coloured threads twisted together and bound it round my neck. Then mixing some dust with spittle, she took it on her middle finger and ignoring my repugnance, marked my forehead with it ... After completing this spell, she instructed me to spit three times and drop down my chest, again three times, some pebbles which she had charmed and wrapped in purple. Then she began to test my virility with her hands. Faster than you could speak, the nerves obeyed the command, and the little old woman's hands were filled with a mighty throbbing. Leaping with joy, she said: "Do you see, my dear Chrysis, do you see how I've started a hare for others to hunt?"

Proselenos' ritual includes several elements which are often found in witchcraft: she begins by creating a *periamma* and places it around the hero's neck; she then proceeds with a superstitious gesture of marking his forehead with her middle finger using mud and saliva.[38] The text becomes fragmented, but the ritual seems to have included an utterance, which, given the context, would resemble a spell.[39] Immediately after, she orders Encolpius to spit thrice on his bosom, and throw three rocks wrapped in purple clothing.[40] Finally, the old lady rubs Encolpius' genitals in order to sexually arouse him, and she initially succeeds. The general structure which follows the pattern of *logos-praxis*, but especially the details, sketch the ritual as witchcraft rather than a mainstream healing rite.[41]

---

37 E.g., Mart. 8.40; Serv. ad Virg. *G.* 4.111.
38 The connection between these elements of Proselenos' ritual and magic has been noted in Schmeling and Setaioli 2011, 499–500, who also cite the relevant studies separately.
39 Schmeling and Setaioli 2011, 500.
40 The use of rocks, and the action of spitting one's bosom are often encountered in magic rituals. For detailed references and related studies see Schmeling and Setaioli 2011, 500–501.
41 For the two-tiered structure of the *PGM* spells (*logos-praxis*), see Martinez 1991, 8.

Proselenos' cure did not have a permanent effect and the malady strikes back. Encolpius gets beaten and kicked out of the house of Circe (132.2–4). He then arrives in a local small temple of Priapus (133.4) where a second healing ritual takes place, this time by the main priestess, Oenothea. The concept of visiting a god's temple to seek cure for an illness (healing pilgrimage) is well-attested in the ancient world, especially in the sanctuaries of Asclepios.[42] Against this first-line god of Graeco-Roman religion, and the popular practice of incubation in his sanctuaries, the Asclepeiia, Petronius juxtaposes the quasi-magical — and therefore marginal — rituals of Oenothea, and the small *delubrum* of the phallic god. The latter resembles more a humble hut rather than a sacred space (the old table, the smoky wall of the room, the broken cup in 135.3–4, as well as the rotten stool in 136.1 point to the poverty of the place), and its simplicity foreshadows the marginal character of the main ritual. Besides, Encolpius calls the inner part of the temple where Proselenos drags him a *cellam sacerdotis* (134.3). The word denotes any main or secondary space in a temple, a small room, but also a room in a brothel.[43] This last definition appears also in Petronius (8.4) and maybe the use of the word would point to the ambiguous character of the main rite.

The use of materials which were encountered in magic rituals during Oenothea's preparations (135.3–6) brings the whole religious process closer to witchcraft. More specifically, the black pitch (*pice temperata*) was among the substances often used in witchcraft due to its color; beans (*faba*) had magical properties, and their binding together is meant to control the time their magic is going to work;[44] after Encolpius killed Priapus' sacred goose, Oenothea cleanses his hands (137.10) with leek (*porris*) and parsley (*apio*) which are both materials used in magic.[45] Afterwards, she throws some hazelnuts (*nuces*) in a vessel while murmuring a prayer, and makes predictions (*conjecturam ducebat*), which can be viewed as an effort to engage in bowl divination, a common magic ritual for predicting the future.[46]

---

42 On Asclepius, his cult, and healing sanctuaries, see Steger 2018.

43 *OLD* s.v. *cella*.

44 For the use of black pitch in witchcraft, and the significance of storing beans together within the context of magic, see Schmeling and Setaioli 2011, 524.

45 For the use of these herbs in magic rituals see the references in Schmeling and Setaioli 2011, 534 as well as the *quasi*-magical recipes of folk medicine in Plin. *HN* 20.112–115.

46 E.g., PGM IV 3209–3254; III 276; IV 154–285.

The climax of the scene is the healing ritual detailed in 138.1–2:

Profert Oenothea scorteum fascinum, quod ut oleo et minuto pipere atque urticae trito cir-
cumdedit semine, paulatim coepit inserere ano meo ... Hoc crudelissima anus spargit subin-
de umore femina mea ... Nasturcii sucum cum habrotono miscet, perfusisque inguinibus meis
viridis urticae fascem comprehendit omniaque infra umbilicum coepit lenta manu caedere ...

Oenothea brought out a leather dildo: this she rubbed with oil and ground pepper and
crushed nettle seed, and began inserting it gradually up my anus ... The vicious old woman then sprinkled my thighs with this liquid ... She mixed the juice of cress with some
southern-wood, and after soaking my genitals in it, she took a green nettle-stalk and began whipping me steadily everywhere below the navel ...

The procedure bears close resemblance to the ritual described in Hipponax fr. 92
W which tended to the cure of male sexual problems.[47] But it also recalls certain
aspects of magic rituals such as smearing the genitals with a mixture of substances (pepper is often included).[48] The links with witchcraft rites establish the
marginality of the rituals of Oenothea, but the rape of Encolpius with the *fasci-*
num enhance it further through the intratextual connection with the Quartilla
episode, and the inversion of the role of Encolpius as an active sexual partner
(with Circe this time) to that of the one getting penetrated.

Conclusion: Marginal title for marginal deity

I will now show that it is possible to interpret the title of the novel within the
context of marginality. Most scholars accept that the *Satyrica* or *Satyricon* point
to the lewd character of the god and the general lasciviousness of the narrative
events, while some suggest that it might be intentionally ambiguous, referring
also to the literary genre of the *Satura* through a clever pun.[49] But it might also
allude to marginality as the main axis of Petronius' work through the connection of its main deity, Priapus, with the Satyrs.[50] The mythological followers of
Dionysus, apart from their lewdness, also share with Priapus the trait of marginality as human-goat hybrids who live outside the boundaries of human habi-
tation, in the woods and mountains. The ithyphallic god is found frequently

---

47 The similarity has been already noted in West 1974, 144.
48 Schmeling and Setaioli 2011, 535.
49 Walsh 1970, 72; Courtney 2001, 14.
50 Jensson 2004, 114 characterizes Encolpius as a "contemporary Satyr".

among their company both in myths as well as in art: In Ovid's *Fasti*, Priapus appears twice among the Satyrs and Silenus, trying to rape either the nymph Lotis or the goddess Vesta, while artistic depictions of the deity among the Dionysiac *thiasos* abound.[51] In fact, the god became a stock figure in the Greco-Roman depictions of Bacchic content.[52] Besides, Encolpius calls the god *Bacchi comes*, and *tutor* in the *preces* he offers by the threshold of Oenothea's temple (133.3). His worship became so closely associated with that of Dionysus to the point that in certain areas the two gods were even assimilated.[53] Since the figure of Priapus was strongly linked with Dionysus and his followers, maybe the word *Satyros* would be used as a general term for all the eponymous and nameless followers of the god, including the ithyphallic deity.[54]

Priapus constant presence in the background or in the fore of the narrative, and the ritual of the *pharmakos* as a trigger for Encolpius' wanderings allow the reading of the *Satyrica* as an account of religious travels. But the salacious character of the risible deity has a broad effect on the novel, establishing both its parodic nature and marginal aspect. The mythological *vita* of the god who belongs to the margins of Roman religious life served as a general model for the adventures of the anti-hero, Encolpius, perhaps reflecting the anxieties of low-class people during the Imperial period who would become marginalized through their wanderings in search of a better future. The important role of this marginal god in the plot might have been inferred from the title since his figure appeared more than often in representations of Satyr-Dionysiac themes in the Greco-Roman world. His lasciviousness could be matched only by that of the Satyrs, in whose company he was often portrayed. On these grounds, we could assume that the word *Satyros* might have pointed to Priapus as a member of the *thiasos*, and thus the title alludes to him.

---

51 Ov. *Fast*. 1.414–440; 6.319–348.
52 Priapus as a member of the Dionysian *thiasos*: *LIMC* VIII Suppl. 36, 58, 63, 99, 120; Priapus with Satyrs: *LIMC* VIII Suppl. 17, 32, 34, 38, 59, 64, 139; Priapus participating in the mysteries of Dionysus: *LIMC* VIII Suppl. 93, 103, 127, 150, 151; Priapus in the company of maenads and nymphs: *LIMC* VIII Suppl. 110, 16, 33, 39, 60.
53 O'Connor 1989, 18–20.
54 Derkyllus' now-lost *Satyrica* was probably dealing with myths relating to Dionysus and his followers: Γεννᾶται δ' ἐν τῷ ποταμῷ τούτῳ (Μαρσύᾳ) βοτάνη, αὐλὸς ὀνομαζομένη, ἣν ἐὰν πρὸς ἄνεμον σείσῃ τις μουσικὴν ἔχει μελῳδίαν, καθὼς ἱστορεῖ Δέρκυλος ἐν α' Σατυρικῶν ("A weed grows in this river, the Marsyas, which is named 'flute', and which produces music, if someone moves it to and fro the wind, as Derkylos in the first book of the Satyrica narrates").

Theodore Antoniadis

Marginalizing Exemplarity? Hercules in Silius Italicus' *Punica*

Abstract: Focusing on the dynamics of marginality and marginalization sur-rounding Hercules' liminal, vulnerable, and ambivalent status in the *Punica* as well as his transgressive heroism, this chapter casts further light on the epic's moralizing mechanism which often invests on ambiguity to evoke the abnormal ethics of the early Empire. It illustrates how the complicated aspects of Hercules as a model for kingship and cosmocracy, square not only with his autocratic twist in Seneca's *Hercules Furens*, but also with his implicit 'marginalization' in the Flavian epics as a result of his emotional instability. More specifically, Her-cules' complex heroic *exemplum* together with his liminal status is best reflected in the polarized portrayal of the major characters of the *Punica* who are con-nected to him either as heroes or villains, while it resonates the emotional in-stability and extreme theatricality of Rome's controversial emperor, Nero, whose disastrous reign left an indelible mark on his age.

Introduction

In the case of a poetic work such as an epic, the product of literary fiction, to identify an individual character or a group of people as 'liminal' entails a set of criteria that may differ from those applied to prose texts relating the lives of real people and their stories. The question of marginality, in terms of class, ethnici-ty, religion, gender, and many other factors embedded in the core of this pro-ject, becomes perhaps more challenging if such issues are addressed in the context of a poem with a historical or even mythological background which reveals a sustained interest in the interactions between literature and politics. This seems to be the case with the epics of Neronian and Flavian literature, which are now thoroughly grounded on their historical context but continue to trigger scholarly interest concerning the multiple ways they reflect upon the atmosphere of violence, political turmoil, and civil strife that marked their era.

I am grateful to Neil Bernstein and John Jacobs for their comments and suggestions on the first draft of this paper as well as to the editors of the volume for their critical remarks which sub-stantively improved its final version.

https://doi.org/10.1515/9783111063942-008

A recent trend among critics is to focus on the moral ambivalence of the main characters of these poems, not only due to their prominent place in the action, but particularly because their portrayal is susceptible to differing assessments and interpretations as well as to varying interconnections to the *Zeitgeist* of the early Roman empire. In this chapter, however, I consider those cases where dominant figures of myth, ritual, and literary imagination are somehow marginalized as a result of their liminal role in the epics or of their ethically irrelevant impact in the course of a narrative.

One of these 'preeminent outsiders', as I would like to call them, is Hercules in the *Punica* of Silius Italicus. From Homer's violent brute (*Od.* 21.26–30; *Il.* 19.103–106) to Virgil's vanquisher of Cacus (*Aen.* 8.174–279), Livy's protector of the world (*vindex terrae*, 10.5.5), Horace's peacemaker (*Carm.* 2.12.6–7, 3.3.9–12, 3.14.1–4, *Epist.* 2.1.10–12) and Seneca's Stoic sage (*Const.* 2.1), Hercules has been showcased as a lasting popular figure of Graeco-Roman cult, philosophy, and politics. His special qualities as an archetypal hero were often appropriated and redefined to shape the ideologies and concerns of different people and ages.[1] Moreover, some of his representations, like those, for example, in the tragedies of Euripides and Seneca bearing his name, expose the volatility of his "exemplary heroism", which led some critics to call him a "congenitally unstable character" or even "the most ambivalent creature in myth".[2]

This chapter illustrates how the complicated aspects of Hercules as a model for kingship and cosmocracy, already apparent not only in Virgil's manifold associations of the deified hero with Aeneas (*Aen.* 8.362–368) and Augustus (*Aen.* 6.801–803),[3] but also in his autocratic twist in Seneca's *Hercules Furens*, square with his implicit 'marginalization' in the Flavian epics as a result of his emotional instability and unbalanced psychology. Focusing on the *Punica*, I shall argue further that Hercules' complex heroic exemplum together with his liminal status is best reflected in the polarized portrayal of the major characters of the epic, who are variably connected to him either as heroes or villains, while it resonates with the emotional instability and extreme theatricality of Rome's

---

1 On the adaptations of Hercules' figure in literature, Galinsky 1972 remains an influential study. On his representation in the Flavian epics, see Bassett 1966; Billerbeck 1986a, and 1986b; Ripoll 1998, 86–163; Asso 2010; Tipping 2010b.

2 See Feeney 1982, 52; Hardie 1993, 66; Tipping 2010a, 14–15. For a comparative analysis of Hercules in the plays of Euripides and Seneca, see Papadopoulou 2004.

3 For many readers, Hercules' frenzied fury in dispatching Cacus is mirrored in Aeneas' refusal to spare Turnus at the end of the poem. See Virg. *Aen.* 8.228–232, 12.946–947 with Hardie 1993, 66–67 and the discussion on *Aen.* 7.791–805, 8.184–279 and *G.* 4.560–562 in Tipping 2010a, 15–16 who supplies the relevant bibliography.

most controversial emperor, Nero, whose disastrous reign left an indelible mark on his age, the subsequent civil strife of 68–69 CE and the Flavian era.

Struggling for Glory: Hercules in Valerius Flaccus' *Argonautica*

In the *Argonautica* of Valerius Flaccus, Hercules' imposing presence as the most distinguished member of Jason's crew exercises a remarkable influence upon his comrades, at least until his separation as a result of Juno's plots. For instance, when Jason and his men are amorously received by the widowed women of Lemnos (2.77–393), Hercules is the only one to chide them for delaying the enterprise in contrast to his own unremitting struggle for glory and immortal fame (2.377–384). He further demonstrates his *rerum ... amor* (2.381) through the rescue of Hesione, the daughter of king Laomedon of Troy (2.445–578), the liberation of Prometheus from his imprisonment in the Caucasus (4.58–81; 5.154–176), and his battle against the Amazons (5.128–139). Even when he is forced to abandon the campaign in search of Hylas (3.459–486) and appears to be generically transformed into an elegiac lover,[4] Valerius' Hercules never ceases to embody the qualities of a divinely sanctioned hero.[5] His 'marginalization' may be part of the Argonautic saga, but does not essentially detract from his exemplarity as a warrior since his courage and bravery are to be sorely missed by his former comrades on several occasions during the rest of their voyage.[6]

---

4 See V. Fl. 3.576–577, and 587–591 with Heerink 2007.

5 On Hercules' figure in Valerius Flaccus, see Feeney 1991, 333–335; Edwards 1999; Buckley 2014, 319–324; Castelleti 2014, 176.

6 Cf. (with Billerbeck 1986b, 3133 n. 85) V. Fl. 4.84: *multa ... deserto memores super Hercule volvunt*; 4.247: *redit Alcidae iam sera cupido*; 5.43 (Jason's lament for losing him): *ubi monstriferae par ille novercae?* See also V. Fl. 3.724; 5.113–115, 171–176 and the comparisons at V. Fl. 7.622–628; 8.124–126 with Edwards 1999, 161–163. Cf. Meleager's devious argument in favor of leaving Hercules behind at V. Fl. 3.649–689.

A Peerless Forebear with Poor Successors: Hercules in Statius' *Thebaid*

Hercules' image with its allegorical connotations is further appropriated by Statius, who appears to have endorsed more intricately the demigod's gradual relegation to his marginal status. This is what one may understand from the equivocating allusions to the hero in the course of another expedition in *Thebaid*. On the surface, it all starts again with an honorary mention of him as an exemplar of *prisca fides* and *virtus*. As they arm themselves against Thebes, a group of Tirynthian soldiers pays tribute to their renowned ancestor by singing a war paean to him (4.145–163). Hercules' ambivalent ancestry, however, posed a kind of a paradox that Statius was keen to exploit in his version of the war of the Seven against Thebes. Having been raised in Thebes by a family from Tiryns, the demigod is not so much concerned with the fate of his Argive kinsmen, but he is rather preoccupied with the survival of the Thebans, who claim him as their foremost god together with Bacchus (10.899–901; 11.223–25). Thus, he appears to do nothing to help the Tirynthian soldiers in battle (11.46–48); on the contrary, he even intervenes to save the Theban Haemon (8.456–520). Likewise, Hercules' sons, Chromis (6.436–438) and Agylleus (6.824–910), who had joined the Argive army, are rather unexpectedly beaten in the funeral games for Opheltes which take place in Nemea, the location of Hercules' first labor.[7] Most importantly, it is Polynices' striking failure to win the prize of the chariot race, which is a crater of great symbolic import, once the property of the Tirynthian champion, depicting Hercules' participation in the fight between Centaurs and Lapiths.[8] Wearing a lion's hide upon his arrival at Argos, the Theban prince is envisaged by Statius as "a Hercules in the making, who still needs though to prove his worth".[9] Leading therefore the race with Arion, a divine steed Hercules had driven against several monsters (6.311–313), Polynices is projected as the absolute favorite to win the mixing bowl. To the readers' surprise, however, he is helplessly thrown from the chariot (6.491–506) when Apollo dispatches a monster from the underworld to scare his horse and steal the victory in favor of

---

7 See further Rebeggiani 2018, 137–139 who notes that Agylleus' failure "reproduces, yet subverts, the outcome of one of Hercules' deeds, namely the fight with the river Achelous". Similarly, in Stat. *Theb.* 2.613–619, Chromis, who has Theban origins and is dressed precisely like the demigod (with lion skin, club etc.), is confronted with Tydeus and is again defeated.
8 For a stimulating reading of the crater's ekphrasis at Stat. *Theb.* 6.531–539, see Rebeggiani 2018, 126–130.
9 Cf. Stat. *Theb.* 1.483–487 with Rebeggiani 2018, 137.

his own protégé, Amphiaraus (6.431–433, 518–530). As a result, Polynices fails to appropriate the role of the exemplary hero and, like Hercules' sons, is eventually stripped of his Herculean identity. Thus, while his desperate self-identification with the demigod may at first seem to counterbalance his shame-faced self-representation in *Thebaid* 1 when he conceals from Adrastus his descent from Oedipus so as to dissociate himself from his ancestral stigma, eventually his affiliation with Hercules is exemplified only in his lust for power as and his *gentilis furor* against his family (1.126). On the contrary, his liminal status as a Herculean revenger and kin murderer is established through the vision of his brother Eteocles being defeated and cast aside, while he himself is seated on the throne (1.316–323) and is further authenticated after Tisiphone's manipulations, in the fratricidal duel of *Thebaid* 11.

Helpless, Ambivalent, Transgressive: Hercules' Marginalization in Silius Italicus' *Punica*

Hercules' heroic figure, together with his proverbial exemplarity, becomes far more complex once we turn to the *Punica* of Silius Italicus, an epic where the gods in general intervene most vigorously in the narrative of an otherwise purely historical event to pursue their own agenda.[10] As Asso has argued, however, Silius' choice of restoring the divine machinery in his account of the Second Punic War "feels inevitably problematic, especially after Lucan's pessimistic exclusion of the gods' design in human affairs".[11] Hercules, in particular, despite his prominent position early in the narrative through his involvement in the aetiological story of the foundation of Saguntum (1.272–295), repeatedly fails to live up to the expectations of both the city's inhabitants as well as Silius' readers. This becomes evident as soon as Hannibal attacks Rome's most revered ally.

For most readers, Silius presents the Carthaginian assault on Saguntum as an outrageous crime against Rome inasmuch as, from the very outset, the two cities are closely identified with each other on the basis of their common herit-

---

10 Consider, for instance, *Pun.* 10.83–90 (Juno drives Hannibal to kill Paulus); 12.605–629 (Jupiter sends down thunderbolts to repel Hannibal from the Capitol); 17.522–553 (Juno disguises herself as Scipio to draw away Hannibal from the battlefield). See also *Pun.* 12.725; 17.236–289.
11 Asso 2010, 179.

age and their present fate as victims of Hannibal's *furor*.[12] Similarly, Hannibal's breaching of Saguntum's walls is cast as an impious act, not only against the Romans, but also against the god himself, who is said to have fortified the city (1.273: *Herculei … muri*; 1.369: *Herculeus labor*). Nevertheless, Hercules remains a mere spectator of the ultimate destruction of the city, which was traditionally depicted as an exemplar of *pietas* and *fides* on account of its inhabitants' determination to die out of their loyalty to Rome.[13] His passivity is evident at the moment when Murrus, a brave warrior of Rutulian, Saguntine, and Greek stock (1.377–379), invokes him before his duel with Hannibal (1.505–507):

> **Conditor** *Alcide, cuius vestigia sacra*
> *incolimus, terrae minitantem averte procellam,*
> *si* **tua** *non segni defenso* **moenia** *dextra.*

> Hercules, **founder** of our city, on our land we tend your holy footsteps. Turn away this threatening storm of battle, if my hand is not lazy as it defends **your walls**.[14]

Murrus supplicates Hercules to support him in the name of the city which honored him as its *conditor* (505) because of the prowess he exhibited himself earlier in defending Hercules' fortifications. His *aristeia* at 1.376–420 substantiates his claim indeed, whereas his triple descent encompasses the voices of people with different ethnic, religious, and cultural backgrounds who revered the demigod.[15] One needs only to recall Pallas' similar invocation of Hercules in the *Aeneid* (10.461: *te precor, Alcide, coeptis ingentibus adsis*). Contrary to the demigod's emotional outburst in Virgil, though, Feeney observes that Silius' Hercules will not even shed a tear ahead of Murrus' *suprema vota* followed by his moral and physical collapse with the prospect of his death (1.504–505).[16]

On top of Hercules' deafening silence, Hannibal's seemingly outrageous claim to the demigod's 'patronage' on account of his own *ausis* (509) and *aemula virtus* (510) follows as a sardonic reply to Murrus' prayer. By raising so provocatively his ambition to emulate Hercules' deeds while attacking a city dear to

---

12 Cf. especially *Pun.* 1.349: *veluti circumfata vallo Roma foret.* On Saguntum's representation as a second or alternative Rome both in cultural and historical terms, see von Albrecht 1964, 172–183; Dominik 2003 *passim.*

13 Cf. Liv. 21.73; Val. Max. 6.6 ext.1 with Feeney 1982, 183. Lucan had paralleled the siege of Massilia by Caesar to that of Saguntum by Hannibal emphasizing the common aspects of *pietas* and *fides.* See BC 3.302, 342, 349–350.

14 All translations of the *Punica* are taken from Augoustakis and Bernstein 2021.

15 See Asso 2010, 180–181.

16 Feeney 1982, 253–254.

the deity, the Carthaginian leader is presented as the successor of his transgressive heroism and his ambitious lifestyle as exemplified in Valerius' epic. While Silius here is probably following a tradition according to which Hannibal used to cast himself as Hercules for propagandistic purposes, the reiteration of this specific claim on several other occasions, particularly with regard to his crossing of the Alps, apart from accentuating Hannibal's hubristic attitude, complicates further the construction of Hercules as a model for mankind.[17] This idea gradually gains more ground in the *Punica* as Hercules' exemplarity will be invariably questioned, before he is projected as a paradigm of human divinity for Scipio Africanus in the course of the 'Scipiad' of Books 12–17 (see below).[18]

As Silius' account of the fall of Saguntum reaches its climax (2.457–707), Hercules' figure is invoked even more vividly in the poetic narrative of a historical event with its own exemplary tradition.[19] Murrus' memorable resistance is now followed by the patriotic display of Theron, the guardian of Hercules' shrine, whose attire and weapons again serve as emblematic icons of the hero's power and labors (2.153–159):

> *atque illi non hasta manu, non vertice cassis,*
> *sed fisus latis umeris et mole iuventae*
> *agmina vastabat claua, nihil indigus ensis.*
> *Exuviae capiti impositae tegimenque leonis*
> *terribilem attollunt excelso vertice rictum.*
> *Centum angues idem **Lernaeaque monstra** gerebat*
> *in clipeo et sectis geminam serpentibus **hydram***

But he did not have a spear in his hand, nor a helmet on his head. He trusted rather in his broad shoulders and his youthful bulk, and in no need of a sword his club devastated the enemy ranks. A lion's skin, spoils worn on his head, lifted a terrible grin from its lofty peak. This same Theron bore a hundred serpents upon his shield and **Lerna's monster**, the **Hydra** redoubling as its snakes were sliced.

---

17 Cf. also *Pun.* 2.334–337, 349–357; 3.91–92; 4.4–5, 63–64; 11.135–136, 218; 15.505–506 with Liv. 21.41.7: *Hannibal ... aemulus itinerum Herculis, ut ipse fert*. On Hannibal's misunderstanding of his chosen model see Feeney 1982, 157 and Asso 2010, 183–185. Note also Hercules' association with Fabius and Scipio, further discussed below.

18 See Asso 2010, 189–192. The term 'Scipiad' for the last five books of the *Punica* was coined by Hardie 1993, 97.

19 Cf. Luc. *BC* 3.349–350; Petron. *Sat.* 140.6; Juv. 15.113–115 where the Saguntines are commemorated as a paradigm of *fides* and *virtus*. See further von Albrecht 1964, 58–59; Bernstein 2016, 229 n. 5.

Theron's fighting method with a club and a shield that bears the Hydra as a Herculean emblem also indicates the demigod's "absent presence" in the whole scene as was the case Statius' Polynices and Chromis discussed above.[20] Meanwhile, the etymological association of Theron's name with the Greek verbs θη-ράω/θηρεύω ("to hunt") has been thought to evoke the bestial side of his patron-god as a hunter and monster-slayer, which the Saguntine profoundly expounds upon in the slaughtering of numerous Carthaginians and, above all, their most eminent ally, Asbyte (2.160–205).[21] This female warrior, fashioned by Silius as an Amazon virgin-huntress and modelled after Virgil's Camilla,[22] meets a cruel end by Hercules' doppelgänger. In a close revival of the Tirynthian's heroic display against the Nemean lion and Hydra, Theron smashes the virgin's head with his club and finally decapitates her.[23] For most readers, such a gruesome death is in stark contrast with the decorous death of Camilla in the *Aeneid* or that of Hippolyte, the queen of the Amazons whom Hercules had killed to seize her girdle.[24] Silius' focus on the 'otherness' of his female warrior, on the one hand, and Theron's Herculean monstrosity, on the other, is not accidental. As Augoustakis observes, throughout the episode Asbyte's virginity is stressed with the repetition of the word *virgo* (2.84, 114, 121, 168, 176, 188, 202) and her commitment to chastity (2.68: *haec ignara viri vacuoque adsueta cubili*).[25] On the contrary, Theron features as the very embodiment of Hercules' fury, which will be showcased on its own terms in the subsequent rape of Pyrene. As a result of his overreaching, Theron eventually fails to secure the support of the god whose shrine he guards and whose excellence he is struggling to emulate. As he is about to confront Hannibal, Theron is described as *caecus fati divumque abeunte favore* (2.207). We may guess that Theron has probably lost Hercules' favor, just like Murrus before him or Polynices in *Thebaid* 6. Consequently, his

---

20 See further Bernstein 2016, 100–101 who refers to Hercules' "absent present" in his discussion of the ekphrasis of his temple at Gades where the lion and Hydra are the first two labors displayed (3.32–34).

21 Cf. Ov. *Met.* 3.11 with Tipping 2010a, 19 n. 23.

22 Cf. especially *Pun.* 2.68–81 with Virg. *Aen.* 7.813–817, 11.567–584. See further Augoustakis 2010a, 123–126 and Bernstein 2017a, 104–105. Asbyte's participation in the siege of Saguntum is not attested by any historian, which makes her an exclusively Silian invention.

23 See *Pun.* 2.196–202 with Augoustakis 2010a, 126–128 and Bernstein 2017a, 99.

24 Neither of the two Amazons is beheaded. On Hippolyte's death, see further Hom. *Il.* 2.649–651; Eur. *HF* 408–424; Sen. *HF* 245–246, 542–545. Note also Bernstein 2017a, 112 and Rawlings 2005, 154, for whom Asbyte's decapitation denotes that Theron has strayed from the Herculean mold.

25 Augoustakis 2010a, 118.

ensuing death might be seen as the outcome not so much of Hannibal's venge-
ance exacted for the loss of Asbyte, but of his own abandonment from the god
he imitated in the battlefield. From this point of view, Theron's downfall serves
as another example of Hercules' marginalization in the epic. After all, it is Hercules who is essentially defeated and sidelined in this episode, not just the
priest of his temple.

More broadly, the fact that Theron's propensity for violence bears a clear
touch of Hercules' restless, self-aggrandizing heroism, which has already been
detected in Hannibal's arrogant response to Murrus' prayer, is indicative of the
predominance of the *furor/ira* theme at the beginning of the *Punica*. As I have
argued elsewhere, the manifestation of the Carthaginian general's overwhelming *anger* as a passion for revenge instigated at Juno's behest is fully consistent
with Seneca's phenomenological description of anger in the *De ira*.[26] In what
follows, I would like to investigate the possible influence of Seneca's dramatic
representation of the demigod's fury on Hercules' marginalization in Silius,
which culminates in the final part of the Saguntines' debacle.

So far, Silius' account of the Saguntum massacre, no matter how gory, has
been viewed as one of the most sophisticated pieces of the epic due to the rich
exploration of the themes of endurance, madness and intrafamilial suicide both
on an intertextual and intratextual level.[27] Significantly, the same themes play
out in Seneca's *Hercules Furens*. What particularly calls our attention here is
Hercules' despondency as he watches his people starve to death due to the pro-
longed siege (2.475–483):

> **Desuper haec caelo spectans Tirynthius alto**
> *inlacrimat fractae nequiquam casibus urbis.*
> *namque metus magnique tenent praecepta parentis*
> *ne saevae tendat contra decreta **novercae**.*
> *sic igitur coepta occultans ad limina sanctae*
> *contendit Fidei secretaque pectora temptat.*

---

26 See Antoniadis 2018; Stocks 2018. For Bernstein 2017a, 128 violent anger (239: *violentior ira*;
242: *ira*) is a standard attribute of Hannibal in the literary tradition. It is noteworthy, however,
that in Book 1 *ira* appears nine times in total, whereas it is found another fourteen times in
Book 2 which is among the highest rates in the epic. Cf. *Pun.* 1.17, 38, 101, 147, 169, 410, 451,
516, 690 and *Pun.* 2. 22, 45, 55, 139, 203, 208, 239, 242, 280, 328, 529, 539, 619, 672.
27 Suicide, in general, is a common theme in Flavian Epic. See further McGuire 1997, 185–248
and especially the Lemnos massacre at V. Fl. 2.98–241. The bibliography on the suicide at
Saguntum is vast: Augoustakis 2010a, 113–136; 2016, 285–287; Vessey 1974, 28–36; Küppers
1986, 164–170; Dominik 2003; Stocks 2014, 106–121, and 150–156; Bernstein 2016, 235–244;
2018.

arcanis dea laeta polo tum forte remoto
caelicolum magnas voluebat conscia curas.
*quam tali adloquitur **Nemeae pacator** honore ...*

Hercules of Tiryns looking down from lofty Heaven wept in vain at the shattered city's misfortune. Fear and his mighty father's instructions held him back from going against his savage **stepmother** Juno's decrees. So, concealing his undertaking, he approached the threshold of holy Loyalty and tested out her secret thoughts. As it happened, at that time in a distant part of the sky, the goddess, happy in her mysteries, was intently considering the gods' mighty cares. Hercules, **Nemea's pacifier**, addressed her with great respect ...

In the epic tradition, the gods' watching of human action on the battlefield is commonly followed by their active intervention in support of their anguished heroes.[28] On the contrary, Hercules' long, silent and sorrowful gaze upon the Saguntines' drama brings to the forefront his helplessness as a result of which he resorts to Fides' assistance.[29] In her influential paper on Stoicism in Flavian epic, Margarethe Billerbeck has characterized the demigod's overall stance as "largely unphilosophical", in contrast to previous Silian readers who had justified it on account of the virtue of *patientia* — which the Stoic sage is expected to practice in the face of hardship.[30] In her own words, "although Silius exploits the exemplary aspect of Hercules in the *Punica,* it should now be clear that he was not concerned to depict the hero consistently as a Stoic *sapiens*". Be that as it may, Hercules' helplessness cannot be merely ascribed to the epic's 'dramatic economy' either, as Billerbeck goes on to argue. Similarly, the concept that from his residence on Olympus Hercules can no longer exercise his traditional power as an 'action hero' does not sufficiently account either for his subordination to Juno's will or for his previous absence in the heat of combat for Murrus and Theron.[31] In my estimation, Hercules' fear to provoke his stepmother might be better approached against the background of the hero's de-stoicization and his ultimate disempowerment in Seneca's *Hercules Furens.*[32]

In modern scholarship, Senecan drama has often been viewed as a wide canvas upon which the Flavian epicists projected the passions and obsessions

---

28 For a detailed account of this motif see Lovatt 2013, 29–77.

29 On Hercules' ambiguous status in this passage, see Bernstein 2016, 236–237, and 240; 2017a, xxx; Dominik 2003, 485; Hardie 1993, 81–82; on *Fides* here, see Bernstein 2018, 188 who argues that her "ambivalent support of her devotees recapitulates the ambivalence of Hercules' support for Silius' Saguntines".

30 See Billerbeck 1986a, 348–349. *Contra* Kißel 1979, 156–157.

31 Note the reservations expressed by Asso 2010, 192.

32 On a brief survey of the play's major themes related to Hercules' morality see Bernstein 2017b, 17–40.

of their protagonists. Silius' preliminary reference to Juno as Hercules' *noverca* (1.478), a well-established way to identify Juno as his stepmother particularly in Seneca's plays,[33] already calls for an exploration of the variety of themes drawn from this play and imported into the narrative of Saguntum's fall.[34] To begin with, both in the *Punica* and the *Hercules Furens* the demigod's capacity to intervene is undermined as a result of Juno's disingenuous plots. In Silius' poem, though, there is a noticeable shift in her final target. While in Seneca's play Juno resolves to summon the Furies from the Underworld in order to drive Hercules mad (95–122; 982–986), in the *Punica* her insidious assault 'materializes' against the Saguntines always with the assistance of a Fury. When Fides reinvigorates the Saguntines (2.513–525) in answer to Hercules' helpless plea, Juno in turn dispatches Tisiphone to madden them under her commands (2.531–534):

> 'Hos' inquit 'noctis alumna,
> hos muros impelle manu populumque ferocem
> dextris sterne suis: Iuno iubet. ipsa propinqua
> effectus studiumque tuum de nube **videbo**'.

Daughter of night, push down these walls by force and lay low this fierce people with their own hands. Juno orders you. I myself **will watch** your efforts and your impact from a cloud close by.

Juno concludes her guidelines to the Erinys with the promise to supervise the undoing of the Saguntines. Similarly, in her lengthy tirade in Seneca, the goddess commits herself to stand beside the maddened Hercules, guiding his weapons against his family (118–121):

> **stabo** at, ut certo exeant
> emissa nervo tela, **librabo manu**,

---

33 Cf. especially Sen. *HF* 19–21: *una me dira ac fera | Thebana tellus matribus sparsa impiis | quotiens novercam fecit* ("How often has this land alone, this desolate and beastly land of Thebes, with its produce of impious mothers, made me a stepmother!"); 111–112: *facere si quicquam apparo | dignum noverca* ("if I am about to act as befits a stepmother") with Fitch's notes. See also 908, 1018, 1201, 1236.

34 Silius also designates Hercules as *Nemeae pacator* (*Pun.* 2.483), a term that bears a strong resemblance with the hero's philosophical portrait as the Stoic sage *par excellence* in Sen. *Ben.* 13.3: *Hercules nihil sibi vicit; orbem terrarum transivit non concupiscendo, sed iudicando, quid vinceret, malorum hostis, bonorum vindex, terrarum marisque pacator* ("Hercules conquered nothing for himself; he crossed the world, not in desiring, but in deciding what to conquer, an enemy of the wicked, a defender of the good, a peacemaker on land and sea"). Note also Ps.-Sen. *HO* 1990: *orbisque simul pacator, ades*.

regam furentis arma, pugnanti Herculi
tandem favebo.

I **shall stand** beside him and **aim** his arrows with my hand, so they fly unerring from the bowstring, I shall guide the madman's weapons, and at last **take** Hercules' **side** in the fight. (transl. Fitch)

The abundance of future tenses in Juno's speech in Seneca, to which her *videbo* in *Pun.* 2.34 looks back, confirms the impression that Silius parlays Hercules' personal and family tragedy in the *Hercules Furens* into the massive catastrophe of an entire city as the madness theme appears now to be taking on even greater proportions.[35] Most of all, once she has inspired the Saguntines to see the virtue of a decorous death through suicide, Tisiphone ascends to the city's most emblematic monument, a tumulus that Hercules had erected in honor of Zacynthus, to proclaim her ringing peroration with symbolic import (2.581–583). In this sense, the snake that instantly emerges from the tomb (2.585–587) represents both Hercules' escape ahead of the city's devastation and his total eclipse from Silius' narrative of Saguntum's fall.[36]

Silius' nods to Hercules' drama in Seneca become more perceptible as the Saguntines are compelled by Tisiphone to murder their families. In the first part of the massacre, unwilling parents are made to kill their children (2.612–619):

inde opus aggressi toto quod nobile mundo
aeternum inuictis infelix gloria servat.
*princeps Tisiphone **lentum** indignata parentem*
*pressit ovans capulum **cunctantemque** impulit ensem*
et dirum insonuit Stygio bis terque flagello.
***invitas** maculant cognato sanguine dextras*
miranturque nefas auersa mente peractum
*et **facto sceleri** inlacrimant.*

---

35 Note also Allecto's attack to Latium in the *Aeneid* (7.323–340) and Tisiphone's raid on Thebes in Ovid's *Metamorphoses* (4.464–480). For the historical background of the Saguntines' collective suicide, see Liv. 31.17; Val. Max. 6.6.5 ext. 1; Polyb. 3.17 with Bernstein 2017a, xviii; Vessey 1974, 29. On the suicidal proclivities of the Iberian tribes and the suicide as a Roman practice see Grisé 1982, 120–122; Voisin 1984, 617–618; van Hoof 1990, 57–59; Roller 2004, 1–7.
36 See Vessey 1974, 33. Note also Marks 2005, 87 who contrasts the snake's departure with the omen of its appearance in the sky (15.138–148) to confirm Jupiter's support for Scipio's election to the consulship and signal the end of the Carthaginian oppression in Spain and the return of Roman rule. Cf. also Virg. *Aen.* 2.210–211; 5.84–103 with Bernstein 2017a, 245. On snake omens in the *Punica* see also Basset 1955.

Then the undefeated people began that course of action which their glory in misfortune renders forever famous. Tisiphone began it: indignant at some father **slow** to kill his offspring, grasping the hilt in triumph, she drove in the **reluctant** sword; and with dire sound flailed with her Stygian lash, twice, three times. **Unwillingly** men stain their hands with the blood of their kin, stunned with this crime committed against their wish, and weeping over the **wickedness they have perpetrated**.

Beside the lines' rich intertext, which recalls similar episodes of civil strife in the Flavian epics and Lucan's *Pharsalia*,[37] our reading so far prioritizes the idea that Silius aim here is to 'immortalize' the Saguntines by aligning their tragedy with that of their guardian deity through an extensive use of paradox. In particular, by killing their families the Saguntines evoke Hercules' frenzy as he is poised to kill his son and his wife (Sen. *HF* 1020: *sed ante matrem parvulum hoc monstrum occidat*).[38] Although they are commemorated as *invicti* (613: *invictis*) after the demigod's most identifiable title inscribed in the Ara Maxima,[39] their glory is infelicitous (613: *infelix gloria*) like that of Hercules. Moreover, their piety is denounced as *sinistra* (632: *pietate sinistra*) and their acts are tellingly labeled as *laudanda monstra* (650) in a close recollection of Hercules' self-portrayal as a *monstrum impium* (*HF* 1280) once he realizes that his crime has negated all his previous laudable deeds (1268: *laudanda feci iussus; hoc unum meum est*).[40] Most of all, it is the Saguntines' reluctance to slaughter their relatives in the above lines (*Pun.* 614: *lentum ... parentem*; 615: *cunctantem ... ensem*; 617: *invitas ... dextras*) that seems to be informed by Hercules' own belated anguish upon his realization of his crimes (1281–1284):

---

37 Note in general the Massilian episode of Lucan's *Bellum Civile*, the Lemnian massacre in Valerius Flaccus' *Argonautica* and the brothers' duel in Statius's *Thebaid* 11. Cf. V. Fl. 2.215: *cunctantibus ingerit ensis*; 3.391: *invito maduerunt sanguine dextrae*; Stat. *Theb.* 5.230: *impellitque minis atque inserit ensem* with Bernstein 2018, 252. Cf. also *BC* 2.156–157 and 3.342–357 where the Massilians plead with Caesar to respect their neutrality by comparing their situation to that of the Saguntines; see further Dominik 2003.

38 In retrospect, the mutilation of Asbyte's body by Theron may now be seen as a reworking of the smashing of Megaera's bones and her decapitation by the maddened Hercules.

39 According to the Roman tradition, *Herculis Invicti Ara Maxima* was erected by Evander in the spot where Hercules slew Cacus and represented the earliest cult-center of Hercules in Rome. See Liv. 1.7.10–11, Serv. ad Virg. *Aen.* 8.269–271. In the pseudo-Senecan *HO*, the epithet *invictus* is ascribed to Hercules four times: 539, 964, 1179, 1266.

40 Cf. also Sen. *HF* 937–939: *si quod etiamnum est scelus | latura tellus, properet, et si quod parat | monstrum, meum sit* ("If the earth is even now to bring about some wickedness, let it come quickly; if she is preparing some monster, let it be mine"). In the *HF monstrum* is found 18 times in total, referring to Hercules' future or previous deeds: 40, 62, 82, 215, 241, 434, 444, 454, 528, 778, 807, 939, 1020, 1029, 1063, 1168, 1254, 1280.

agedum, **dextra**, conare aggredi
ingens opus, labore bis seno amplius.
ignaue, cessas, fortis in pueros modo
pavidasque matres?

Come, my **right hand**, attempt to undertake a gigantic task greater than all twelve labours.
Are you hesitating coward-brave only against boys and trembling mothers? (trans. Fitch)

While Hercules lacks the Stoic courage to put an end to his life and regrets only
too late his overreaching, his people at Saguntum, being also at a loss to understand and unable to withstand Fury's instigations, abhor the crimes they are
about to commit against their beloved ones (see especially 618–619). Vessey
(1974, 34) has argued that by erecting their own funeral pyre to immolate themselves, the Saguntines are indeed replicating Hercules' passion on Mt. Oeta
(*Pun.* 2.599–600). Since however the context is now different, in my view it is
Hercules' tragic fate that the Saguntines are reflecting in their vigorous resistance against another macabre ritual prescribed for them again by Juno. Even
so, the act of suicide, 'pronounced' by the Stoics as an efficient way forward to
escape from adversity and suffering, is questioned in both works in terms of its
moral value/potential and its very usefulness.[41] In the final act of *HF*
(1138–1344), Hercules' attempt to commit suicide suggests an outward crime in
the eyes of his father (1300–1301: *Ecce iam facies scelus | volens sciensque*) and
is eventually averted after Theseus' intervention who offers his kingdom of
Athens to harbor and rehabilitate his exiled friend (1272–1277). Like *monstrum*,
scelus is featured some 16 times in Seneca's play referring to Hercules' murder
of his family. Most characteristically, when Hercules comes to his senses, he
painfully admits that *saepe error ingens sceleris obtinuit locum* ("a great mistak-
en action often stands for a crime", 1238).[42] A similar wording is adduced by
Silius in his dramatic sketch of Saguntum as a city once fortified by Hercules
that has now turned into a site of serial crime (2.654–658):

---

41 In his *Epistulae*, however, Seneca is not an enthusiastic advocate under all circumstances
of the Stoic *libertas moriendi/recedendi* traditionally associated with Cato's suicide (*Ep.* 24.7;
26.10; 70.14; see also *Prov.* 2.10). Edwards 2007, 104–105 discusses a number of passages where
the philosopher explicitly criticizes those obsessed with death among whom he counts some
aristocrats of his own age (*Ep.* 24.25; 104.3). On this issue, see Hill 2004, 146–157; van Hoof
1990, 190; Grisé 1982, 206–217.
42 In most cases the context is similar to that of Saguntum. Cf. especially Sen. *HF* 96–99,
121–122, 251–252, 1199, 1300–1301, as well as 271, 746, 937, 1004, 1134, 1237, 1278, 1300, 1313,
1336.

urbs, habitata diu Fidei caeloque parentem
murorum repetens, ruit inter perfida gentis
*Sidoniae tela atque **immania facta** suorum,*
iniustis neglecta deis: furit ensis et ignis,
*quique caret flamma, **scelerum est locus.***

A city long inhabited by Loyalty that recalled its walls' founder in heaven was collapsing. Amid the Carthaginian race's treacherous missiles and its own people's **savage deeds**, the unjust gods neglected Saguntum. Sword and fire raged, and wherever fire was lacking, **there was the place for crime**.

Locating *scelus* in the plural (658: *scelerum ... locus*), the poet presents the Saguntines' *immania facta* (656) as a kind of metaliterary 'legacy' from their founder's drama in Seneca. It appears, indeed, as if Hercules' pathetic subservience to Juno's plots in the *Punica* is adapted directly from Seneca.

At the end of the day, the result of the mass suicide in *Punica* 2 remains dubious and the Saguntines' carnage is stigmatized as a *scelus* in Senecan/Herculean fashion. From this aspect, their struggle to obliterate their communal and personal identity by burning heirlooms (clothing, weapons, images of gods), eloquently discussed by Augoustakis in his reading of 2.599–608, may convey the dramatic effect of Hercules' loss of his own identity in Seneca, where Amphitryon orders his servants to strip his son of his weapons (1053: *removete, famuli, tela, ne repetat*), which are presented as his iconic attire in both works.[43] On the whole, the Saguntines' resolution to preserve through their collective death their exemplary fides in the Roman literary and historical tradition may now be seen as their ultimate response to their guardian deity who, in his negligence for them (657: *iniustis neglecta deis*), succumbs to the most ambivalent of his literary representations.

As Book 2 comes to an end, Hercules' persistent demotion appears as a *variatio in imitando*, if not an extreme makeover of his drama in Seneca, as the consequences of his marginalization are being transferred to the Saguntines who fall upon their weapons after having slain their own families. However, the side-effects of Hercules' ambivalent standing in the *Punica* do not end here. Following his provocative identification with the demigod in the first books of the epic, at the beginning of *Punica* 3 the Carthaginian leader pays a visit to the temple at

---

43 Augoustakis 2010a, 131. On Hercules' disarmament as a symbolic denudation of his own identity, see Bernstein 2017b, 15.

Gades to honor the god for his victory at Saguntum.[44] While his worship belongs to a long tradition of heroic pilgrimage,[45] Silius' reader is once again struck by the scene's inherent irony. This is not merely because a ritual celebrating Saguntum's fall takes place in the temple of the city's founder and protector. It is rather Silius' ekphrasis of the decorated doors of the temple, which feature a selection of Hercules' labors giving prominence to the annihilation of female monsters such as the Hydra (3.32–33) and Megaera (3.37).[46] In particular, the reference to the slaying of these mythical monster, which precedes even that of the Nemean lion, undermines Hercules' synecdochic portrait as *Nemeae pacator* thereby casting him not only as a monster slayer, but also as a persecutor of female beings. What is more, as Augoustakis has argued, the ekphrasis' violence prefigures the rape of Pyrene in the aetiological story – a concept that further points to the hero's liminal status so far in the epic.[47]

In Silius' version of this tale, Pyrene is the daughter of Bebryx, a cruel Mediterranean king who offers hospitality to the hero on his way to confront Geryon. However, the visit ends in a very unfortunate way as Hercules becomes intoxicated (423: *possessus Baccho*) and robs the maiden of her virginity. The latter gives birth to a serpent and in fear of her father's anger runs away to the woods, only to fall prey to wild animals which kill her and mutilate her body. The lines that matter here read as follows (3.420–426):

> *nomen Bebrycia duxere a virgine colles,*
> *hospitis Alcidae* **crimen**, *qui, sorte laborum*

---

44 On the programmatic importance of this episode for Hannibal's characterization in the *Punica* and the epic's overall structure, see Kißel 1979, 154; Vessey 1982; Gibson 2005; Augoustakis and Littlewood 2022, 147–149.

45 See further Gibson 2005, 181–183.

46 See Augoustakis 2003, 244 who further points to the defeat of Antaeus, whose power derived from his mother Tellus. For a detailed discussion of the ekphrasis, see also Harrison 2010, 285–286 who adduces the relevant scholarship; detailed commentary is now provided in Augoustakis and Littlewood 2022, 155–159.

47 Augoustakis 2010a, 131–134. Silius' short digression on the origin of the name of the mountain range, which stands as the first natural barrier for Hannibal (3.417–419) ahead of his crossing of the Alps, has often been found in the core of the scholarly debate regarding the general's complex portrayal as a counter-Hercules in *Pun.* 1–3. Vessey 1982, 332 has long observed that Hercules' offence is drawing on the Carthaginian's proverbial audacity, whereas Augoustakis 2003, 248–253 has illustrated how the transformation of the landscape as a result of Pyrene's dismemberment absorbs her woes and sufferings in a way that foreshadows the anguish of the Carthaginian soldiers during their imminent march over the Alps that is also assimilated to nature. See also Keith 2000, 56–57 and the detailed commentary in Augoustakis and Littlewood 2022, 246–252.

Geryonae peteret cum longa tricorporis arva,
possessus Baccho *saeva Bebrycis in aula*
lugendam formae sine virginitate reliquit
Pyrenen, **letique** *deus, si credere fas est,*
causa fuit **leti** *miserae deus.*

The Pyrenees took their name from Pyrene, a virgin maiden, Bebryx's daughter, **a girl who fell victim** to Hercules, her father's guest. When Hercules came to Geryon's wide fields as part of his labors, he was **overtaken by wine** in Bebryx's savage court and robbed Pyrene of her virginity, leaving her to be pitied because of her beauty. If it is right to believe this, the god was the cause of Pyrene's **death.**

Silius' aetiology appears to have been largely adapted so as to bring together Hercules' and Hannibal's uncontrolled and uncontrollable portraits as violent intruders.[48] However, it is Hercules' misdemeanor that is solely condemned as a crime (421) and as the ultimate reason for the pitiful girl's death (note the anaphora of *leti* at 425–426). At the same time, as Keith notes, Silius suppresses the details of the rape to focus on the maiden's loss of virginity (420; 424) and her ensuing dismemberment and decapitation (433: *laceros … artus*; 435: *palluit invento dilectae virginis ore*).[49] These most appalling aspects of the story, though, point to previous instances of female body mutilation related to Herculean liminality both in the *Punica* and the *Hercules Furens*. Most relevant are the abuse of Asbyte's corpse by Theron and the slaughter of female monsters in the ekphrasis of the temple at Gades discussed above, as well as the smashing of Megaera's bones and her beheading in Seneca.[50] In addition, Pyrene's frantic lament of her desertion by her ungrateful lover and her subsequent laceration may further evoke the Saguntines' distress at Hercules' abandonment, which led to their carnage. On this basis, Ripoll is right to argue that Hercules' failure to protect the dishonored princess from her father's rage (*Pun.* 3.430–433) makes another case for his persistent vulnerability in the *Punica*.[51] Be that as it

---

48 Tipping 2010a, 20.

49 Keith 2000, 56.

50 See especially *HF* 1024–1026: *in coniugem nunc claua libratur gravis:* | *perfregit ossa, corpori trunco caput* | *abest nec usquam est* ("against his wife now his heavy club is leveled, smashing her bones; her head is gone from her truncated body, totally destroyed") with *Pun.* 2.200–202: *disiecto spargit conlisa per ossa cerebro,* | *ac rapta properans caedem ostentare bipenni amputat e curru revolutae virginis ora* ("he spattered fragments of brain amid shattered bones, and hurrying to display his kill, he snatched up her axe and cut off the virgin's head, thrown down from the chariot"). Note also Keith 2000, 62 with Augoustakis 2003, 252.

51 Ripoll 1998, 117. Augoustakis 2003, 236 has also discerned in the darker side of Hercules, that is apparent in the rape and death of Pyrene, a *Hercules furens* figure, without elaborating

may, Silius' exclamation *si credere fas est* (425) may not simply ponder on the validity of the story and its outrageous character, but metapoetically challenge — as a kind of reversed 'Alexandrian footnote' — the demigod's overall exemplarity in the literary tradition. From this point of view, what actually Silius might be wondering here is "How far could a god like Hercules go, particularly after his literary criminal record in Seneca's play?"

Nevertheless, Hercules' sorrow and regret in the aftermath of his wrongdoings both in Pyrene's tale and Seneca's play indicate that these are not stories of rape and death only, but also of expiation as a result of crime and violence.[52] That said, Silius does not so much exculpate the demigod's misconduct as he applies the slipperiness of his composite figure to the epic's destabilizing mechanism. One way or another, Hercules' ambivalence is reflected in the fragmented and complex representation of the epic's main protagonists. This is evident not only in Hannibal's portrayal as Hercules' foil, as has been seen so far, but also — and perhaps more intricately — in the display of the major Roman generals, whose flaws invite Silius' readers to think about both the instability of power and the vulnerability of the human condition which sustain the ambiguities surrounding Hercules' *virtus* in the *Punica* and the Senecan play.

To pursue this point further, we may turn to another case of rape which Silius inserts in *Pun.* 6.627–636, where Hercules is again found in the role of a *hospes* and a seducer but is now spared of any potentially negative associations. This is the far more celebrated story of the demigod's union with Evander's daughter from which the famous *genus* of the Fabii had sprung, among whom by far the most distinguished descendant was the Roman statesman and general Fabius Maximus, Hannibal's main opponent in the first half of the *Punica*.[53] This is the first time in the epic when Hercules' moral ambivalence is given positive, if not auspicious, connotations. However, Tipping is right to observe that this rape renders the demigod incompatible with society — an idea that may be applied to Pyrenes' ravishment as well. To illustrate his point, Tipping detects the same concept even in Fabius' well-established portrait as a synecdochic hero in the *Punica*.[54] Indeed, by displaying caution and hesitance in contrast to the public demand for warfare, Fabius is both spiritually and practically isolat-

---

further on this idea. The mutilation theme and the macabre element are also inherent in Seneca's *Thyestes*, *Phaedra*, and *Medea*.

52 Tipping 2010a, 117–118.

53 For a comparative reading of the related passages, see Augoustakis 2003, 246–248 who approaches them as a "contrasting pair".

54 Tipping 2010a, 116–117. On this concept, see further Hardie 1993, 3–10 and 66–69; Cowan 2007, 16–38.

ed from his rash comrades and soldiers (7.1: *trepidis Fabius spes unica rebus*) as a result of his superhuman wisdom (7.5: *mens humana maior*) or his unpopular policy (7.7–8: *tot in agmina solus ibat*). At the same time though, Fabius' sketch in the *Punica* is also checkered since his autocratic elements may not be irrelevant to the "solo and socially excluded heroism" of his ancestor, as Tipping fittingly puts it.[55]

If we now move to the much-disputed ending of the *Punica*, we shall see that scholars are often at pains to apply a fitting translation to Scipio's status as *securus sceptri* (17.627) that complicates Silius' description of his triumphal entrance into Rome after the conquest of Africa (17.625–642).[56] As is the case with Senecan tragedy, readers have also noticed that in the *Punica*, *sceptrum* is mostly associated with monarchical power, thereby hinting at Scipio's possible repressive qualities as a proto-emperor. Of course, this is not the only instance in which Silius is concerned with tyrannical figures in the *Punica*. Hannibal himself is fashioned as *tyrannus* at 2.239 and elsewhere in the epic, although such a characterization does not correspond to his status as leader of the Punic army.[57] Sibyl's emphasis on the punishment awaiting tyrannical kings in the Underworld at 13.601–612 has been also considered as a moralizing lesson for Scipio which, not coincidentally, has been found to draw on Theseus' account about the adjudication of ruthless tyrants and their crimes in Seneca (731–747).[58]

Yet, Raymond Marks among other scholars has made use of Silius' likening of Scipio to Bacchus and Hercules in the double simile at 17.645–650 to speculate on Scipio's possible apotheosis at the end of the epic.[59] However, despite their divinization and their similar juxtaposition as world conquerors in Anchises' speech in *Aen.* 6.801–805, Bacchus and Hercules tend to problematize readers for their own liminal aspects in terms of their susceptibility to drunken-

---

55 See Tipping 2010a, 120–131, and note the reservations expressed by Marks 2011, 483–485.

56 On the positive connotations of *securus sceptri* regarding Scipio's kingship in the epic, see Marks 2005, 201–206 who bases his argumentation on Scipio's rejection of kingship in *Pun.* 16. Most reservations have been expressed by McGuire 1997, 101–102 and Tipping 2010a, 182–185 who point further to his characterization as *rector* at *Pun.* 17.534, 586, 625, a term which is also applied to Hannibal several times in the epic (*Pun.* 10.188, 251; 11.210, 320, 494, 521; 13.514).

57 Silius refers to Hannibal as tyrant also at 1.239, 4.707, 5.202, 10.487, 11.31. The noun is rarer in the *Aeneid* while in the *Metamorphoses* Ovid restricts its application to hated rulers. See further Bernstein 2017a, 128. Note also Hasdrubal's representation as another Atreus at 1.149: *metui demens credebat honorem.*

58 Tipping 2010b, 183–185.

59 Marks 2005, 224–228.

ness and degeneracy in the *Punica* and other works.[60] In my view, what is particularly intriguing here is Scipio's identification with Hercules on account of
their shared parentage as products of Jupiter's rapes. Even more, despite his
choice of Virtue instead of Voluptas at the famous Crossroads episode in *Pun.*
15,[61] when the Roman general enters Rome dressed in purple and gold (17.391,
395) to celebrate his triumph, his outfit recalls Voluptas' appearance before him
in a glowing purple dress suffused with tawny gold (15.21–25).[62] Likewise, when
Silius famously hails Scipio as *invictus* at 17.651 (*salve, invicte parens*), the general's identification with the demigod on account of his unmatched qualities in
leadership is somehow undermined by the previous, and most ironic, application of this most recognizable Herculean epithet to Hannibal in the Saguntines'
obituary which predicates the bitter fate of the "once unconquered warrior"
(2.706: *invictus quondam … bellator*). Thus, limitless ambition together with uncontrollable leadership could be lurking behind *securus sceptri* as a warning on
the poet's part to Scipio in the sense of "be careful what you wish for". Hercules
ended up killing his own family and dying by immolation atop Mt. Oeta and,
even though he retained his heroic (even divine) status on account of all those
trials and tribulations he went through, his life and death may still seem quite
awful to many of his advocates.[63]

Conclusions: Hercules and Nero

All in all, Hercules may now be best described as an 'effectively' marginal figure
in the *Punica* due to his composite figure and his much ambivalent standing,
which reflects upon the fragmented selves and complex identities of the epic's
main protagonists. In light of the preceding analysis, a distinction may be further drawn between the demigod's liminal status in terms of his very limited

---

60 Taking as the most characteristic example Bacchus' representation at *Pun.* 3.101–105, Tipping 2010a, 208–209 notes that Silius "portrays his not as benefactor but as conqueror, associ-
ating him not with the blessings of wine, but with Maenadic violence and the lust of one of his
satyr sons, whose horny resemblance to Bacchus the poet emphasizes. Bacchus' traditional
feature as a drunkard god is also apparent in the Falernus episode (*Pun.* 7.157–214), but there
the god is cast as a benefactor of Italy in contrast to Hannibal's prefiguration as a violent in-
truder".
61 For different approaches to this identification, see Marks 2005, 222–226; Tipping 2010a, 167
and 175.
62 Jacobs 2021, 107.
63 I would like to thank John Jacobs for sharing with me his thoughts on Hercules' portrait.

involvement in the battlefield in the first half of the epic and his customary representation as a model of kingship in the rest of the poem. The latter is never devoid of some of the aspects of his transgressive heroism, in the fashion of Seneca's *Hecules Furens*, that still confuse even those readers who consider the hero as a paradigm of Roman heroism and the absolute model-hero for Scipio in the second half of the epic.[64] The question that still needs to be addressed is why is the demigod in the *Punica* lacking the symbolic import that complements his standard exemplary status in literature and philosophy? Could it be that Silius was making use of the inconsistencies of Hercules' character to imply that historical figures are also influenced by identity issues?

To approach such questions in a comprehensive way, we must not fail to bear in mind that Silius emerged as a public figure in Roman politics under Nero's reign, actually being one of the last consuls of 68 CE, the year that marked the emperor's downfall. As Rebeggiani notes, the emperor himself was "the most vocal aspirant to the role of Hercules in the years leading up to the principate of Domitian".[65] From Suetonius' account of Nero's extreme theatricalities (*Ner.* 53), we learn that the emperor was particularly fond of staging Hercules' labors in his 'one-man shows'. Judging further from Vespasian's avoidance of any connection to Hercules (Suet. *Vesp.* 12.1), we may understand that his predecessor courted ridicule with his performances to such a degree that it might even account for Hercules' liminal, and sometimes even mock-heroic, status in the Flavian epics.[66]

If the poor performances of Hercules' sons and Polynices in the *Thebaid* and particularly the latter's self-destructive impetuosity indeed serve as a kind of commentary on the theatricality of the emperor, as Rebeggiani has recently argued, this idea might be further traced in Hercules' liminal status in the *Puni-*

---

64 This skepticism is best framed by Asso 2010, 192 who observes the hero's marginalization in his failure to behave as the archetypal "action-hero" both in the siege of Saguntum and his hapless fighting on the side of the Romans at the battle of Cannae (9.290–295) and captures it in a single sentence: "In Silius, Hercules weeps the only time he speaks and loses in battle the only time he fights".

65 Rebeggiani 2018, 138.

66 In his rewarding reading of the *Thebaid*, Rebeggiani 2018, 138–140 has explicitly shown how Nero's doomed impersonations of the gaming Hercules are reflected in Polynices' failure to live up to Hercules in the context of Statius' Nemean games. In particular, the mode of his failure, falling from a chariot, is reminiscent of Nero's famous failure in one of his exploits in the games at Olympia. For Rebeggiani, Polynices' Herculean/Neronian nature is exhibited at the time of his arrival in Argos, where he catches sight of the Heraion of Argos, the temple where Nero made his offerings to Hercules.

ca and his much ambiguous identification with minor and major figures of the epic such as Theron, Hannibal or even Scipio as seen so far.[67] Even more, in the eyes of learned men, like Seneca and Silius, who from their public posts experienced the emperor's atrocities and demeanors first hand, Nero's ill-fated embodiment of Hercules perhaps was not restricted to his ventures on the stage (to his staginess), but could be further confirmed in his sexual aberrations and his crimes against his family. His ravishing of a Vestal Virgin (Suet. *Ner.* 28), the murdering of his wives, Octavia and Poppaea (*Ner.* 35) and his mother Agrippina (*Ner.* 34), his implication in the deaths of Claudius and Britannicus (*Ner.* 33) and, above all, the mass-suicide of some of the most reputable members of the Roman aristocracy (*Ner.* 37) are all re-enacted in the Saguntum debacle and Pyrene's rape. Silius, therefore, might have had his own agenda by casting most of his protagonists (the Saguntine warriors, Hannibal, Fabius, and Scipio) in a Herculean mold that bears recognizable influences from Seneca's *Hercules Furens*. Recently, Bernstein has persuasively argued that the Saguntines' hesitance to commit suicide (*Pun.* 2.617) may point to the drama of the marginalized Neronian courtiers (Lucan, Petronius, Seneca, and prominent senators like Thrasea Paetus and Barea Soranus), who took their lives at the emperor's behest or lacked the courage to do so.[68] If Suetonius is to believed, even Nero in his last moments barely managed to take his life (*Ner.* 59). At any rate, his multilayered connection with murder and suicide during his reign (*Ner.* 35.4: *nullum adeo necessitudinis genus est, quod non scelere perculerit*), made him look like a caricature of Silius' and Seneca's Hercules if not a monster and a killer at the same time. While he himself never lived at the margin, there is no doubt that, one way or another, he marginalized his family and the Roman aristocrats.[69]

To sum up. Consistency of character and characterization is seldom the strong point of ancient literary works which do not aspire to realism in our modern sense of the word — nor did their readers expect such consistency, as modern readers do. This is particularly true regarding the portraits of mythological and historical figures as well, while it becomes even more apparent when religion is involved. Hercules' marginalization as part of his overall moral am-

---

67 Rebeggiani 2018, 138–140.

68 Bernstein 2018, 184–185.

69 See further Gallia 2012, 21–22. Significantly, Nero's identification with Hercules was the target of Vindex's propaganda in 68 CE. When the Gauls revolted against Nero, their governor issued coins portraying Hercules with the legend *Hercules Adsertor*, "Hercules the Liberator". As Rebeggiani 2018, 130–131 notes: "The message was clear: Hercules displaced the monster Cacus from his home on the Palatine on his way back from the West; Vindex too was on his way to displace the monster Nero from Rome".

bivalence in the *Punica* could actually fit to what Paul Veyne in his ground-breaking study *Les Grecs ont-ils cru à leurs mythes?* labelled as "balkanisation des cerveaux" ("brain balkanization") in the post-classical world[70] — a concept that has been employed to explain the widely differing functions and unstable identities of gods in ancient literary works, sometimes even within the limits of a single work. Not accidentally at all, Hercules has already been taken as an example of this kind of contextual understanding authors and readers apply to many mythical figures of literature and religion.[71] As we have seen, Hercules is so multifarious that he persistently demands contextualization perhaps, else his ambivalent portrayal is often inexplicable, if not meaningless. Thus, even if in the second half of his epic Silius partially 'corrects' the Herculean imagery through Scipio's persistent identification with the demigod and the prospect of his divinization, we must concede that such a 'correction' may not be irrelevant to the fact that at the time of the final output of the *Punica* Domitian was re-envisaged as Hercules. Both Martial's epigrams and Statius' *Silvae* point to this idea in a mostly lavish and servile manner.[72] Silius' closure to his panegyric of the Flavian regime in *Pun.* 3.570–629 and his casting of the triumphant Scipio in *Pun.* 17.651 (*salve, invicte parens*) as an embodiment of the emperor and the demigod may also reflect Domitian's apotheosis at the beginning of the *Thebaid* (1.21–45) in return for his service to mankind. However, Hercules' 'criminal impact' on the first part of the *Punica* as showcased in the atrocities of the Saguntines and the rape of Pyrene, will always cast a shadow of doubt over every scholarly attempt at identifying his unmatching virtue with Scipio and/or Domitian. Silius' implementation of Seneca's 'poetics of marginalization' in the *Hercules Furens* marks not just a literary shift from tragedy to epic, but a political one as well from collective authority to absolutism. If in the era of Trajan, whose accession to the throne Silius lived to see, Juvenal called Domitian a *calvus Nero*

---

70 Veyne 1983, 103.

71 Note especially Feeney 1998, 14–15: "Brain-balkanization captures the capacity of educated Greeks and Romans of the post-classical era to entertain different kinds of assent and criteria of judgement in different contexts, in ways that strike the modern observer as mutually contradictory. These people are involved in very different activities when they sacrifice outside a temple, talk to the custodian of a temple, read the aretalogy inscribed outside the temple, ... read an epic on Heracles, or read about Heracles the supreme commander in a history. Expressions of scepticism are always potentially part of the procedure, for the participants' assent may be provisional, self-consciously in tension with dissent".

72 Note, again Stat. *Silv.* 4.2.46–51 (with Rebeggiani 2018, 123–132), where Domitian is compared to the triumphant Mars, Pollux, Bacchus, and Hercules, as he himself is reclining at his table, as well as Mart. 9.101.11–16.

on account of his atrocities, and Pliny the Younger castigated his sexual excesses and rapes,[73] we may then understand why Hercules' transgressive qualities never ceased to entice the Roman emperors and the Flavian epicists, who saw the demigod's flux between world conqueror and monster in the works and days of their emperors.

---

73 See Tac. *Ann.* 13.25.47; Cass. Dio 61.8.1–9.4; Plin. *Ep.* 4.11, and *Pan.* 52.3, 63.7 with Betzig 2014, 61–62.

Angeliki Nektaria Roumpou
Between Life and Death: Hannibal at the Center of the Margins in Silius Italicus' *Punica* 17

Abstract: This chapter focuses on the question of whether or not Hannibal is a marginalized figure within the epic narrative of Silius Italicus' *Punica*. If he is, then his position at the center of the *Punica*'s action encourages numerous questions. By showing that Hannibal, in the final book of the epic, is marginalized in spatial (if not in narrative) terms, Roumpou argues that Silius signals the end of his epic by highlighting Hannibal's displacement from the battlefield and his own homeland. The *Punica*'s very *raison d'être* is thus revealed to be a thing of the margins, a *raison d'autre*.

Introduction

In this paper, I discuss the subject of marginality by exploring the elusive nature of Hannibal's personality. I will first show that in the *Punica* Silius depicts Hannibal as the core and center of the whole epic narrative, to the extent that his absence from the battlefield in the final book of the epic immediately signals the end of the epic — the *Punica* loses its *raison d'être*. I will then move on to show the different occasions that reveal Hannibal's liminality between life and death, and between the frames of this epic and beyond, which metapoetically reflect the literary liminality between closure and new beginnings. Hannibal's liminal condition at his final appearance in the epic and the references to his possible return will lead to the examination of the significance of closure as a powerful narrative space. Hannibal's displacement at the margins of the epic battle and the references to his future return reveal an open-ended *Punica* which offers the audience a different sense of liminality, an uncertainty and anticipation of what follows next.

https://doi.org/10.1515/9783111063942-009

The Center of the Narrative

It has already been discussed in scholarship that the *Punica* contrary to the *Aeneid* lacks a central hero around whom is built a nexus of relationships that drives the narrative forward.[1] Hannibal is the Carthaginian protagonist who throughout the epic faces multiple Roman leaders at different stages of the war: Regulus (Book 6), Fabius (Book 7), Paulus (Books 9 and 10) Marcellus (Book 12) and finally Scipio (Books 13, 16, 17) who terminates the Second Punic War and thus the epic.[2] Hannibal's personality captures the whole epic narrative from the first book until the final one. Although he is a peripheral character in identity, he comes from the East to conquer Rome and thus to impose himself on "the centre".[3] He becomes the central character due to his continuous presence in the epic, with almost all the *Punica*'s books surrounding his achievements. In the *Punica*, Hannibal is a character who crosses the geographical and moral boundaries, a man who is challenging the divine and aspires to become a god. Despite his centrality, at the final lines of the epic he is led away from the center of the action to a marginal space, forced to abandon the poem. As the antagonist of the epic, he recalls the antagonist in the second part of the *Aeneid*, Turnus, who, despite being the principal agent of the war and the center of the action, is often displaced by deities to the margins of the fighting.

The *Punica* begins with Hannibal's desire to initiate the war against the Romans. Urged first by Juno, his protectress, and then by his father Hamilcar, he is the character who sets the epic in motion (1.35–39):

> ... *iterum instaurata capessens*
> *arma remolitur; dux agmina sufficit unus*
> *turbanti terras pontumque movere paranti.*
> *Iamque deae cunctas sibi belliger induit iras*
> *Hannibal (hunc audet solum componere fatis).*

---

1 See Augoustakis 2010b, 16 who offers significant bibliographical references about the *Punica*'s heroism.
2 Most recently Stocks 2014; Kortmann 2018.
3 Augoustakis 2010a, 3; he extensively discusses center and periphery in Flavian epic and the *Punica* in particular.

... And yet Juno took up renewed arms and tried once more. One leader, Hannibal, provided all for her as she troubled the earth and prepared to roil the sea. And now warlike Hannibal took on all of the goddess' anger. Juno dared to set him alone against fate.[4]

Hannibal is the *dux unus*, the sole leader (1.36) chosen by Juno to cause turmoil to land and sea (1.36–37).[5] From the beginning of the epic, he envisions the conquest of the Capitol at the heart of Rome (*Pun.* 1.64): *nocturno penetrat Capitolia visu | aut rapidis fertur per summas passibus Alpes* ("Even then, he penetrated the Roman Capitol in his nightly visions or headed with rapid marching across the highest Alps"). Jupiter Ammon prophecies that no one other than him will be able "to penetrate deeper into the entrails of the Roman populace" (*Pun.* 3.709 *altius Ausoniae penetrare in viscera gentis*), an indication that Hannibal's actions from the beginning aimed at the heart of Rome.[6] Hannibal's central position can be viewed from his relationship with his army: at his first battle in Book 1, it is clear that without Hannibal the Punic army cannot continue fighting (1.581–583), which indicates that his presence on the battlefield is necessary for the war in the *Punica*, even if he is absent from the audience's view.[7] At 16.17–22 he keeps the Carthaginian side together and simply his name is enough to unite and rally the disparate and defeated troops (19: *Hannibalis sat nomen erat*). This shows that Hannibal is the character who drives the narrative forwards. At the end of the epic, when Hannibal disappears from the battle of Zama, Carthage is ready to collapse; she has lost all her leaders, and only Hannibal's name keeps her from ruin (17.149–151): *stabat Carthago truncatis undique membris | uni innixa viro, tantoque fragore ruentem | Hannibal absenti retinebat nomine molem* ("Carthage was still standing, even though her limbs were truncated everywhere, relying on one man's strength. Even in his absence, Hannibal supported the empire which was collapsing in such a crash"). Carthage's complete reliance on Hannibal alone posits a synecdochic relationship between the city and its leader, in the same way we observed with Hector in the *Iliad*, Priam in the *Aeneid* for Troy, and Pompey for the Roman Republic in Lucan.[8] Later in

---

4 All Latin passages of the *Punica* come from Delz 1987, and the translations come from Augoustakis and Bernstein 2021.

5 The phrase *Hannibal unus* occurs only three times in the *Punica*, at 10.568; 17.197, 512.

6 In the end, Hannibal will only penetrate Rome figuratively as he surveys the city (*Pun.* 12.569–570): *penetraret in omnes | spectando partes* ("he would have penetrated into all its parts with his gaze"). On Hannibal's gaze, see Lovatt 2013, 94–98.

7 See Stocks 2014, 11.

8 Hardie 1993, 4 describes Hannibal as the individual "who stands for the totality of his people present and future, part for whole". For the synecdochic relationship between Hannibal and

the book, Silius explains how Hannibal is the surviving hope of a Carthage that is ready to fall apart; if Hannibal survives, then Rome will have gained nothing, but if he falls, then everything will be under Roman domination (17.512–516):

> *Hannibal unus*
> *dum restet, non, si muris Carthaginis ignis*
> *subdatur caesique cadant exercitus omnis,*
> *profectum Latio. contra, si concidat unus,*
> *nequiquam fore Agenoreis cuncta arma virosque.*

> While *Hannibal alone* remained, even if the Romans set Carthage's walls on fire and the whole Carthaginian army lay dead, there would be no success for Latium. By contrast, if Hannibal alone should fall, all the remaining men and weapons would be futile for the Carthaginians.

At the end of the epic, Hannibal disappears from the battlefield, and Carthage loses the war. Scipio loots Carthage and burns her fleet. At this particular point in the narrative, Silius makes the disappearance of Hannibal coincide with the end of the war: *hic finis bello* (618). But before he totally disappears, Silius allows him, even in defeat, to become the prevailing character as the poem reaches its end, something that is confirmed by his reference to the fact that during Scipio's triumphal procession, the eyes of the spectators are focused on Hannibal's image as a fugitive who has just been taken to a hill by Juno (17.643–644): *sed non ulla magis mentesque oculosque tenebat, | quam visa Hannibalis campis fugientis imago* ("But no other image attracted more people's minds and eyes than Hannibal's as he left the field"). In this sense, the end of the poem resembles both the Iliadic and the Virgilian epic endings, both focusing on the defeated antagonist, and not the protagonist (see *Il.* 24.804 and *Aen.* 12.952).[9] In the *Punica*, the focus is on the live but absent antagonist, but, at the same time, in contrast to the present and triumphant protagonist.[10] Having an alive, but absent, antagonist does not create a sense of finite closure as in the *Iliad* and the *Aeneid* but rather postpones the confrontation indefinitely.[11]

Carthage, see: Hardie 1993, 51; Marks 2008, 76–85. On the "synecdochic" epic hero generally, the one man who represents many, see Hardie 1993, 3–11, 27–35, and 49–56.

9 In the last 22 lines of the *Iliad*, Achilles is not mentioned at all, whereas the poet concentrates on Hector, where his name appears 3 times. The last line is again about Hector.

10 For discussion about whether Hannibal is an antagonist or a protagonist, and on the protagonist of the *Punica* in general, see Stocks 2014.

11 Other scholars find the closure at the end of the *Iliad* and the *Aeneid* to be highly problematic and in fact, not at all really closural on several levels. For the problems of closure and anti-

In order to reach to the center, Rome, Hannibal breaks the boundaries of the world: he crosses the Pyrenees and the Alps in 218 BCE, he invades Italy and returns back to Africa to face the Roman army in the decisive battle of Zama in 202 BCE. He is a man too big for Africa (cf. Juv. 10.148: *hic est quem non capit Africa*) that starts from the southeast, passing by the west and ending up in the east, though this time he will be exiled from his fatherland. In the *Punica* he is known for the violation and transgression of borders from spatial, geographical, and ethical points of view (e.g., at 1.1–11, 648–649; 2.297, 451; 11.559).[12] Jupiter in the *Punica* characterizes Hannibal as a fierce youth who knew no bounds (*Pun.* 12.693–695: *Nullane Sidonio iuveni, coniunxque sororque | cara mihi, non ulla umquam sine fine feroci | addes frena viro?* "My dear wife and sister, won't you ever restrain the Carthaginian youth, a man so endlessly fierce?"), and it is this divinity who will eventually impose a *finis* at his actions at the end of the epic (17.356: *ad finem ventum. Claudenda est ianua belli*, "now we've reached the end. The war's door must be closed"), acknowledging that during the years of the war the power of Hannibal's myth has shaken Rome's walls and made him the 'first', not just of his own men but of all humanity (17.353–355): *tremuerunt moenia Romae | perque bis octonos primus fuit Hannibal annos | humani generis*, "Rome's walls trembled, and Hannibal has been the human race's leader for sixteen years").[13] In Book 1, he is ready to cause cosmic chaos, and by the final book he has achieved it. Hannibal is Rome's sublime enemy, and the Second Punic War is thus framed on a cosmic scale. Hannibal's transgressions and breaking of the borders shows that he cannot bear the confinement. The cosmos cannot contain him who breaks the boundaries of the world and crosses the threshold of the riverbanks. At the end of the epic, Jupiter's desire is to *componere gentes* (17.355) and to close the gates of war (17.356). And Juno must obey, as she did in the *Aeneid* with Turnus. But in contrast to the *Aeneid*, she saves Hannibal to escape and remain alive, not to be killed by Scipio, who is deliberately looking to confront Hannibal, the originator of the war and the bastion of his city. If Scipio exterminates Hannibal, then the war is over; if Hannibal remains alive, then all the victories are insignificant (17.512–516). This episode prepares the reader for the forthcoming battle of Hannibal and Scipio

---

closure in Greek and Roman epic, see Zissos 2019. On the many endings of the *Aeneid*, see also Hardie 1997, 142–151.

12 The act of violating boundaries is a characteristic of civil war, as Lucan clearly shows. Lucan's Caesar is the poem's ultimate boundary violator; on boundary violation in Lucan, see Myers 2011. For Livy's Hannibal as an oath-breaker, see Liv. 21.4.3.

13 See Stocks 2014, 215 who analyses how the audience gives validity and power to Hannibal's mythic identity.

and implies that the extermination of Hannibal brings the end of the war and of the epic: there is no epic narrative without the antagonist.

Between Life and Death: Hannibal's Displacement into a Non-epic World •

Hannibal's actions in the epic are sometimes organized and manipulated by Juno. In order to protect him, she saves him from imminent death or employs other minor divinities, such as Somnus or Anna Perenna, to carry out her tasks. Her intervention in the *Punica* contributes to grand scenarios on the battlefield; for example, at 10.45–48 Juno disguised as Metellus dissuades Paulus from killing Hannibal at Cannae; at 10.83–90 Juno disguises herself as Gelesta the Moor to urge Hannibal to kill Paulus; at the end, she again displaces him and leads him to a different combat (91: *iuvenem diversa ad proelia raptat*) showing again her manipulation of the Punic leader; at 10.326–387 she sends Somnus to dissuade Hannibal from marching on Rome; at 12.701–328, when she intervenes and shows Hannibal that his mission is impossible, she hinders him from attacking Rome. Her intervention in the final book of the epic is to some extent different from her role in the previous ones, as she removes Hannibal completely from the epic action. Hannibal's actions during the final episodes of the epic show him in a liminal condition, marginalized in non-epic spaces, struggling to re-enter the epic narrative. He is in a liminal situation between life and death, existence and non-existence within the frames of this epic and beyond. His transgressive character does not allow him to remain in one specific space, depicting him always in motion. At 17.522–580 Scipio seeks to confront Hannibal for the final battle but Juno intervenes and removes him from the battlefield, as Juturna, impersonating Metiscus at *Aen.* 12.623–625, had directed Turnus at the (safer) margins of the battlefield. At the end of *Punica* 17, Juno creates a sham battle with a false image of Scipio on a fake horse that leads Hannibal away from the battle (522–553), she destroys his horse, so that he cannot ride back onto the battlefield (553–557), and she disguises herself as a shepherd in order to remove him not only from the conflict but also from the epic world (567–580), and to disempower him (17.529–531):

> *tum par effigies fallacis imagine vana*
> *cornipedis moderanda cito per **devia passu***
> *belligerae datur **ad speciem certaminis** umbrae*

Then she also gave to the phantom warrior a similarly insubstantial phantom image of a fake horse *to be ridden quickly away from the battle* in a mock fight.

This move to the trackless area of the battle, *devia passu*, displaces Hannibal and leads him to a resemblance of a battle, not to a real one (*ad speciem certaminis*). The vocabulary illustrates the dark and blurred atmosphere in which Hannibal is guided. The resemblance of the battle shows that for Hannibal there is a negation of warfare with Scipio at Zama, as happens in history, but instead Silius prefers to invent a duel between Hannibal and Scipio at Cannae, when there is no historical one. The sham battle at the end of the epic postpones its conclusion indefinitely; Hannibal will flee and there will be no duel, defeating the expectations of readers. When Hannibal realizes the deceit, he is desperate and ready to commit suicide (566). Juno takes pity upon him, and in the guise of a shepherd she meets him, feigns ignorance of his identity, and claims to give him directions back to the battle of Zama, though in reality, she misdirects him out of the battle. Hannibal will never enter the battlefield again. By means of this delay within the epic narrative, Silius removes Hannibal from the epic world and places him in an un-epic, rural one (17.567–580):

> *Tunc Iuno miserata virum pastoris in ora*
> *vertitur ac **silvis** subito procedit **opacis***
> *atque his alloquitur versantem ingloria fata:*
> *'Quaenam te **silvis** accedere causa subegit*
> ***armatum** nostris? num dura ad proelia tendis,*
> *magnus ubi Ausoniae reliquos domat Hannibal armis?*
> *si velox gaudes ire et compendia grata*
> *sunt tibi, vicino in medios te tramite ducam.' ...*
> *praecipitem et vasto superantem proxima saltu*
> *circumagit Iuno ac fallens regione viarum*
> *non gratam invito servat celata salutem.*

Then pitying the man, Juno transformed herself into a shepherd and suddenly set out from a *shady forest*, addressing him as he turned such an inglorious destiny in his head: "What reason in the world forced you to come near my *forest* with your weapons? You are surely heading to the savage battle where great Hannibal is defeating the Romans' remaining army? If you are happy to go quickly, and if you like a good shortcut, I'll take you there by a nearby path" ... Juno took him in a circle, as Hannibal moved quickly and leapt forward passing by the neighbouring places. So the goddess in disguise deceived him about the region and roads, and she preserved his life, even though Hannibal did not want it and was not grateful.

Previously a hunter, Hannibal is now hunted by Scipio, hiding in a pastoral environment that is beyond the traditional heroic epic genre. The use of *silvis* ...

opacis (568) further blurs the atmosphere where Hannibal — as well as the reader — is unsure of the events taking place at this moment. Hannibal's suicidal thoughts at 17.566 reveal his desire to leave the epic immediately, reflected in this generic escape into the rural world. The condensation of the displacement within a few lines, as well as the inclusion of *subito, praeceps, vasto superantem saltu*, and the lines 573–574 with the 'short path' to exodus suggest a speedy flight outside the epic, perhaps a Silian invention to illustrate Hannibal's speedy flight into exile. The fast escape from the battlefield contrasts historical reports which narrate that after the war was over, Hannibal remained in Carthage for a few years until he left to the East in 196/195 BCE for fear of being handed over to Rome.[14] In contrast to the speed of the action, the pastoral escape works as a narrative delay in the epic's ending with anti-closural effects. Hannibal is shown in flight, unavailable for any further action, which is a sign of anti-closure, differing from the 'closural' duel of Aeneas-Turnus where Turnus' shade flees to the Underworld (*sub umbras* at 12.952), or of Achilles-Hector in the *Iliad* with Hector's death or of Eteocles-Polynices in the *Thebaid*. The pastoral episode of the sham battle is anti-closural for one more reason: it connects the final book of the *Punica* with the opening book of the *Aeneid*, where Aeneas is in the forests and Venus disguised as a huntress, offers him instructions on how to leave the uncivilized landscape and integrate himself back to civilization (*Aen.* 1.314–342). Similarly, Athena in the *Odyssey* (13.221–440) is welcoming Odysseus to Ithaca in the guise of a shepherd and is directing him on how to reach the center through a set of gradual moves from the periphery inwards. Aeneas' and Odysseus' situation is the reversed from Hannibal's one, as Venus and Athena point Aeneas and Odysseus respectively to the center rather than the periphery. On the contrary, the pastoral world to which Hannibal is displaced will be the place of his disempowerment and eventually of his disappearance. This generic plurality in the end of the *Punica* characterizes the whole epic poem, in which, according to Littlewood, the fact that Hannibal slips from the national arena of historical epic to the tragic fate of individuals manipulated by the gods resembles Ovid's heroes in the *Metamorphoses* who constantly step from one genre to another.[15] To this extent, this scene is a very powerful moment that forces the central character into a marginal space but puts him in a liminal condition between two generic realms: an epic and a non-epic one (or rural more specifically). At the end of the epic, after his displacement to a non-epic

---

14 Nep. *Han.* 11; Just. *Epit.* 32.4.

15 See Littlewood 2018, 254. Silius, on several occasions, uses generic tension or instability as a means to explore a fundamental theme in his epic (7.409, 493; 11.385, 482; 15.18, 127).

world by Juno, Hannibal will once again be abandoned on the top of a hill, away from his army, powerless and unable to act. The external enemy, Hannibal, is now transformed into an 'external' viewer of the epic narrative. He becomes a simple spectator of the progress of the narrative (17.597–603):

> *At fessum tumulo tandem regina propinquo*
> *sistit Iuno ducem, facies unde omnis et atrae*
> *apparent admota oculis vestigia pugnae.*
> *qualem Gargani campum Trebiaeque paludem*
> *et Tyrrhena vada et Phaethontis viderat amnem*
> *strage virum undantem, talis, miserabile visu,*
> *prostratis facies aperitur dira maniplis.*

> But Queen Juno at last made exhausted Hannibal sit down on a hill nearby, from where he had a clear view of the whole picture and could trace with his eyes every detail in the destructive battle. Just as he had once seen Mount Garganus' field and Trebia's marshes, Trasimene the Tuscan lake, and Phaethon's River Po overflow with a pile of corpses, such was now the dreadful sight that opened before his eyes — sad to behold. Then Juno returned to her heavenly abode disturbed.

Hannibal is led from a world of martial action into the un-epic world that Juno created for him, and can only watch powerless to intervene. This decentering creates a sense of confusion: despite his absence, Hannibal is able to hear the sufferings of his followers (17.562–564: et *absens | accipio gemitus vocesque ac verba vocantum | Hannibalem*, "and even though I am not present, I hear their groans and voices and their words calling me, Hannibal"), although physically he cannot reach them, just like Turnus at 10.672–675. From the moment when Juno intervenes to impose her control over Hannibal, he is deprived of his military advantage fairly won throughout the epic, and becomes a vulnerable individual caught under the wheels of Rome's destiny.[16] He is "trapped perpetually in the role of an isolated Turnus",[17] but he is not killed to provide a sense of finite end. Hannibal's disappearance becomes a sudden and swift event at the end of the epic, and under conditions not aligned with the military glory he has gained over the past sixteen books. Hannibal is already deprived of his military activity after his luxurious stay at Capua at book 11, where both himself and his army face the degenerative effects and a sluggish behaviour when it is time for them to resume the fighting, as Silius describes at 12.15–26 and in particular at 12.18–19: *molli luxu madefacta meroque | illecebris somni, torpentia membra*

---

16 See Littlewood 2018, 254.
17 Stocks 2014, 233.

fluebant ("soft luxury and wine had drenched the soldiers' limbs. They were moving sluggishly, dulled by sleep"). Their armoury was felt heavy and inefficient (12.25–26: *tum grave cassis onus maioraque pondera visa | parmarum ac nullis fusae stridoribus hastae*, "now their helmets became a heavy burden, and the weight of their light shields seemed heavier; they threw their spears making no hissing sound").[18] A few lines later in the same book, Hannibal's status as a "viewer" of various sites in Campania causes a sense of marginalization which foreshadows his departure from Italy at the end of the epic, where he will join a band of fugitives and will flee to the mountains to hide (17.616–617: *sic rapitur paucis fugientum mixtus, et altos | inde petit retro montis tutasque latebras*, "Then he joined a band of fugitives who took him away. And he sought a safe hiding-place in the high mountains to the rear").[19] Hannibal's submissiveness is once again indicated by the word of *rapitur* being in passive voice and is culminated when he becomes a passive image in Scipio's triumph at the end of the epic narrative (643–644).

At the final lines of the epic, before Hannibal joins a band of fugitives and disappears, as if he cannot accept his displacement from the epic so abruptly, he gives a long speech addressing Rome, announcing that for as long as he is alive, the Romans will remain in fear of his return (605–618). The closure of *Punica* 17 has been foreshadowed by the closure of *Punica* 12; it is the moment where Hannibal's attempts to conquer the Capitol and fight with Jupiter are proved futile. Juno once again intervenes and leads his actions, until she finally removes him from his task at 12.726–728: *sic affata virum indocilem pacisque modique, | mirantem superum vultus et flammea membra | abstrahit* ("With these words she spoke, and as Hannibal was in awe before the gods' faces and fiery limbs, she removed him from his undertaking, a man unable to be taught neither peace nor moderation"), echoing Jupiter's future demand to Juno to remove him from the battle of Zama at 17.376–377: *aetherias … trahat Hannibal auras | ereptus pugnae* ("let Hannibal enjoy life … by being snatched away from battle"). When Hannibal leaves the battle and the narrative at *Punica* 12, he performs it in the same way as in book 17, by looking back and threatening that he would return (12.729–730); and the people watching him departing, were unsure

---

18 Also, at 12.83–84 Hannibal was trying to rouse his soldiers' hearts and minds because luxury and continuous success has worn them out. For Campania as the site of Hannibal's own decline and eventual defeat, see Stocks 2014, 135 and n. 6–7 on Capua's association with *luxus*, and Augoustakis 2015, 160–167 on Campania's and Capua's *luxuria* and oriental otherness function.

19 Livy reports that Hannibal joined a crowd of horsemen who fled to Hadrumetum at 30.35.3.

whether this is reality (733–738), and even at the moment of the absolute celebration of Jupiter's victory, the eyes of some spectators focused at the place
where Hannibal had set up his tents (746–747), exactly as in 17.643–644.

Titania desine bella: Liminality, Transgression, and Monstrosity

The narrative edges have been used by authors as the narrative space of defeat
and enervation.[20] Hannibal's move to *devia passu* at 17.530 will eventually become the space of his elimination, just as Statius' Parthenopaeus when he is
removed to the edge of the battle for his dying moments at the end of *Thebaid* 9
(877–879). At the end of the *Punica*, at the narrative edge of the epic, Hannibal
is shown defeated, almost feminized, which aligns him with female-focused
heroes within the epic, such as Dido, Juno, Anna, and the feminized and defeated East where he comes from.[21] Liminality is not only about thresholds, but it
can also describe a transition from one world to another.[22] Just like Anna Perenna in the *Punica*, who, despite her central role in the epic to inspire Hannibal to
begin the battle of Cannae, remains unplaced and ambiguous, on the margins
and in-between two warring nations and two identities,[23] similarly Hannibal
"fights" between two worlds. Anna Perenna's ambiguity, starting from Carthaginian origins and ending up as a Roman goddess reflects this ambiguity in
Hannibal's Punic identity and his failed Romanity. Hannibal is thus shown in a
liminal situation between "death" and "life", between the frames of this epic
and beyond: he is too glorious to be marginalized in a non-epic world, and he is
too alive to abandon the epic in such a humiliating way. Additionally, this liminality inevitably connects him with Hercules, one of the most ambivalent heroes
in Greco-Roman culture, whose representations are full of contradictions: he is
strong, masculine and virile whereas at the same time he is bestial, transgressor
and feminine, enslaved by females, such as Omphale; he was *heros* and *theos*,
receiving divine and heroic sacrifice in cult, on the margins between human

---

20 See Lovatt 2015.

21 See Keith 2010, 372.

22 See Lovatt 2015, 74 where she discusses the narrative edges as a space of defeat.

23 See McIntyre 2019, 37 and 52 who connects Anna Perenna's dual identity between Rome
and Carthage with Silius' choice to place her story at a central position in the *Punica*, at the
battle of Cannae. Despite her marginality and her otherness, Anna Perenna in the *Fasti* and the
Punica eventually becomes a figure of stability and renewal connected to Rome's origins.

and divine, an interstitial figure.[24] All the above characteristics recall Hannibal whose ambivalent personality makes him also a transitional figure. He is at the service of female will, as he embodies Juno's bellicose desires as well as materializing Dido's curse. At *Pun.* 11.134–137 Hannibal's cross of the Alps is compared to that of Hercules.[25] In her recent work on Hannibal's multidimensional character, Stocks revealed the opposition between monstrous/transgressive and divine elements in *Pun.* 12 at Hannibal's sojourn at Capua and Campania. Stocks argues that Hannibal in *Punica* 12 resembles gods, such as Jupiter, monsters, such as Cacus and the giants, and monstrous demigods, such as Hercules.[26]

Hannibal's liminal condition at the closure of the epic, and the fact that he remains alive leaves open the possibility of his return, and creates an image of him, who does not belong within the frames of this epic anymore, but one who has stepped to another one, an allusion to a possible new beginning. At the end of the poem, Silius leads his external antagonist outside the frames of his epic narrative by exploiting the historical reality of Hannibal's disappearance from the battle, his flight to the East (Polyb. 3.11; Liv. 33.47) and his later attempts from Syria to conquer Rome. Hannibal again breaks the frames of the narrative space of closure with this reference of his future return simply implying that an alive antagonist can always return for revenge. And indeed, he will come back to be defeated by Scipio Aemilianus in the third Punic war. Jupiter at 17.378 has prophesied *terras implere volet redeuntibus armis* that Hannibal 'will want to stir stars and sea and fill the land with a returning army'. But another Scipio, Scipio Aemilianus (17.374: *venietque pari sub nomine ductor*), will prevent him and will destroy Carthage entirely. With the emphasis on renewal and continuation, Silius again resists complete and absolute closure.

Hannibal's struggle to impose himself in the center throughout the epic made him entangled with his target, Rome, and caused him an identity imbalance. In his final monologue before his departure from the epic world, Hannibal's focalization through the eyes of the Romans when he refers to himself by

---

24 See Feeney 1987, 51–52. Loraux 1990 also discusses Hercules' personality and gender and shows that the effort to construct a super-male hero in Hercules' case reveals also a strong feminine side of his.

25 At 3.512–517, Silius shows a historical figure pushing beyond Hercules, the greatest hero of all. On Hercules as a model for Hannibal, see Asso 2010, 179–189 and Antoniadis in this volume.

26 See Stocks 2019, 234. Stocks broader argument is that through this transgressive depiction of Hannibal's personality in book 12, Silius puts a gigantomachic threat to the previous established epic tradition. Feeney 1987, 63 has argued on Hercules' liminality at the end of Apollonius' *Argonautica*, as a sign of the hero's passing into the world of gods.

his name, *facta Hannibalis sileant* (17.610), is a sign of this removal from the *Punica*. Additionally, before Hannibal disappears, at the moment of his transition from Italy to Carthage in the final book, in order to defend Africa from Scipio, he is again shown in a liminal condition. Silius describes him pursuing a reunion with the Italian soil until the very end; he is attached to the Italian *tellus*, which he finds hard to abandon, just as if he were abandoning his own fatherland (17.211–217):[27]

> omnis in altum
> Sidonius visus converterat undique miles;
> ductor defixos Itala tellure tenebat
> intentus vultus, manantesque ora rigabant
> per tacitum lacrimae, et suspiria crebra ciebat,
> haud secus ac patriam pulsus dulcesque penates
> linqueret et tristes exul traheretur in oras.

All the Carthaginian soldiers everywhere turned their eyes to the sea, but their leader Hannibal held his face intensely fixed on Italian soil in silence, while tears flowed down and wetted his cheeks. He frequently sighed, just as if he were leaving his own country and his sweet home and was being dragged into a grim place in exile.

Hannibal is struggling between two worlds: one Roman and one Carthaginian. This liminality in identity is reflected in the liminal geographical space in which he acts: when Hannibal faces the sea storm, he is not in Carthage, not in Rome, which reveals himself as neither a Carthaginian, as he is attached to his new, hostile country, Rome, neither Roman by identity. Hannibal was holding his eyes steady at Italy (17.213: *ductor defixos Itala tellure tenebat*), as he realizes what he has left behind: after his crushing victory at the battle of Cannae in 216 BCE, he was in control of most (but not all) of Italy. But now, in the middle of the sea, he is *haud secus ... exul* (216–217) an ironic reference to his real exile and displacement at the end of the epic, dragged in sad areas, where *traheretur* is one more instance of his submissiveness. Hannibal has the status of a proper migrant who is displaced and constantly in motion. He is an *exul* led outside his fatherland, reminding also of exiled Medea who, manipulated by forces outside of her control, is always in motion fleeing Corinth and Athens due to her crimes; her status as *exul* or φυγάς (Eur. *Med.* 12; 400) portrays her always in motion, displaced and seeking for asylum.[28] Therefore, Hannibal's liminality can be

---

27 See Augoustakis 2010a, 152–154.
28 For Medea the exile, see Ennius' tragedy titled *Medea exul*, Hyg. *Fab.* 25, 26; Sen. *Med.* 459. For Medea's displacement in Ovid, see Newlands 1997.

viewed in different terms: he is at the *limen* of being Roman although he is Carthaginian, of being feminine although he is masculine, and of being hunted although he is the hunter.[29] Apart from transcending geographical spaces he also transcends literary spaces: when the fight for Rome is over, Hannibal withdraws from the epic and historiographical world into a rural one. As we approach the end of the *Punica*, the Carthaginian "other" is about to become Roman, and Hannibal's liminal condition and his tendency to transcend every boundary blurs the distinction of what counts as Roman and Carthaginian, what as center and what as periphery: in his final moments, Hannibal is removed from the center of the action and from the central signs of epic genre. Although he continues to draw the attention at these peripheral areas, he is unable to act. He becomes a spectator of the progress of the narrative still anticipating his return. The frames of this epic cannot contain him who continuously in the *Punica* breaks the boundaries of this world and the treaties between the nations.

Center and Periphery

The above internal battle in Hannibal's epic character and the blurred distinction of what is central and what peripheral, reflects the continuous geographic battle between center and periphery which fight for dominance. Similarly, Rome's centrality and Hannibal's withdrawal into an un-epic, rural world when the fight for Rome is over reflects the dialogue between the urban and the rural space. In the Roman world, the relationship between center and periphery is altered in Lucan due to civil war, through his narrative on the transgression of boundaries and systemic collapse. The war between Caesar and Pompey has global consequences: it distorts the relationship between internal and external, altering the fabric of Roman and non-Roman space.[30] Just as Lucan's Caesar has boundless and global ambitions (1.200–202), aiming at a world occupation, similarly in the *Punica*, the Punic War has global effects, with Scipio and Hannibal, the two principal leaders, fighting for world conquest (17.389–390: *discriminis alta | in medio merces, quicquid tegit undique caelum*, "the price of the contest to be decided was high, namely everything the wide sky covers"). The

---

29 For Hannibal's multiple roles paralleled with monstrous individuals both divine and gigantomachic in *Pun.* 12 as a reflection of Campania's volatility and Capua's dubious moral status, see Stocks 2019.
30 See the discussion on Myers 2011, 415.

discussion on the central and marginal position of Hannibal in a Roman epic, reflects in turn the relationship between the Empire's center and periphery in Silius' times with its cultural and political transformation; the Empire's expansion accentuated the significance of peripheral locations and the relationship between center, edges and beyond; the very existence of the periphery gives power to the center. This means that the center cannot exist without the periphery. However, because of interdependence, this state of affairs ensures that the periphery has the potential to subvert the power of those in the center and this is what Hannibal managed to achieve in the *Punica*. The peripheral character has become the center of the action, who despite his transformation into a marginal character, he leaves open the possibilities for the continuation of the story. But we should not forget Silius' announcement in the epic's *exordium*: this epic poem will narrate only the second out of the three Punic Wars. Endings that can also be beginnings for something new is something of a mannerism in epic of the 1st century CE.[31] Hannibal's tendency to break the *fines* and the limit of the world is visualized in the closure of the epic where Hannibal's disappearance does not give a finite end in the epic but rather postpones the war indefinitely. It creates expectations for further engagement and for further narrative. Although the *Punica* is a complete epic, in the sense that it offers a terminal closure in the story, as the historical truth compels, there are other narratives in motion that do not close. Hannibal's character is such that transcends every boundary, every limit, every threshold. Even the *Punica* itself is not enough for him.[32]

---

31 See Zissos 2019, 534 n. 17.

32 I would like to thank the library of the Université de Genève as well as the Fondation Hardt in Geneva for providing me with the necessary resources to complete this article.

List of Contributors

Theodore Antoniadis is currently Assistant Professor of Latin at the Aristotle University of Thessaloniki (Greece). He studied Classics at the Universities of Thessaloniki (BA, PhD) and Toronto (MA). A revised version of his doctoral dissertation, *The Rhetoric of Belatedness: A Running Commentary on Ovid's Amores* as well as a translation of Lucretius' *De Rerum Natura* and an *Anthology of Latin Love Elegy from Catullus to Ovid* (e-book) have been published in modern Greek. He has also written various articles on Neronian Literature and Flavian Epic in peer-reviewed journals and conference proceedings, while his current research focuses primarily on the *Punica* of Silius Italicus.

Konstantinos Arampapaslis holds a PhD in Classical Philology from the University of Illinois at Urbana-Champaign (USA). His research interests lie in Imperial Latin literature, especially Neronian epic and prose, with particular focus on the depiction of the religious reality of the 1st century CE in the literature of the period. He has published an article on Cicero's use of antiquarian material in *De Haruspicum Responsis*, and a book chapter on religion in Lucan's *Bellum Civile* (co-authored with Antony Augoustakis). Forthcoming articles include an examination of Eteocles' dream in *Thebaid* 2 from the reader's perspective, and an analysis of doctor-related narratives in the *Annals*, illustrating Tacitus' prejudice against Greeks. He is currently working on the publication of his thesis "*Hostes Deum*: Magic in the Literature of the Neronian Period".

Antony Augoustakis is Professor of Classics at the University of Illinois at Urbana-Champaign (USA). He is the author of *Silius Italicus, Punica 3* (with R.J. Littlewood; Oxford, 2022), *Silius Italicus' Punica. Rome's War with Hannibal* (with N.W. Bernstein; London, 2021), *Statius, Thebaid 8* (Oxford, 2016), *Motherhood and the Other: Fashioning Female Power in Flavian Epic* (Oxford, 2010) and *Plautus' Mercator* (Bryn Mawr, 2009). He has edited many volumes on various topics in Latin literature.

Stephen Froedge received his PhD in Classical Philology from the University of Illinois at Urbana-Champaign (USA) and is currently a Latin Teacher at Northwest Ohio Classical Academy (USA). His research focuses on Neronian and Flavian literature, especially epic poetry. In particular, his work treats monsters and monstrosity. Additionally, he has an interest in Classical reception in television. He has co-authored a chapter (with Antony Augoustakis, Adam Kozak, and Clayton Schroer) on death and ritual in epic poetry. Additionally, he is preparing an article on hair in Statius' *Thebaid* from his dissertation as well as a pedagogical article concerning his experience teaching epic poetry at Danville Correctional Center.

Eleni Hall Manolaraki is Associate Professor of Classics at the University of South Florida (USA). She holds a PhD in classics from Cornell University and is the author of *Noscendi Nilum Cupido: Imagining Egypt from Lucan to Philostratus* (Berlin, 2013), and the co-author and editor of *A History of Rome* (Wiley-Blackwell, 2009). She has published several journal articles and book chapters on Roman epic (Lucan, Statius, Silius Italicus), historiography (Tacitus, Pliny the Younger), and natural history (Pliny the Elder).

Jonathan Master is Associate Professor of Classics at Emory University (USA). His research focuses on early imperial prose, especially historiography. He is the author of *Provincial Soldiers and Imperial Instability in the Histories of Tacitus* (Michigan, 2016). He has also published articles on Tacitus and Seneca and is co-authoring a commentary on Seneca's *Consolation to Marcia*. His current book project examines Seneca's views on historiography and the educational value of the past.

Victoria Emma Pagán is Professor of Classics at the University of Florida (USA). She is the author of *Conspiracy Narratives in Roman History* (Austin, 2004), *Conspiracy Theory in Latin Literature* (Austin, 2012); *Rome and the Literature of Gardens* (London, 2006); *Tacitus* (London, 2017); and *A Sallust Reader* (Bolchazy-Carducci, 2009). She edited the Wiley *Companion to Tacitus* and co-edited *Disciples of Flora: Gardens in History and Culture* (Cambridge Scholars, 2015) with Judith Page and Brigitte Weltman-Aron, and *Tacitus' Wonders: Empire and Paradox in Ancient Rome* (London, 2022) with James McNamara. She is the author of over two dozen publications on Tacitus, Statius, and Latin literature. She is sole editor of the *Tacitus Encyclopedia*, due to appear in 2022.

Paul Roche is Associate Professor in Latin at the University of Sydney (Australia). His research focusses on the literature of the Roman empire. He has authored two commentaries on Lucan's epic poem, *De Bello Civili*: Book One (2009) and Book Seven (2019). He has also edited or co-edited volumes of essays on politics in imperial literature (2009), Pliny the Younger (2011) and Lucan (2020). He is currently writing commentaries on Lucan, *De Bello Civili* Book Ten and Tacitus, *Annals* Book One.

Angeliki Nektaria Roumpou is a Swiss government post-doctoral fellow in Latin language and literature at the University of Geneva. Her research focus is on Flavian epic, and she is currently writing a commentary on Silius Italicus' *Punica* 17. She is also working on a project exploring the connection between ritual and textual closure in Flavian literature.

Clayton Schroer earned his PhD in Classical Philology from the University of Illinois at Urbana-Champaign (USA) and is currently Visiting Assistant Professor of Classics at Emory University (USA). His research focuses on Augustan and Imperial Latin poetry, especially epic, as well as postcolonial theory. He has authored numerous forthcoming and published articles and book chapters on Silius Italicus, Vergil, Ovid, and Propertius, and he has co-authored (with Antony Augoustakis, Stephen Froedge, and Adam Kozak) a chapter on the development of funerary rituals in Greco-Roman epic. His book project (*"Quid restat profugis?* Exile, the Roman Imperial Imagination, and Silius Italicus' *Punica"*) is under contract with Oxford University Press, and he is also at work on an article concerning Statius' *Silvae* 4.5 and creolization.

Christopher Star is Professor of Classics at Middlebury College (USA). He is the author of *The Empire of the Self: Self-Command and Political Speech in Seneca and Petronius* (Baltimore, 2012), *Seneca* (London, 2017), and *Apocalypse and Golden Age: The End of the World in Greek and Roman Thought* (Baltimore, 2021).

Bibliography

Abdy, R. and Harling, N. (2005), "Two Important New Roman Coins", in: *The Numismatic Chronical* 165, 175–178.

Acton, K. (2012), "Vespasian and the Social World of the Roman Court", in: *AJP* 132, 103–124.

Adams, J.N. (1982), *The Latin Sexual Vocabulary*, London.

Agamben, G. (1998), *Homo Sacer: Sovereign Power and Bare Life* (trans. D. Heller-Roazen), Stanford.

Al-Ati, T. (2011), "Assyrian Plum (*Cordia myxa L.*)", in: E.M. Yahia (ed.), *Postharvest Biology and Technology of Tropical and Subtropical Fruits. Acai to Citrus*, Oxford, 116–124, 125e–126e.

Ando, C. (2000), *Imperial Ideology and Provincial Loyalty in the Roman Empire*, Berkeley, CA.

Antoniadis, T. (2018), "Intratextuality via Philosophy: Contextualizing ira in Silius Italicus' *Punica* 1–2", in: S. Frangoulidis, S.J. Harrison, and T.D. Papanghelis (eds.), *Intratextuality and Roman Literature*, Berlin, 377–396.

Asso, P. (2010), "Hercules as a Paradigm of Roman Heroism", in: A. Augoustakis (ed.), *Brill's Companion to Silius Italicus*, Leiden, 179–192.

Aubert, J.-J. (1999), "Du noir en noir et blanc: éloge de la dispersion", in: *MH* 56.3, 159–182.

Augoustakis, A. (2003), "*Lugendam formae sine virginitate reliquit*: Reading Pyrene and the transformation of landscape in Silius' *Punica* 3", in: *AJP* 124, 235–257.

Augoustakis, A. (2010a), *Motherhood and the Other: Fashioning Female Power in Flavian Epic*, Oxford.

Augoustakis, A. (2010b), "Introduction: Silius Italicus, A Flavian Poet", in: A. Augoustakis (ed.), *Brill's Companion to Silius Italicus*, Leiden, 1–23.

Augoustakis, A. (2015), "Campanian Politics and Poetics in Silius Italicus' *Punica*", in: *ICS* 40.1, 155–169.

Augoustakis, A. (2016), "Burial and Lament in Flavian Epic: Mothers, Fathers, Children", in: N. Manioti (ed.), *Family in Flavian Epic*, Leiden, 276–300.

Augoustakis, A. and Bernstein, N.W. (2021), *Silius Italicus' Punica: Rome's War with Hannibal*, London.

Augoustakis, A. and Littlewood, R.J. (2022), *Silius Italicus, Punica 3: Text, Translation, and Commentary*, Oxford.

Bakhtin, M. (1981), *The Dialogic Imagination: Four Essays* (trans. Caryl Emerson and Michael Hoquist), Austin, TX.

Baldwin, B. (2005), "Roman Emperors in the Elder Pliny", in: *Scholia* 4, 56–78.

Barchiesi, A. and Cucchiarelli, A. (2005), "Satire and the Poet: The Body as Self-referential Symbol", in: K. Feudenburg (ed.), *The Cambridge Companion to Roman Satire*, Cambridge, 207–223.

Barr, W. and Lee, G. (1987), *The Satires of Persius*, Liverpool.

Barrett, A. (1989), *Caligula: The Corruption of Power*, New York.

Barringer, J.M. (2001), The *Hunt in Ancient Greece*, Baltimore, MD.

Bartsch, S. (2012), "Persius, Juvenal, and Stoicism", in: S. Braund and J. Osgood (eds.), *A Companion to Persius and Juvenal*, Malden, MA, 217–238.

Bartsch, S. (2015), *Persius: A Study in Food, Philosophy and the Figural*, Chicago, IL.

Bassett, E. (1955), "Regulus and the Serpent in the *Punica*", in: *CP* 50, 1–20.

Bassett, E. (1966), "Hercules and the Hero of the Punica", in: L. Wallach (ed.), *The Classical Tradition. Studies in Honor of Harry Caplan*, Ithaca, NY, 258–273.

https://doi.org/10.1515/9783111063942-011

Bauer, J. (1983), "Semitisches bei Petron", in: P. Händel and W. Meid (eds.), *Festschrift für Robert Muth zum 65. Geburtstag*, Innsbruck, 17–23.

Beard, M. (1998), "Imaginary *horti*: or up the garden path", in: M. Cima and E. La Rocca (eds.), *Horti Romani*, Rome, 23–32.

Bellandi, F. (1996), *Persi: Dai "verba togae" al solipsismo stilistico*, 2nd ed., Bologna.

Bernstein, N. (2016), *"Mutua vulnera*: Dying Together in Silius' Saguntum", in: N. Manioti (ed.), *Family in Flavian Epic*, Leiden, 228–247.

Bernstein, N. (2017a), *Silius Italicus, Punica 2: Text, Translation, and Commentary*, Oxford.

Bernstein, N. (2017b), *Seneca: Hercules Furens*, London.

Bernstein, N. (2018), "*Invitas maculant cognato sanguine dextras*: Civil War Themes in Silius's Saguntum Episode", in: L.D. Ginsberg and D.A. Krasne (eds.), *After 69 C.E. – Writing Civil War in Flavian Rome*, Berlin, 179–198.

Betzig, L. (2014), "*Suffodit inguina*: Genital Attacks on Roman Emperors and Other Primates", in: *Politics and the Life Sciences* 33, 54–68.

Bexley, E.M. (2009), "Replacing Rome: Geographic and Political Centrality in Lucan's *Pharsalia*", in: *CP* 104.4, 459–475.

Billerbeck, M. (1986a), "*Aspects* of *Stoicism in Flavian Epic*", in: *PLLS* 5, 341–356.

Billerbeck, M. (1986b), "Stoizismus in der römischen Epik neronischer und flavischer Zeit", in: *ANRW* 2.32.5, 3116–3151.

Bispham, E. (2007), "Pliny the Elder's Italy", in: *BICS* 100, 41–67.

Bonner, S.F. (1977), *Education in Ancient Rome: From the Elder Cato to the Younger Pliny*, London.

Bouby, L., Bouchette, A., and Figueiral, I. (2011), "Sebesten Fruits (*Cordia myxa* L.) in *Gallia Narbonensis* (Southern France): a trade item from the Eastern Mediterranean?", in: *Veget Hist Archaeobot* 20, 397–404.

Bovey, M. (1999), "La greffe de l'olivier sur le figuier: Columelle, Virgile et la greffe des arbres", in: *REL* 77, 184–204.

Bowersock, G.W. (1973), "Syria under Vespasian", in: *JRS* 63, 133–140.

Bradley, M. (ed.) (2015), *Smell and the Ancient Senses*, New York.

Bramble, J.C. (1974), *Persius and the Programmatic Satire*, Cambridge.

Braund, S. (2004), *Juvenal and Persius*, Cambridge, MA.

Braund, S. and Osgood, J. (eds.) (2012), *A Companion to Persius and Juvenal*, Malden, MA.

Bremmer, J.N. (2010), "Hephaistos Sweats or How to Construct an Ambivalent God", in: J.N. Bremmer and A. Erskine (eds.), *The Gods of Ancient Greece: Identities and Transformations*, Edinburgh, 193–208.

Briggs, W. (1999), "Petronius and Virgil in *The Great Gatsby*", in: *IJCT* 6, 226–235.

Briscoe, J. (2008), *A Commentary on Livy, Books 38–40*, Oxford.

Bruère, R.T. (2016), "*Color Ovidianus*", in: A. Augoustakis (ed.), *Oxford Readings in Flavian Epic*, Oxford, 345–387.

Bücheler, F. and Heräus, G. (eds.) (1862), *Petronii Saturae et Liber Priapeorum ... adiectae sunt Varronis et Senecae saturae similesque reliquiae*, Berlin.

Buckley, E.L. (2014), "Valerius Flaccus and Seneca's Tragedies", in: G. Manuwald and M. Heerink (eds.), *The Companion to Valerius Flaccus*, Leiden, 307–325.

Burgos, L., Petri, C., and Badenes, M.L. (2007), "Prunus spp.", in: E.-C. Pua and M. Davey (eds.), *Transgenic Crops V. Biotechnology in Agriculture and Forestry, Vol 60*, Berlin, 283–307.

Burkert, W. (1979), *Structure and History in Greek Mythology and Ritual*, Berkeley, CA.

Burkert, W. (1985), *Greek Religion* (trans. J. Raffan), Cambridge, MA.

Cary, E. (1924), *Dio Cassius: Roman History Books LVI–LX*, Cambridge, MA.

Castelletti, C. (2014), "A Hero with a Sandal and a Buskin: The Figure of Jason in Valerius Flac-cus' Argonautica", in: G. Manuwald and M. Heerink (eds.), *The Companion to Valerius Flaccus*, Leiden, 171–191.

Champlin, E. (1991), *Final Judgments: Duty and Emotion in Roman Wills, 200 B.C. – A.D. 250*, Berkeley, CA.

Charry-Sánchez, J.D., Velez-van-Meerbeke, A., and Palacios-Sánchez, L. (2021), "Caligula: A Neuropsychiatric Explanation of his Madness", in: *Arquivos de Neuro-Psiquiatria* 79.4, 343–345.

Christoforou, P. (2021), "'An Indication of Truly Imperial Manners': The Roman emperor in Philo's *Legatio ad Gaium*", in: *Historia* 70.1, 83–115.

Cima, M. and Talamo, E. (2008), *Gli horti di Roma antica*, Rome.

Classen, C. (2012), *The Deepest Sense: A Cultural History of Touch*, Urbana, IL.

Clausen, W. (1994), *Virgil Eclogues*, Oxford.

Clausen, W. and Zetzel, J.E.G. (2004), *Commentum Cornuti in Persium*, Leipzig.

Clément-Tarantino, S. (2006), "La poétique romaine comme hybridation féconde. Les leçons de la greffe (Virgile, *Géorgiques*, 2, 9-82)", in: *Interférences – Ars Scribendi* 4 (http://ars-scribendi.ens-lyon.fr/article.php3?id article=37var affichage=vf, accessed March 10, 2022).

Cofer, C.M. (2015), *The Ara Pacis Augustae and the Ancient Understanding of Grafting*, Ph.D. diss., Bryn Mawr College.

Coffey, M. (1989), *Roman Satire*, 2nd ed., London.

Collins, A.W. (2009), "The Palace Revolution: The Assassination of Domitian and the Accession of Nerva", in: *Phoenix* 63, 73–106.

Colson, F.H. (1941), *Philo: Every Good Man is Free; On the Contemplative Life; On the Eternity of the World; Against Flaccus; Apology for the Jews; On Providence*, Cambridge, MA.

Colson, F.H. (1963), *Philo: On the Embassy to Gaius*, Cambridge, MA.

Corbin, A. (1986), *The Foul and the Fragrant: Odor and the French Social Imagination*, Cambridge, MA.

Cosci, P. (1980), "Quartilla e l'iniziazione ai misteri di Priapo (Satyricon 20,4)", in: *MD* 4, 199–201.

Courtney, E. (2001), *A Companion to Petronius*, Cambridge.

Cowan, R. (2007), "The Headless City: The Decline and Fall of Capua in Silius Italicus' *Punica*", in: ORA 1542, (https://ora.ouls.ox.ac.uk/objects/uuid:dceb6b5a-980c-46ca-ac9e-088 615e7fbea/download_file?file_format=pdf&safe_filename=The%2BHeadless%2BCity%2 B%28PDF%2BVersion%29&type_of_work=Book+section, accessed April 2, 2022).

Crook, J.A. (1967), *Law and Life at Rome*, London.

Csapo, E. (1997), "Riding the Phallus for Dionysus: Iconology, Ritual, and Gender-Role De/Construction", in: *Phoenix* 51, 253–295.

Cucchiarelli, A. (2012), *Publio Virgilio Marone, Le Bucoliche*, Rome.

Dabrowa, E. (2011), "The Date of the Census of Quirinius and the Chronology of the Governors of the Province of Syria", in: *ZPE* 178, 137–142.

Decharneux, B. (2003), "Entre le pouvoir et sacré: Philon d'Alexandrie, ambassadeur près du 'divin' Caius", in: A. Dierkens and J. Marx (eds.), *La Sacralisation du Pouvoir: Images et mises en scène*, Brussels, 21–27.

Dehon, P.-J. (2018), "Les notations hivernales dans le *Moretum*: Emprunts virgiliens et inten-tions parodiques", in: *Hermes* 146.3, 341–348.

Delz, J. (1987), *Silius Italicus: Punica*, Stuttgart.

Den Hollander, W. (2014), *Josephus, the Emperors, and the City of Rome: From Hostage to Historian*, Leiden.

Dench, E. (2005), *Romulus' Asylum: Roman Identities from the Age of Alexander to the Age of Hadrian*, Oxford.

Deremetz, A. (2009), "The Question of the Marvellous in the *Georgics* of Virgil", in: P. Hardie (ed.), *Paradox and the Marvellous in Augustan Literature and Culture*, Oxford, 113–125.

Dinter, M.T. (2012), "The Life and Times of Persius: The Neronian Literary 'Renaissance'", in: S. Braund and J. Osgood (eds.), *A Companion to Persius and Juvenal*, Malden, MA, 41–58.

Dominik, W.J. (2003), "Hannibal at the Gates: Programmatizing Rome and *Romanitas* in Silius Italicus' *Punica* 1 and 2", in: A.J. Boyle and W.J. Dominik (eds.), *Flavian Rome: Culture, Image, Text*, Leiden, 469–497.

Doody, A. (2007), "Virgil the Farmer? Critiques of the *Georgics* in Columella and Pliny", in: *CP* 102, 180–197.

Doody, A. (2011), "The Science and Aesthetics of Names in The Natural History", in: R. Gibson and R. Morello (eds.), *Pliny the Elder: Themes and Contexts*, Leiden, 113–130.

Dougherty, C. (2001), *The Raft of Odysseus: The Ethnographic Imagination of Homer's Odyssey*, New York.

Dowden, K. (2010), "The Gods in the Greek Novel", in: J.N. Bremmer and A. Erskine (eds.), *The Gods of Ancient Greece: Identities and Transformations*, Edinburgh, 362–374.

Dyck, A.R. (2003), "Evidence and Rhetoric in Cicero's 'Pro Roscio Amerino': The Case against Sex. Roscius", in: *CQ* 53, 235–246.

Eck, W. (1991), "Sulpicii Galbae Und Livii Ocellae – Zwei Senatorische Familien in Tarracina", in: *Listy Filologické* 114, 93–99, III.

Edmunds, L. (2010), "Toward a Minor Roman Poetry", in: *Poetica* 42.1–2, 29–80.

Edwards, C. (1993), *The Politics of Immorality in Ancient Rome*, Cambridge.

Edwards, C. (2007), *Death in Ancient Rome*, London.

Edwards, M.J. (1999), "The Role of Hercules in Valerius Flaccus", in: *Latomus* 58, 150–163.

Elsner, J. and Rutherford, I. (2010), "Introduction", in: J. Elsner and I. Rutherford (eds.), *Pilgrimage* in *Graeco-Roman* and *Early Christian Antiquity: Seeing the Gods*, Oxford, 1–40.

Évrard, É. (1982), "Quelques traits quantitatifs du vocabulaire du 'Moretum'", in: *Latomus* 41.3, 550–565.

Farrell, J. (2007), "Horace's Body, Horace's Books", in: S.J. Heyworth (ed.), *Classical Constructions: Papers in Memory of Don Fowler, Classicist and Epicurean*, Oxford, 174–193.

Fear, A.T. (1996), *Rome and Baetica: Urbanization in Southern Spain c. 50 BC – AD 150*, Oxford.

Fear, A. (2011), "The Roman's Burden", in: R. Gibson and R. Morello (eds.), *Pliny the Elder: Themes and Contexts*, Leiden, 21–34.

Feeney, D.C. (1982), *A Commentary on Silius Italicus Book 1*, D.Phil., Oxford University.

Feeney, D.C. (1987), "Following after Hercules, in Virgil and Apollonius", in: *PVS* 18, 47–85.

Feeney, D.C. (1991), *The Gods in Epic: Poets and Critics of the Classical Tradition*, Oxford.

Feeney, D.C. (1998), *Literature and Religion at Rome: Cultures, Contexts, and Beliefs*, Cambridge.

Fitch, J.G. (1987), *Seneca's Hercules Furens: A Critical Text with Introduction and Commentary*, Ithaca, NY.

Fitch, J.G. (2018), *Seneca: Tragedies*, 2 vols., Cambridge, MA.

Fitzgerald, W. (1996), "Labor and Laborer in Latin Poetry: The Case of the *Moretum*", in: *Arethusa* 29.3, 389–418.

Fitzgerald, W. and Spentzou, E. (eds.) (2018), *The Production of Space in Latin Literature*, Oxford.

Formisano, M. (2018), "Introduction: Marginality and the Classics, Exemplary Extraneousness", in: M. Formisano and C.S. Kraus (eds.), *Marginality, Canonicity, Passion*, Oxford, 1–28.

Frass, M. (2006), *Antike römische Gärten: Soziale und wirtschaftliche Funktionen der Horti Romani*, Horn.

Freudenburg, K. (1993), *The Walking Muse: Horace on the Theory of Satire*, Princeton.

Freudenburg, K. (2001), *Satires of Rome: Threatening Poses from Lucilius to Juvenal*, Cambridge.

Freudenburg, K. (2021), *Horace: Satires Book II*, Cambridge.

Fulkerson, L. (2016), *Ovid: A Poet on the Margins*, London.

Galinsky, K. (1972), *The Herakles Theme: The Adaptations of the Hero in Literature from Homer to the Twentieth Century*, Oxford.

Gallia, A.B. (2012), *Remembering the Roman Republic: Culture, Politics and History Under the Principate*, Cambridge.

Gambetti, S. (2009), *The Alexandrian Riots of 38 C.E. and the Persecution of the Jews: A Historical Reconstruction*, Leiden.

Garner, R.J. (1979), *The Grafter's Handbook*, New York.

Garnsey, P. (1980), *Non-Slave Labor in the Greco-Roman World*, Cambridge.

Genette, G. (1997), *Paratexts: Thresholds of Interpretation* (trans. Jane E. Lewin), Cambridge.

Gervais, K. (2020), "*Dominoque legere superstes?* Epic and Empire at the End of the *Thebaid*", in: *HSPh* 111, 385–420.

Gibson, B. (2005), "Hannibal at Gades: Silius Italicus 3.1–60", in: *PLLS* 12, 177–195.

Glass, L. (2017) "Obscenity Trials", in: I. Takayoshi (ed.), *American Literature in Transition, 1920-1930*, Cambridge, 449–458.

Gowers, E. (1993), *The Loaded Table: Representations of Food in Roman Literature*, Oxford.

Gowers, E. (2005), "Talking Trees: Philemon and Baucis Revisited", in: *Arethusa* 38, 331–365.

Gowers, E. (2011), "Trees and Family Trees in the *Aeneid*", in: *ClAnt* 30, 87–118.

Gowers, E. (2012), *Horace: Satires Book I*, Cambridge.

Grainger, J.D. (2018), *Syrian Influences in the Roman Empire to AD 300*, London.

Graver, M. (2007), *Stoicism & Emotion*, Chicago, IL.

Griffin, M. (1976), *Seneca: A Philosopher in Politics*, Oxford.

Grimal, P. (1984), *Les jardins romains*, 3rd ed., Paris.

Grisé, Y. (1982), *Le suicide dans la Rome antique*, Montreal.

Gruen, E. (2004), *Diaspora: Jews amidst Greeks and Romans*, Cambridge, MA.

Gruen, E. (2016), *Constructs of Identity in Hellenistic Judaism: Essays on Early Jewish Literature and History*, Berlin.

Haley, E.W. (2003), *Baetica Felix: People and Prosperity in Southern Spain from Caesar to Septimius Severus*, Austin, TX.

Hall, J. (2005), "Politeness and Formality in Cicero's Letter to Matius (*Fam.* 11.27)", in: *MH* 62, 193–213.

Hall, J. (2014), *Cicero's Use of Judicial Theater*, Ann Arbor, MI.

Hardie, P. (1993), *The Epic Successors of Virgil: A Study in the Dynamics of Tradition*, Cambridge.

Hardie, P. (1997), "Closure in Latin Epic", in: H. Roberts, M. Dunn, D. Fowler (eds.), *Classical Closure. Reading the End in Greek and Latin Literature*, Princeton, 142–151.

Harland, P.A. (2010), "Pausing at the intersection of Religion and Travel", in: P.A. Harland (ed.), *Travel and Religion in Antiquity*, Waterloo, ON, 1–26.

Harrison, S.J. (2008), "Laudes Italiae (*Georgics* 2. 136 – 175): Virgil as a Caesarian Hesiod", in: G. Urso (ed.), *Patria diversis gentibus una? Unità, politica e identità etniche nell'Italia antica (Atti del convegno internazionale, Cividale del Friuli, 20–22 settembre 2007)*, Pisa, 231–242.

Harrison, S.J. (2010), "Picturing the Future Again: Proleptic Ekphrasis in Silius' *Punica*", in: A. Augoustakis (ed.), *Brill's Companion to Silius Italicus*, Leiden, 279–292.

Hartog, F. (2001), *Memories of Odysseus* (trans. J. Lloyd), Chicago, IL.

Harvey, R.A. (1981), *A Commentary on Persius*, Leiden.

Haubold, J. (2013), "Ethnography in the *Iliad*", in: M. Skempis and I. Ziogas (eds.), *Geography, Topography, Landscape: Configurations of Space in Greek and Roman Epic*, Berlin, 19–36.

Heerink, M. (2007), "Going A Step Further: Valerius Flaccus' Metapoetical Reading of Propertius' Hylas", in: *CQ* 57, 606–620.

Heinze, R. (1899), "Petron und der Griechische Roman", in: *Hermes* 34, 494–519.

Heinze, R. (1960), "Das Kräuterkäsegericht (Moretum)", in: E. Burck (ed.), *Vom Geist des Römertums: Ausgewählte Aufsätze*, Stuttgart, 404–416.

Hellmann, O. (2004), "Tristes Leben auf dem Lande? Das pseudo-vergilische Moretum und die poetische Darstellung des Landlebens in der römischen Literatur", in: *Gymnasium* 111, 1–14.

Henkel, J. (2014), "Vergil Talks Technique: Metapoetical Arboriculture in *Georgics* 2", in: *Vergilius* 60, 33–66.

Hersch, K.K. (2010), *The Roman Wedding: Ritual and Meaning in Antiquity*, Cambridge.

Hill, T. (2004), *Ambitiosa Mors: Suicide and Self in Roman Thought and Literature*, New York.

Hinds, S. (1998), *Allusion and Intertext. Dynamics of Appropriation in Roman Poetry*, Cambridge.

Holzberg, N. (2005), "Impotence? It Happened to the Best of Them! A Linear Reading of the *Corpus Priapeorum*", in: *Hermes* 133, 368–381.

Hooley, D.M. (1997), *The Knotted Thong: Structures of Mimesis in Persius*, Ann Arbor, MI.

Hopkins, K. (1983), *Death and Renewal*, Cambridge.

Horsfall, N. (2001), "*The Moretum Decomposed*", in: *C&M* 52, 303–318.

Höschele, R. (2005), "Moreto-Poetik: Das Moretum als intertextuelles Mischgericht", in: N. Holzberg (ed.), *Die Appendix Vergiliana: Pseudepigraphen im literarischen Kontext*, Tübingen, 244–269.

Hottes, A.C. (1950), *The Book of Shrubs*, New York.

Houston, G.W. (1977), "Vespasian's Adlection of Men in Senatum", in: *AJP* 98, 35–63.

Howes, D. (2003), *Sensual Relations*, Ann Arbor, MI.

Hoyos, B.D. (1979), "Pliny the Elder's Titled Baetican Towns: Obscurities, Errors and Origins", in: *Historia* 28, 439–471.

Hunt, A. (2010), "Elegiac Grafting in Pomona's Orchard: Ovid, *Metamorphoses* 14.623–771", in: *MD* 65, 43–58.

Hunt, A. (2016), *Reviving Roman Religion: Sacred Trees in the Roman World*, Cambridge.

Hurlet, F. (1993), "La 'Lex de imperio Vespasiani' et la légitimité augustéenne", in: *Latomus* 52, 261–280.

Jacobs, J. (2021), *An Introduction to Silius Italicus and the Punica*, New York.

Jensson, G. (2004), *The Recollections of Encolpius: The Satyrica of Petronius as Milesian Fiction*, Groningen.

Jones, F.M.A. (2014), "Roman Gardens, Imagination, and Cognitive Structure", in: *Mnemosyne* 67, 781–812.

Keay, S. and Earl, G. (2011), "Towns and Territories in Roman Baetica", in: A. Bowman and A. Wilson (eds.), *Settlement, Urbanization, and Population*, Oxford, 276–316.

Keith, A. (2000), *Engendering Rome: Women in Latin Epic*, Cambridge.

Keith, A. (2002), "Ovidian Personae in Statius's *Thebaid*", in: *Arethusa* 35, 381–402.

Keith, A. (2004–5), "Ovid's Theban Narrative in Statius' *Thebaid*", in: *Hermathena* 177/178, 177–202.

Keith, A. (2010), "Engendering Orientalism in Silius' *Punica*", in: A. Augoustakis (ed.), *Brill's Companion to Silius Italicus*, Leiden, 356–373.

Keller, M.L. (2009), "The Ritual Path of Initiation into the Eleusinian Mysteries", in: *Rosicrucian Digest* 2, 28–42.

Kennedy, D.L. (1996), "Syria", in: A.K. Bowman (ed.), *The Cambridge Ancient History Volume 10: The Augustan Empire, 43 B.C – A.D. 69*, Cambridge, 703–736.

Kennedy, R.F., Roy, C.S., Goldman, M.L. (eds.) (2013), *Race and Ethnicity in the Classical World: An Anthology of Primary Sources in Translation*, Indianapolis, IN.

Kenney, E.J. (1984), *The Ploughman's Lunch*, Bristol.

Kenney, E.J. (2012), "Satiric Structures: Style, Meter, and Rhetoric", in: S. Braund and J. Osgood (eds.), *A Companion to Persius and Juvenal*, Malden, MA, 113–136.

Kerremans, B. (2016), "*Metus Gallicus, Tumultus Cimbricus?* The Possible Promulgation of a 'Tumultus' in the Cimbrian War (105–101 BCE)", in: *Mnemosyne* 69, 822–841.

Khobnya, S. (2013), "'The Root' in Paul's Olive Tree Metaphor", in: *Tyndale Bulletin* 64, 257–273.

Kißel, W. (1979), *Das Geschichtsbild des Silius Italicus,* Frankfurt am Main.

Kißel, W. (1990), *Aules Persius Flaccus: Satiren*, Heidelberg.

Klebs, E. (1889), "Zur Composition von Petronius Satirae", in: *Philologus* 47, 623–635.

Knapp, R. (2011), *Invisible Romans*, Cambridge, MA.

Kortmann, J.R.T.G. (2018), *Hannibal ad portas: Silius Italicus, 'Punica' 12.507–752. Einleitung, Übersetzung und Kommentar*, Heidelberg.

Küppers, J. (1986), *Tantarum causas irarum. Untersuchugen zur Enleitenden Bücherdyade der Punica des Silius Italicus*, Berlin.

Laehn, T.R. (2015), *Pliny's Defense of Empire*, London.

Lao, E. (2008), *Restoring the Treasury of Mind: The Practical Knowledge of the Natural History*, Ph.D. Diss., Princeton University.

Lattimore, R.A. (2011), *The Iliad of Homer*, Chicago, IL.

Laudani, C. (2004), *Moretum*, Naples.

Lavan, M.P. (2013), *Slaves to Rome: Paradigms of Empire in Roman Culture*, Cambridge.

Lavan, M.P. (2016), "'Father of the Whole Human Race': Ecumenical Language and the Limits of Elite Integration in the Early Roman Empire", in: M. Lavan, R. Payne, and J. Weisweiler (eds.), *Cosmopolitanism and Empire: Universal Rulers, Local Elites and Cultural Integration in the Ancient Near East and Mediterranean*, Oxford, 153–168.

Lavan, M.P. (2020), "Beyond Romans and Others: Identities in the Long Second Century", in: A. König, R. Langlands, and J. Uden (eds.), *Literature and Culture in the Roman Empire, 96–235: Cross-Cultural Interactions*, Cambridge, 37–57.

Lavery, G.B. (1997), "Never Seen in Public: Seneca and the Limits of Cosmopolitanism", in: *Latomus* 56, 3–13.

Leigh, M. (2010), "The Garland of Maecenas (Horace, Odes 1.1.35)", in: *CQ* 60, 268–271.

Lennon, J. (2018), "The Contaminating Touch in the Roman World", in: A. Purves (ed.), *Touch and the Ancient Senses*, New York, 121–133.

Lentz, A. 1867. *Grammatici Graeci. Vol. 3.1: Herodiani Technici Reliquiae*, Leipzig.

Levick, B. (1999), *Vespasian*, London.

Lindsay, H. (2010), "Vespasian and the City of Rome: The Centrality of the Capitolium", in: *AC* 53, 165–180.

Littlewood, C. (2017), "Post-Augustan Revisionism", in: S. Bartsch, K. Freudenburg, and C. Littlewood (eds.), *The Cambridge Companion to the Age of Nero*, Cambridge, 79–92.

Littlewood, J. (2018), "Epic on the edge: generic instability at the pivotal centre of Silius' *Punica* (10.336–371)", in: F. Bessone and M. Fucecchi (eds.), *The Literary Genres in the Flavian Age. Canons, Transformations, Reception*, Berlin, 253–268.

Loraux, N. (1990), "Herakles: The Super-Male and the Feminine", in: D. Halperin, J. Winkler, and F. Zeitlin (eds.), *Before Sexuality: The Construction of Erotic Experience in the Ancient Greek World*, Princeton, 21–52.

Lovatt, H. (2013), *The Epic Gaze: Vision, Gender and Narrative in Ancient Epic*, Cambridge.

Lovatt, H. (2015), "Death on the Margins: Statius and the Spectacle of the Dying Epic Hero", in: A. Bakogianni and V. Hope (eds.), *War as Spectacle: Ancient and Modern Perspectives on the Display of Armed Conflict*, London, 73–89.

Lowe, D. (2010), "The Symbolic Value of Grafting in Ancient Rome", in: *TAPA* 140, 461–488.

Lowrie, M. (2015), "*Rege incolumi*: Orientalism, Civil War, and Security at *Georgics* 4.212", in: P. Fedeli and H.-C. Günther (eds.), *Virgilian Studies: A Miscellany Dedicated to the Memory of Mario Geymonat (26.1.1941 – 17.2.2012)*, Nordhausen, 322–344.

Luke, T. (2010a), "A Healing Touch for Empire: Vespasian's Wonders in Domitianic Rome", in: *G&R* 57, 77–106.

Luke, T. (2010b), "Ideology and Humor in Suetonius' 'Life of Vespasian' 8", in: *CW* 103.4, 511–527.

Majić, B., Šola, I., Likić, S., Cindrić, I.J., and Rusak, G. (2015), "Characterisation of *Sorbus domestica* L. Bark, Fruits and Seeds: Nutrient Composition and Antioxidant Activity", in: *Food Technology and Biotechnology* 53, 463–471.

Malkin, I. (1987), *Religion and Colonization in Ancient Greece*, Leiden.

Manolaraki, E. (2015), "*Hebraei Liquores*: The Balsam of Judaea in Pliny's *Natural History*", in: *AJP* 136, 633–667.

Manolaraki, E. (2017), Review of Master 2016, in: *CP* 112, 506–511.

Marks, R. (2005), *From Republic to Empire. Scipio Africanus in the Punica of Silius Italicus*, Frankfurt am Main.

Marks, R. (2008), "Getting Ahead: Decapitation as Political Metaphor in Silius Italicus' *Punica*", in: *Mnemosyne* 61.1, 66–88.

Marks, R. (2011), "The Exemplary *Punica*", in: *CR* 61, 483–485.

Marks, R. (2020), "Searching for Ovid at Cannae: A Contribution to the Reception of Ovid in Silius Italicus' *Punica*", in: N. Coffee, C. Forstall, L. Galli Milić, and D. Nelis (eds.), *Intertextuality in Flavian Epic Poetry: Contemporary Approaches*, Berlin, 87–106.

Marks, R. (2022), "Silius Italicus and Ovid's Roman History", in: A. Augoustakis and M. Fucecchi (eds.), *Silius Italicus and the Tradition of the Roman Historical Epos*, Leiden, 77–102.

Martinez, D.G. (1991), *P. Michigan XVI: A Greek Love Charm from Egypt*, Atlanta, GA.

Mason, S. (2016), "Updates on an Emperor's Death", in: *Histos* 10: CXXXIX-CLIV.

Master, J. (2009), "Nobody Knows You Like Your Mother. Tacitus, *Histories* 2.64 on Vitellius' True Identity", in: *MD* 63, 191–194.

Master, J. (2016), *Provincial Soldiers and Imperial Instability in the 'Histories' of Tacitus*, Ann Arbor, MI.

Mayer, R. (2012), *Horace: Odes Book I*, Cambridge.

McCoskey, D.E. (2012), *Race, Antiquity, and its Legacy*, New York.

McGuire, D.T. (1997), *Acts of Silence. Civil War, Tyranny, and Suicide in the Flavian Epics*, Hildesheim.

McIntyre, J. (2019), "Calendar Girl: Anna Perenna Between the *Fasti* and the *Punica*", in: G. McIntyre and S. McCallum (eds.), *Uncovering Anna Perenna: A Focused Study of Roman Myth and Culture*, London, 37–53.

McNelis, C. (2012), "Persius, Juvenal and Literary History after Horace", in: S. Braund and J. Osgood (eds.), *A Companion to Persius and Juvenal*, Malden, MA, 239–261.

Meghwal, P. and Singh, A. (2015), "Lasoda or Gonda (Cordia myxa L.)", in: S.N. Ghosh (ed.), *Breeding of Underutilized Fruit Crops*, New Delhi, 247–253.

Merkelback, R. (1979), "Des Josephus Prophezeiung für Vespasian", in: *RhM* 122, 361.

Milns, R.D. (2010), "Suetonius and Vespasian's Humor", in: *AC* 53, 117–123.

Montiglio, S. (2005), *Wandering in Ancient Greek Culture*, Chicago.

Morgan, T. (2011), "*Ethos*: The Socialization of Children in Education and Beyond", in: B. Rawson (ed.), *A Companion to Families in the Greek and Roman Worlds*, Malden, MA, 504–520.

Mudge, K., Janick, J., Scofield, S., and Goldschmidt, E. (2009), "A History of Grafting", in: *Horticultural Reviews* 35, 437–487.

Muecke, F. (1993), *Horace: Satires II*, Warminster.

Müller, K. (2009), *Petronius: Satyricon Reliquiae*, 4th ed., Munich.

Munson, R.V. (2001), *Telling Wonders: Ethnographic and Political Discourse in the Work of Herodotus*, Ann Arbor, MI.

Myers, M.Y. (2011), "Lucan's Poetic Geographies: Centre and Periphery in Civil War Epic", in: P. Asso (ed.), *Brill's Companion to Lucan*, Leiden, 399–415.

Munson, R.V. (2009), "Who Are Herodotus' Persians?", in: *CW* 102, 457–470.

Neudecker, R. (2005), "Die Pyramide des Cestius", in: L. Giuliani (ed.), *Meisterwerke der antiken Kunst*, Munich, 94–113.

Newlands, C. (1997), "The Metamorphosis of Ovid's Medea", in: J. Clauss and S. Johnston (eds.), *Essays on Medea in Myth, Literature, Philosophy, and Art*, Princeton, 178–208.

Nicols, J. (1978), *Vespasian and the Partes Flavianae*, Wiesbaden.

Niehoff, M. (2018), *Philo of Alexandria: An Intellectual Biography*, New Haven, CT.

Nisbet, R.G.M. and Hubbard, M. (1970), *A Commentary on Horace Odes, Book I*, Oxford.

Nussbaum, M. (1995), *Poetic Justice: The Literary Imagination and Public Life*, Boston.

O'Connor, E.M. (1989), *Symbolum Salacitatis: A Study of the God Priapus as a Literary Character*, Frankfurt am Main.

Onelli, C. (2014), "Freedom and Censorship: Petronius' *Satyricon* in Seventeenth-Century Italy", in: *Classical Receptions Journal* 6, 104–130.

Orlin, E.M. (2010), *Foreign Cults in Rome: Creating a Roman Empire*, Oxford.

Panoussi, V. (2019), *Brides, Mourners, Bacchae: Women's Rituals in Roman Literature*, Baltimore, MD.

Papadopoulou, T. (2004), "Herakles and Hercules: The Hero's Ambivalence in Euripides and Seneca", in: *Mnemosyne* 57, 257–283.

Passavanti, L. (2009), *Laudes Italiae: L'idealizzazione dell'Italia nella letteratura latina di età augustea*, Trento.

Pearce, S. (2007), *The Land of the Body: Studies in Philo's Representation of Egypt*, Tübingen.

Perutelli, A. (1983), *Moretum*, Pisa.

Perutelli, A. (1985), "I 'bracchia' degli alberi. Designazione tecnica e imagine poetica", in: *MD* 15, 9–48.

Petsalis-Diomidis, A. (2005), "The Body in Space: Visual Dynamics in Graeco-Roman Healing Pilgrimage", in: J. Elsner and I. Rutherford (eds.), *Pilgrimage in Graeco-Roman and Early Christian Antiquity: Seeing the Gods*, Oxford, 183–218.

Pfeiffer, R. (1968), *A History of Classical Scholarship from the Beginnings to the End of the Hellenistic Age*, Oxford.

Pinna, T. (1978), "Un'ipotesi sul rituale di Quartilla (Satyricon, XVI–XXVI)", in: *AFMC* 3, 215–259.

Plaza, M. (2005), *The Function of Humour in Roman Verse Satire: Laughing and Lying*, Oxford.

Pogorzelski, R. (2016), "Centers and Periphery", in: A. Zissos (ed.), *A Companion to the Flavian Age of Imperial Rome*, Malden, MA, 223–238.

Pollard, E.A. (2009), "Pliny's *Natural History* and the Flavian *Templum Pacis*: Botanical Imperialism in First-Century C. E. Rome", in: *Journal of World History* 20, 309–338.

Posner, R. (2009), *Law and Literature*, Cambridge, MA.

Potter, D. (1999), "Odor and Power in the Roman Empire", in: J.I. Porter (ed.), *Constructions of the Classical Body*, Ann Arbor, 169–189.

Pucci, J.M. (1998), *The Full-Knowing Reader: Allusion and the Power of the Reader in Western Literary Tradition*, New Haven, CT.

Rawlings, L. (2005), "Hannibal and Hercules", in: L. Rawlings and H. Bowden (eds.), *Herakles and Hercules. Exploring a Graeco-Roman Divinity*, Swansea, 153–184.

Rebeggiani, S. (2018), *The Fragility of Power: Statius, Domitian and the Politics of the Thebaid*, New York.

Reckford, K.J. (1962), "Studies in Persius", in: *Hermes* 90, 476–504.

Richlin, A. (1992), *The Garden of Priapus: Sexuality and Aggression in Roman Humor*, New York.

Rieker, J.R. (2005), *Arnulfi Aurelianensis* Glosule *Ovidii Fastorum*, Florence.

Rimell, V. (2002), *Petronius and the Anatomy of Fiction*, Cambridge.

Rimell, V. (2015), *The Closure of Space in Roman Poetics: Empire's Inward Turn*, Cambridge.

Ripoll, F. (1998), *La morale heroïque dans les épopées latines d'époque Flavienne: Tradition et innovation*, Louvain.

Roche, P.A. (2003), "The Execution of L. Salvius Otho Cocceianus", in: *CQ* 53, 319–322.

Roche, P.A. (2012), "Self-Representation and Performativity", in: S. Braund and J. Osgood (eds.), *A Companion to Persius and Juvenal*, Malden, MA, 190–216.

Roller, M. (2004), "Exemplarity in Roman culture; the Cases of Horatius Cocles and Cloelia", in: *CP* 99, 1–56.

Ross, D.O. (1975), "The Culex and Moretum as Post-Augustan Literary Parodies", in: *HSPh* 79, 235–263.

Ross, D.O. (1980), "*Non Sua Poma*: Varro, Virgil, and Grafting", in: *ICS* 5, 63–71.

Rudd, N. (1976), *Lines of Enquiry*, Cambridge.

Said, E.W. (1979), *Orientalism*, New York.

Sartori, F. (1995), "'Laudes Italiae' in scrittori greci e latini", in: N. Criniti and L. Allegri (eds.), *Sermione mansio. Società e cultura della 'Cisalpina' tra tarda antichità e altomedioevo*, Brescia, 5–16.

Scafuro, A. (1997), *The Forensic Stage: Settling Disputes in Graeco-Roman New Comedy*, Cambridge.

Schiavone, A. (2012), *The Invention of Law in the West* (trans. J. Carden and A. Shugaar), Cambridge, MA.

Schiebinger, L. and Swan, C. (eds.) (2005), *Colonial Botany: Science, Commerce, and Politics in the Early Modern World*, Philadelphia.

Schmeling, G. and Setaioli, A. (2011), *A Commentary on the Satyrica of Petronius*, Oxford.

Scholer, D.M. (1993), "Foreword: An Introduction to Philo Judaeus of Alexandria", in: C.D. Yonge (tr.), *The Works of Philo: Complete and Unabridged*, Peabody, MA, ix–xvii.

Schroer, C.A. (2022), "*Exul in orbe toto*, or, How to Map Future Power in Silius Italicus", in: A. Augoustakis and M. Fucecchi (eds.), *Silius Italicus and the Tradition of the Roman Historical Epos*, Leiden, 210–231.

Sellars, J. (2007), "Stoic Cosmopolitanism and Zeno's Republic", in: *History of Political Thought* 28, 1–29.

Skinner, J. (2012), *The Invention of Greek Ethnography*, Oxford.

Slater, N. (1990), *Reading Petronius*, Baltimore.

Snowden, F. (1983), *Before Color Prejudice: The Ancient View of Blacks*, Cambridge, MA.

Sosin, J.D. (1999), "Lucretius, Seneca and Persius", in: *TAPA* 129, 281–299.

Star, C. (2012), *The Empire of the Self: Self-Command and Political Speech in Seneca and Petronius*, Baltimore.

Steger, F. (2018), *Asclepius: Medicine and Cult*, Stuttgart.

Stephens, S.A. (2015), *Callimachus: The Hymns*, Oxford.

Šterbenc Erker, D. (2013), "Religion", in: E. Buckley and M. Dinter (eds.), *A Companion to the Neronian Age*, Malden, MA, 118–133.

Stevenson, T.R. (2010), "Personifications on the Coinage of Vespasian", *AClass* 53, 181–205.

Stocks, C. (2014), *The Roman Hannibal: Remembering the Enemy in Silius Italicus' Punica*, Liverpool.

Stocks, C. (2018), "Anger in the Extreme? Ira, Excess, and the Punica", in: *Phoenix* 72, 293–311.

Stocks, C. (2019), "In a Land of Gods and Monsters: Silius Italicus' Capua", in: A. Augoustakis and J. Littlewood (eds.), *Campania in the Flavian Poetic Imagination*, Oxford, 233–247.

Sullivan, J.P. (1968), *The Satyricon of Petronius: A Literary Study*, London.

Sullivan, J.P. (2011), *Petronius: The Satyricon*, Revised ed., London.

Syme, R. (1969), "Pliny the Procurator", in: *HSPh* 73, 201–236.

Syme, R. (1991), "Consular Friends of the Elder Pliny", in: A.R. Birley (ed.), *Ronald Syme: Roman Papers, Vol. 7*, Oxford, 496–511.

Talbert, T.J. (1938), "Top and Double Working, and Bridge Grafting of Fruit Trees", in: *Missouri Agricultural Experiment Station* 196, 1–16.

Taub, L.C. and Doody, A. (2009), *Authorial Voices in Greco-Roman Technical Writing*, Trier.

Taylor, N.H. (2001), "Popular Opposition to Caligula in Jewish Palestine", in: *JSJ* 32.1, 54–70.

Telford, W.R. (1991), "More Fruit from the Withered Tree: Temple and Fig-Tree in Mark from a Graeco-Roman Perspective", in: W. Horbury (ed.), *Templum Amicitiae: Essays on the Second Temple Presented to Ernst Bammel*, Sheffield, 264–304.

Thomas, R.F. (1988a), *Virgil: Georgics*, Cambridge.

Thomas, R.F. (1988b), "Tree Violation and Ambivalence in Virgil", in: *TAPA* 118, 261–273.

Thomas, R.F. (1992), "The Old Man Revisited: Memory, Reference and Genre in Virg., *Geo.* 4.116-48", in: *MD* 29, 35–70.

Tipping, B. (2010a), *Exemplary Epic. Silius Italicus' Punica*, Oxford.

Tipping, B. (2010b), "Virtue and narrative in Silius Italicus' Punica", in: A. Augoustakis (ed.), *Brill's Companion to Silius Italicus*, Leiden, 193–218.

Toner, J. (2009), *Popular Culture in Ancient Rome*, Cambridge.

Totelin, L. (2012), "Botanizing Rulers and Their Herbal Subjects: Plants and Political Power in Greek and Roman Literature", in: *Phoenix* 66, 122–144.

Tuori, K. (2021), "Between the good king and the cruel tyrant: The *Acta Isidori* and the perception of Roman emperors among provincial litigants", in: K. Berthelot, N. Dohrmann, and C. Nemo-Pekelman (eds.), *Legal Engagement: The reception of Roman law and tribunals by Jews and other inhabitants of the Empire*, Rome, 109–132.

Udoh, F. (2005), "Taxation of Judea under the Governors", *To Caesar What Is Caesar's: Tribute, Taxes, and Imperial Administration in Early Roman Palestine (63 B.C.E – 70 C. E.)*, Providence, RI.

Van der Horst, P. (2003), *Philo's Flaccus: The First Pogrom. Introduction, Translation and Commentary*, Atlanta, GA.

Van Hoof, A.J.L. (1990), *From Autothanasia to Suicide: Self-killing in Classical Antiquity*, London.

Vessey, D. (1974), "Silius Italicus on the Fall of Saguntum", in: *CP* 69, 28–36.

Vessey, D. (1982), "The Dupe of Destiny: Hannibal in Silius, *Punica* III", in: *CJ* 77, 320–335.

Veyne, P. (1983), *Les Grecs ont-ils cru à leurs mythes? Essai sur l'imagination constituante*, Paris.

Voisin, J.L. (1984), "Tite Live, Capoue et les Bacchanales", in: *MEFRM* 96, 2601–2653.

Von Albrecht, M. (1964), *Silius Italicus. Freiheit und Gebundenheit römischer Epik*, Amsterdam.

Von Jan, L. and Mayhoff, K. (eds.) (1870–1909), *C. Plini Secundi Naturalis Historiae Libri XXXVII*, 6 vols., Leipzig.

Von Stackelberg, K.T. (2009), "Performative Space and Garden Transgressions in Tacitus' Death of Messalina", in: *AJP* 130.4, 595–624.

Von Stackelberg, K.T. (2014), "Garden Hybrids: Hermaphrodite Images in the Roman House", in: *ClAnt* 33, 395–426.

Walker, B. (1952), *The Annals of Tacitus: A Study in the Writing of History*, Manchester.

Walsh, P.G. (1970), *The Roman Novel*, Cambridge.

Weitzman, S. (2005), *Surviving Sacrilege: Cultural Persistance in Jewish Antiquity*, Cambridge, MA.

West, M.L. (1974), *Studies in Greek Elegy and Iambus*, Berlin.

White, K.D. (1970), *Roman Farming*, Ithaca, NY.

Wiegels, R. (1978), "Das Datum der Verleihung des Ius Latii an die Hispanier: Zur Personal- und Municipalpolitik in den ersten Regierungsjahren Vespasians", in: *Hermes* 106, 196–213.

Wilson, M. (2012), "Bastard Grafts, Crafted Fruits: Shakespeare's Planted Families", in: J.E. Feerick and V. Nardizzi (eds.), *The Indistinct Human in Renaissance Literature: Early Modern Cultural Studies*, New York, 101–117.

Wimmel, W. (1960), *Kallimachos in Rom*, Wiesbaden.

Wiseman, T.P. (1965), "Mallius", in: *CR* 15, 263.

Wiseman, T.P. (1971), *New Men in the Roman Senate, 139 B.C. – A.D. 14*, Oxford.

Wiseman, T.P. (1991), *Flavius Josephus: Death of an Emperor*, Exeter.

Wiseman, T.P. and Wiseman, A. (2011), *Ovid, Times and Reasons: A New Translation of Fasti*, Oxford.

Woodside, M. St. A. (1942), "Vespasian's Patronage of Education and the Arts", in: *TAPA* 73, 123–129.

Zetzel, J.E.G. (1977), "Lucilius, Lucretius, and Persius 1.1", in: *CP* 72, 40–42.

Zetzel, J.E.G. (1980), "Horace's *Liber Sermonum*: The Structure of Ambiguity", in: *Arethusa* 13, 59–77.

Ziogas, I. (2021), *Law and Love in Ovid: Courting Justice in the Age of Augustus*, Oxford.
Zissos, A. (2019), "Closure and Segmentation: Endings, Medial Proems, Book Divisions", in:
     C. Reitz and S. Finkmann (eds.), *Structures of Epic Poetry. Vol. I: Foundations*, Berlin,
     531–564.

General Index

References are to page numbers. This index is selective.

https://doi.org/10.1515/9783111063942-012

Index Locorum

https://doi.org/10.1515/9783111063942-013